KADMOS THE PHOENICIAN

KADMOS THE PHOENICIAN

A Study in Greek Legends
and the
Mycenaean Age

RUTH B. EDWARDS

ADOLF M. HAKKERT — PUBLISHER — AMSTERDAM
1979

I.S.B.N. 90-256-07969

Phototypeset by Fotron S.A., Athens, Greece

To Patrick,
Hilary and Nicholas

CONTENTS

PREFACE

What relationship, if any, do the stories preserved in ancient Greek legendary traditions have to real events and circumstances of the periods and places to which they ostensibly refer? A wide range of answers to this question is to be found in the works of both popular and scholarly writers, not only where it has been debated explicitly but also —and more frequently— where some kind of answer seems to be presupposed in the course of their general discussions of Greek literature and history. The present book sets out to study the development and interpretation of a substantial group of Greek legends associated with one well-known figure, who was said to have originated in the East. It is intended that it should be of interest to oriental specialists as well as to classicists, prehistorians and students of mythology.

The book is based upon my Ph.D. thesis (*Greek Legends and the Mycenaean Age*, Cambridge, 1968): the revision took into account work appearing up to early 1973, when the typescript was completed and submitted for publication. It is regretted that this has been unavoidably delayed, but fortunately the work which has appeared since then does not affect my main arguments, though there are a few matters of detail and emphasis which I should now have preferred to treat differently. Among recent publications the most directly relevant are S. Symeonoglou's report on his excavation of a workshop area, including many ivories, at Thebes (*Kadmeia* I, 1973), and the full publication, by Th. G. Spyropoulos and J. Chadwick, of the new Linear B tablets mentioned on p. 104 (*The Thebes Tablets II. Minos*, Supplement 4, 1975). Symeonoglou's study emphasises both the Cretan and Near Eastern connexions of Thebes (cf. my Chapters V and VI); that of Spyropoulos and Chadwick suggests that the Linear B tablets are probably LH III B (rather than III A.2), and tends to confirm the lower dating for the destructions at Thebes. Further work has also been published on the Ugaritic texts, illustrating the variety of interpretation possible: I may mention in particular P. Xella's study of the myth of Shachar and Shalim (Rome, 1973). The full publication of the oriental seals from Thebes is still awaited.

I am glad to have this opportunity of thanking all who have helped me, most especially Dr. F.H. Stubbings of Emmanuel College, Cambridge, who supervised the original research and has continued to give me much encouragement, and Professor John Gray and Mr. William Johnstone, of the Department of Hebrew and Semitic Languages in the University of Aberdeen, for initiating me into their mysteries and for discussing some of the Near Eastern questions with me. The help given me by Aberdeen University Library over many years has been indispensable. A book like this owes much to previous work in the same general field, and I readily acknowledge my debt to the many scholars whose writings are mentioned in these pages: even where they are cited for criticism, I have learnt much from them.

I should like also to thank Mr. A.M. Hakkert for accepting this work for publication at what proved to be a difficult time; Dr. J.G.P. Best of the Henri Frankfort Foundation, Amsterdam; Mrs. Margaret Gerrie, who typed the whole manuscript with characteristic conscientiousness and cheerfulness; Miss D. Harvey and all who have been concerned with the setting and printing of the text; Mrs. A. Sandison for drawing the maps; and Miss Teresa Clark for typing the index.

Finally I want to express my warmest thanks to my own family, and especially to my husband, Dr. G.P. Edwards, for his constructive criticism and practical help at all stages of the work. This book is dedicated to them in gratitude and affection.

R.B.E.

King's College,
Old Aberdeen.
August, 1978.

ABBREVIATIONS

This list includes only journals and multi-author works: for abbreviated titles of books and articles see the Bibliography under the names of their authors.

AA	Archäologische Anzeiger.
AAA	Ἀρχαιολογικὰ Ἀνάλεκτα ἐξ Ἀθηνῶν (= Athens Annals of Archaeology).
AAS	Annales archéologiques de Syrie.
AD	Ἀρχαιολογικὸν Δελτίον.
AE	Ἀρχαιολογικὴ Ἐφημερίς or Ἐφημερὶς Ἀρχαιολογική.
AIRRS	Acta Instituti Romani Regni Sueciae (= Skrifter utgivna av Svenska Institutet i Rom).
AJA	American Journal of Archaeology.
AJPh	American Journal of Philology.
ANET	Ancient Near Eastern Texts relating to the Old Testament(ed. J.B. Pritchard). Ed. 3, Princeton, 1969.
AR	Archaeological Reports (JHS Suppl.).
ArchClass	Archeologia Classica.
ASAA	Annuario della Scuola Archeologica di Atene.
Ath. Mitt.	Mitteilungen des Kaiserlich Deutschen Archäologischen Instituts. Athenische Abteilung.
BASO	Bulletin of the American Schools of Oriental Research in Jerusalem and Baghdad.
BCH	Bulletin de Correspondance Hellénique.
BICS	Bulletin of the Institute of Classical Studies of the University of London.
BSA	Annual of the British School at Athens.
CAH	The Cambridge Ancient History Vols. I and II, Cambridge. Ed. 1 (ed. J.B. Bury and others) 1923-24; ed. 2 (ed. I.E.S. Edwards and others) appearing in fascicles from 1961 onwards; ed. 3 (bound volumes

	with new pagination) Vol. I, 1970-71; Vol. II, 1973-75.
CH	A Companion to Homer (ed. A.J.B. Wace and F.H. Stubbings). London, 1962.
CPh	Classical Philology.
CR	Classical Review.
CRAI	Comptes Rendus de l'Académie des Inscriptions et Belles-Lettres.
CVA	Corpus Vasorum Antiquorum.
EGF	Epicorum Graecorum Fragmenta I (ed. G. Kinkel). Leipzig, 1877.
FGrH	Fragmente der griechischen Historiker (ed. F. Jacoby). Berlin and elsewhere, 1923 onwards.
FHG	Fragmenta Historicorum Graecorum (ed. C. Müller and T. Müller). Paris, ed. 2, 1841-70.
GGM	Geographici Graeci Minores (ed. C. Müller). Paris, 1855-61.
G&R	Greece and Rome.
HSPh	Harvard Studies in Classical Philology.
IEJ	Israel Exploration Journal.
ILN	Illustrated London News.
JA	Journal Asiatique.
JAOS	Journal of the American Oriental Society.
JDAI	Jahrbuch des Deutschen Archäologischen Instituts.
JHS	Journal of Hellenic Studies.
JNES	Journal of Near Eastern Studies.
JPOS	Journal of the Palestine Oriental Society.
JSS	Journal of Semitic Studies.
M-W	Fragmenta Hesiodea (ed. R. Merkelbach and M.L. West). Oxford, 1967.
Nestor	Nestor. Mycenaean Bibliography (ed. E.L. Bennett Jr., Madison, Wisconsin).
OCD	The Oxford Classical Dictionary, Oxford. Ed. 1 (ed. M. Cary and others) 1949; ed. 2 (ed. N.G.L. Hammond and H.H. Scullard) 1970.
PAAH	Πρακτικὰ τῆς ἐν ᾿Αθήναις ᾿Αρχαιολογικῆς ῾Εταιρείας.

PalEQ	*Palestine Exploration Quarterly.*
PBA	*Proceedings of the British Academy.*
PCA	*Proceedings of the Classical Association.*
Peake	*Peake's Commentary on the Bible* (ed. M. Black and H.H. Rowley). London, 1962.
PP	*La Parola del Passato.*
PPS	*Proceedings of the Prehistoric Society.*
PRU	*Le Palais Royal d'Ugarit* (for Vols. II-VI see Bibliography under Nougayrol and Virolleaud; Vol. I, a proposed history of the Palace, is still forthcoming).
RA	*Revue Archéologique.*
RE	*Paulys Real-Encyclopädie der classischen Altertumswissenschaft* (ed. A. Pauly, G. Wissowa and others). Stuttgart and elsewhere, 1894 onwards.
REG	*Revue des Études Grecques.*
RhM	*Rheinisches Museum.*
RHPh	*Revue d'Histoire de la Philosophie et d'Histoire Générale de la Civilisation.*
RHR	*Revue de l'Histoire des Religions.*
Roscher	*Ausführliches Lexikon der griechischen und römischen Mythologie* (ed. W.H. Roscher and others). Leipzig, 1894-1937.
RPh	*Revue de Philologie.*
SMA	*Studies in Mediterranean Archaeology* (ed. P. Åström).
TPhS	*Transactions of the Philological Society.*
Teiresias	*Teiresias. A Review and Continuing Bibliography of Boiotian Studies* (ed. J.M. Fossey and A. Schachter, Montreal).
TGF	*Tragicorum Graecorum Fragmenta* (ed. A. Nauck). Ed. 2, Leipzig, 1889.
YWCS	*The Year's Work in Classical Studies.*
ZASA	*Zeitschrift für ägyptische Sprache und Altertumskunde.*
ZS	*Zeitschrift für Semitistik und verwandte Gebiete.*

CHAPTER I

INTRODUCTION: CHANGING ATTITUDES TOWARDS GREEK LEGEND AND PREHISTORY

"All we know about the earliest inhabitants of Greece, is derived from the accounts of the Greeks themselves." These words of Connop Thirlwall (*A History of Greece*, Vol. I (1835) p.32) well illustrate how, as recently as the early nineteenth century, the ancient traditions were still of paramount importance in the study of Greek prehistory. Such independent sources of information as were available were few and inadequate for assessing the reliability of these traditions: all that could be done was to take the stories as they had been transmitted and to discard or explain away what seemed to be impossible or historically implausible. Naturally scholars varied in the extent to which they trusted the picture thus gained: some were willing to give credence to all that was left after the removal of fantastic and supernatural elements, and frequently made elaborate chronological calculations, attempting to correlate the results of their study of the Greek traditions with data obtained from the Old Testament;[1] others made thorough-going rationalisations of the stories, explaining the supernatural and miraculous as having an ultimate origin in historical fact, and often supposing these parts of the traditions to have arisen from verbal misunderstandings.[2] But not all scholars were so confident

---

1. The discussions of chronology are numerous: see esp. the works of Usher, Newton, Blair, Hales and Clinton cited in the Bibliography. For a notable attempt to write a connected history from the myths and legends see W. Mitford, *HGMit* I (ed. 1, 1784). Mitford himself was doubtful of the value of such elaborate chronological calculations: see esp. op. cit. ed. 2 (1789) pp.155f.

2. A systematic rationalisation of the stories was, for example, put forward by Abbé Banier in *The Mythology and Fables of the Ancients explain'd from History* (1739-40). Banier's explanations, some of which may be paralleled in classical writers, include the idea that Pasiphae's union with the bull was "an Intrigue of the Queen of *Crete* with a Captain named *Taurus*", that Herakles' slaying of the hydra was but the draining of

1

of a historical basis for the legends: one notable sceptic was Jacob Bryant, who published towards the end of the eighteenth century *A Dissertation concerning the War of Troy, and the expedition of the Grecians, as described by Homer; shewing that no such expedition was ever undertaken, and that no such city of Phrygia existed* (ed. 1, 1796), and who in his large work entitled *A New System, or, an Analysis of Antient Mythology* (ed. 1, 1774-6) repeatedly expressed sceptical views about the historical value of the legends, saying that there were very few events before the Olympiads to which he could give credence.[3]

Bryant's method of criticism had been to show how ridiculous the legends were in many of their details, such as the tale of Helen's birth from an egg; he paid no regard to the date or nature of the *sources* for different versions which he criticised, but simply conflated the varying ancient accounts into a whole, which he then showed to be incredible. Early in the nineteenth century however we see the beginning of a new type of scepticism arising out of the growth of historical criticism with an emphasis on the study of sources. In Germany this more scientific method of study is especially associated with the name of K.O. Müller, who in his *Orchomenos und die Minyer* (1820) and *Prolegomena zu einer wissentschaftlichen Mythologie* (1825; English translation by J.Leitch, 1844) stresses the need to distinguish different types of material, and examines the authorities for the traditions, rejecting for example many of the stories of migrants from the East, upon which whole theories of oriental origins of civilisation in Greece had been based, because they were not to be found in Homer and the early poets. In Britain a critical contribution of outstanding importance was made by George Grote, who had thought deeply about the problem of establishing history from the traditions. He rejected the old method of

---

some marshy land, that the dolphin which led the Cretans to Kirrha was in reality a ship named the *Dolphin,* and that the story of Athamas' children and the ram arose from a misunderstanding about their tutor named Krios (see *MFA* I, esp. pp.29, 60, 68).

3. See Bryant, *NSAM* (ed. 3, 1807) I p. xxxvi. Other scholars who minimised the historical content of Greek mythology were those who interpreted the stories in allegorical fashion. For a discussion of this view, which goes back to ancient times, see Grote, *HGGro* I (1846) pp.558-68, 579-85; cf. also Banier, *MFA* I, Ch. II, "In which 'tis proved that Fables are not mere Allegories, but comprehend several ancient facts".

2

taking plausibility as a criterion of truth, and believed that there was no means of distinguishing plausible fiction from fact, and no outside source for checking the validity of the legends. Grote writes: "I really know nothing so disheartening or unrequited as the elaborate balancing of what is called evidence — the comparison of infinitesimal probabilities and conjectures all uncertified — in regard to these shadowy times and persons" (Preface to *A History of Greece,* Vol. I (1846) p.xi). In his monumental work he therefore simply related the stories as the Greeks told them, maintaining an agnostic view about their historicity. The heroic age, he argued, must be kept strictly separate from historical Greece, since it is the "age of historical faith, as distinguished from the later age of historical reason" (op. cit. p.xiii).

By the end of the nineteenth century the position was radically altered. No longer were scholars almost entirely dependent on what the Greeks themselves had to say about their early past: a new type of evidence had been discovered which at once became the prime source for prehistoric Greece. This new source was archaeology, the first use of which for the study of Greek prehistory will always be associated with the name of Heinrich Schliemann. Schliemann was motivated by the desire to prove the traditions true; he believed in Homer "like the Creed", and set out to discover by study of the sites famous in Homer — Troy, Mycenae, Orchomenos, Ithaka, Tiryns — what truth lay behind the stories. The results of his work are well known: he thought that he had discovered the very city and treasures of Priam, the very tombs and remains of Agamemnon and his retinue. The work of his successors showed that the destruction of the city which Schliemann first believed to be Homer's (what is now known as Troy II) was to be dated about a millennium earlier than the earliest of the ancient dates for the fall of Troy, and even the graves which he ascribed to Agamemnon and his company at Mycenae were some two or three hundred years too early. But this was not to undo Schliemann's work; in the application of systematic excavation to the problem of Greek prehistory he had, in Virchow's words, opened up "an entirely new science" (Preface to Schliemann's *Ilios* (1880) p.xiv).

Since Schliemann much progress has been made in the archaeological study of prehistoric Greece. Site after site has been excavated, not only on the mainland but also in Crete and the other islands, and our knowledge has been extended and enriched in ways that were inconceivable early in the last century. Along with the advent of dating by the radio-carbon method has come the discovery of palaeolithic cultures in Greece. Naturally the physical survivals of such a remote period are scanty, consisting of stone tools and a few skeletal remains, but by Late Neolithic times much more material evidence is available in the form of tombs, pottery and other artefacts, and habitation sites have been excavated. Our picture is even fuller for the Bronze Age, which, thanks to the large number of sites known and the higher level of culture, can be studied in considerable detail in its different phases.

Nor is archaeology the only source for prehistoric Greece. For the Bronze Age — especially its latter part — there are others available, again hardly known to Grote and his predecessors. First there is the evidence of the Greek language. Two centuries ago exceedingly little was understood about its affinities: there was indeed speculation about its relation to the other languages of Europe and the Near East, but the lack of real knowledge about the true position may be seen in William Mitford's treatment of the question at the end of the eighteenth century (see Vol. I of *The History of Greece,* first published in 1784).[4] Then came the discovery of Sanskrit and the realisation that Greek (and Latin) must be related to the old language of India. At first the new evidence was misunderstood: it was, for example, believed that Sanskrit was the parent of the Greek language, and that many of the Greek myths and legends were derived directly from the Indian. These ideas were soon shown to be false; but the scientific study of languages which has developed since the early nineteenth century has continued to have important consequences for our understanding of prehistory. The fact that Greek is a member of the Indo-European family, combined with the evidence of non-Greek place-names in the Aegean, now allows the deduction that at least some of the ancestors of the Greeks must have entered Greece from outside by migration, and that

4. Mitford writes that "we find strong reason to suppose that, in the early ages, the difference of language over Asia, Africa, and Europe, as far as their inhabitants of those ages are known to us, was but a difference of dialect", and he comments on the close analogy between "the Celtic dialects" and Hebrew and on the particular resemblance in certain forms between Welsh and Arabic *(HGMit* I (ed. 2, 1789) esp. p.90 with n. 40)!

4

they were not the first inhabitants of the country. Moreover the distribution of the classical Greek dialects enables inferences to be drawn about the stages in this immigration.[5]

Secondly the study of the ancient orient has been revolutionised. Two centuries ago, apart from the references in classical and Old Testament writers, the only sources of information were travellers' reports of the monuments and undeciphered inscriptions occasionally visible above ground. Then came the discovery and decipherment of a long series of oriental documents beginning with the Rosetta Stone found in 1799 during Napoleon's expediton to Egypt. This provided the clue for the decipherment of the Egyptian demotic and hieroglyphic scripts in the first decades of the nineteenth century, and the same period saw also the decipherment of numerous Babylonian documents from excavation in Mesopotamia. Since then rapid progress has been made in both the excavation of sites and the interpretation of texts: Sumerian, Hittite, Ugaritic and other languages have been deciphered in their turn. As a result of all this work, not only the material culture but also the history of many persons and events in the Near East is now known, sometimes in remarkable detail. The consequence of this for the prehistory of Greece is the provision of a historical setting for its Bronze Age culture, the establishment by cross-dating of a more detailed chronological scheme than that obtainable from scientific analysis in the laboratory, and the identification (often disputed) of a number of specific references in the oriental texts to the peoples of the Aegean.[6]

Finally, there has been the discovery of Bronze Age documents in

5. On the evidence of language in general see Albright and Lambdin, *CAH* ed. 2, fasc. 54 (1966); and for the progress of scholarly ideas up to the present century see Pedersen, *LSNC.* On the Greek dialects as evidence for prehistory see esp. Chadwick in *G&R* 3 (1956) pp.38-50, and id., *CAH* ed. 2, fasc. 15 (1963), though some scholars have disagreed with the historical deductions there expressed: for some dissentient views see n. 8.

6. For the history of the Near East see esp. the relevant chapters in *CAH* ed. 2, Vols. I and II. The progress of excavation and of the discovery and decipherment of the documents is described conveniently in the various Pelican books on archaeology, most notably Albright, *AP*, Gurney, *The Hittites*, Lloyd, *Early Anatolia* and Roux, *AI*; for Egypt see Gardiner, *EP*. A useful collection of texts is that of Pritchard, *ANET*, with copious references to further literature.

Greece itself. Less than a century ago it was thought that Mycenaean Greece was entirely illiterate. Thus G. Perrot and C. Chipiez in their major work entitled *History of Art in Primitive Greece* (1894) wrote: "What most strikes the historian who sets about to define pre-Homeric culture, is its having been a stranger to writing. .... throughout the whole of this period, naught with a semblance of any kind of script has been seen in Peloponnesus, Central Greece, or on the thousand and one objects found in the tombs, which were designed for domestic or ornamental uses. This culture, then, is a dumb culture, so that the voice of its authors will never fall directly on our ear" (op. cit. Vol. II, pp.462f.). Yet in the same year as these words were published, Arthur Evans paid his first visit to Crete, collecting evidence which proved the existence there of pictographic and linear writing which had been in use many centuries before the time when the Phoenician alphabet was introduced into Greece (see his article in *The Athenaeum* No. 3478 for June 23rd, 1894, pp.812f.). Six years later Evans was able to begin excavating at Knossos, and within a week there was brought to light the first example of a clay tablet in the Linear B script. The story of further discoveries of similar documents both at Knossos and at various sites on the mainland, of their decipherment in 1952 as an early form of Greek, and of the stimulus which this provided to Mycenaean studies, is now well known and need not be recapitulated here.[7]

What then are the main facts about the Greek Bronze Age which may be taken as reasonably well established by a synthesis of these new sources? The following may be regarded as a fair summary of what is most widely accepted, though there is still disagreement today even over some of the more fundamental questions.[8]

---

7. For the decipherment of Linear B see Ventris and Chadwick, *DMG* (1956), with bibliography to 1955, and Chadwick, *DLB* (1958), with a discussion of criticisms of the decipherment; for further details of progress see B. Moon's works cited in the Bibliography. Bibliographical information about more recent work is given monthly in *Nestor* (ed. E.L. Bennett, Jr.).

8. For surveys of Greek prehistory setting out views which are widely accepted see Blegen in *BSA* 46 (1951) pp.16-24; Wace in *Historia* 2 (1953-4) pp.74-94; id. in *CH* pp.331-61; Dow, *TGBA;* and the relevant chapters of the revised *CAH* Vols. I and II. More detailed studies of Crete are Hutchinson, *PC,* and Hood, *The Minoans;* for the

The Greek mainland, Crete and the Cyclades were inhabited in the Early Bronze Age by peoples of similar, but by no means homogeneous, culture. During the Middle Bronze Age in Crete this culture developed into the highly advanced Middle Minoan (MM) civilisation; palaces were built, great progress was made in both practical and decorative arts, writing came into use (hieroglyphic and Linear A scripts), and trade was exercised with the Cyclades, parts of the mainland, and, in the East, as far as Egypt and Syria. Some settlements or colonies seem to have been founded in the Aegean, and in spite of setbacks through several earthquakes a remarkably high level of civilisation was maintained, which continued into the Late Bronze Age, with the palaces as important administrative and artistic centres, and many flourishing private houses and mansions.

Mainland Greece on the other hand appears to have been invaded at the end of the second Early Helladic period (EH II) by a culturally less advanced people, probably of Indo-European origin. It is thought by many scholars that these are likely to have been the first Greek speakers to enter Greece, or at any rate to have spoken a language which later became Greek. A second wave of related invaders may have followed at the end of the EH III period and have been responsible for the destructions which appear to have occurred then. The first two centuries of the succeeding Middle Helladic (MH) culture see few material advances, with mainland Greece in comparative isolation; but towards the end of the period, around 1600 B.C., trade with Crete becomes intensified, Minoan cultural influence is very strong, and there is a striking increase of wealth at certain sites, most notably at Mycenae, where the splendour of the Shaft Graves discovered by Schliemann has never ceased to astonish. During the Late Helladic (LH or Mycenaean) period, relations are maintained

mainland see Vermeule, *GBA*, with useful bibliography of sites; for the Aegean, esp. in the third millennium, cf. also Renfrew, *ECCA;* further references to the extensive literature on the subject will be found in the bibliographies mentioned in n. 7. Among those scholars who do not accept the conventional views are Palmer, who places the coming of the Greeks about 1600 B.C. and postulates an earlier Luwian invasion of Greece (see *M&M* Ch. VII, with Mylonas' criticisms in *Hesperia* 31 (1962) pp.284-309, esp. pp.296ff.), Hood (*HH* pp.126-30) and Grumach (*TCG*), who believe that the first Greeks did not arrive till about the late thirteenth century B.C. (see Chadwick's criticisms in *Antiquity* 41 (1967) pp.271-5).

not only with Crete but also with the West (South Italy and Sicily) and with the orient. Raw materials are imported from the East, and Mycenaean pottery is exported in increasing quantities into the LH IIIB period. By this time there were established palaces comparable with those of Crete, and writing was adopted in the form of the Linear B script.

Mainland relations with Crete from the MM III period onwards are a matter of uncertainty. It is now generally thought that at the period of intensive Minoanisation on the mainland (MM III/LM I) Cretan influence was purely cultural and not political; some scholars even believe that people from mainland Greece raided Crete in MM IIIB after an earthquake there. It is widely believed that a mainland Greek power conquered Knossos at the beginning of LM II and was responsible for the use there of the Greek language (as indicated by the Linear B tablets). By this date many of the major Cretan settlements had been destroyed, probably as a result of the cataclysmic explosion of the volcano of Thera (Santorini), situated only 70 miles from the north coast of Crete. Knossos seems to have survived longer than the other palaces, but it too suffered a violent destruction, most plausibly to be dated early in the fourteenth century.[9] Thereafter mainland Greece continued to be dominant in the Aegean, and for the rest of the Bronze Age Minoan culture was maintained at a lower level.

Mainland Greece too suffered destructions, though at a later date; some are attested as early as LH IIIB, the latest at the end of LH IIIC (ca. 1100 B.C., at Mycenae).[10] The most likely cause of these destructions is thought to be invasions, the latest of them usually being

9. On the eruption of Thera see esp. Luce, *EAt,* Page, *SVDC* and Marinatos' continuing series *Excavations at Thera.* There is some problem over chronology, as the pottery from the destruction levels at Thera is in the LM IA floral style, while that of the main Cretan destructions is in the LM IB marine style; for a possible solution see Money in *Antiquity* 47 (1973) pp.50-3. For the controversy over the fall of Knossos see esp. Palmer and Boardman in *OKT;* the most likely date for its fall would now appear to be LM IIIA.1 or the beginning of LM IIIA.2, i.e. 1400-1375 B.C. or soon thereafter: see Popham, *DPK* esp. p.85 and Hood, *The Minoans* esp. pp.149f. with useful bibliography (p. 166).

10. On the mainland destructions see esp. Ålin, *EMFF* and Desborough, *LMS.* At Thebes the first destruction may be as early as LH IIIA, but it is clear that the final destruction of the palace was not till IIIB (see n. 105 below).

associated by scholars with the arrival of Doric-speaking Greeks, who established themselves in Crete and certain other islands as well as most of the Peloponnese. By about 1100 B.C. Mycenaean and Minoan civilisation had collapsed, and the following period, though perhaps not quite so destitute as once imagined, is still a Dark Age. It is not until the ninth to seventh centuries B.C. that a high level of material civilisation appears again in Greece with the reopening of trade with East and West, the introduction of the Phoenician alphabet and the beginnings of classical literature and archaic art.

Thus our new sources, and above all the archaeological discoveries, make it possible to construct a picture of prehistoric Greece quite independently of the traditions. But a fundamental problem remains: what is the relationship of the material contained in the legendary stories, ostensibly about the Greeks' own past, to the picture of Greece in the Bronze Age which can now be built up from archaeological and other evidence? Here we must retrace our steps and consider something of the development of scholarly ideas since Grote.

In the latter part of the nineteenth century, though there were some scholars besides Schliemann who attempted to use the traditions for the study of prehistoric Greece,[11] we find a strong tendency towards scepticism about their value as a historical source. There now came into popularity a method of interpreting mythology by a means which had nothing to do with history at all, namely by solar symbolism. The scholars who adopted this approach may be grouped for convenience under the name of the "comparative" school, and the most celebrated among them were F. Max Müller and G.W. Cox. Their method was to take the traditional stories of ancient India, Greece and Northern Europe, and interpret them as referring in large part to natural phenomena, especially to the rising and setting of the sun, and from this a picture was painted of a primitive "Aryan"

---

11. Schliemann was exceptional in adopting such a literal interpretation of the legends, but certain other scholars, though they expressed doubts about the details of the stories, nevertheless made extensive use of the more historical-looking elements in their reconstructions of prehistory: see for example Curtius, *HGCur* I (1868) esp. pp.60ff., 73ff., 97ff., and Duncker, *HGDun* I (1883) esp. Bk. I, Chs. V-VI and VIII.

mythology concerned with this one subject. Such was the enthusiasm of the adherents of solar symbolism that it was spoken of as "this key, which has unlocked almost all the secrets of mythology" (Cox, *A Manual of Mythology* (ed. 6, 1892) p.xiv), and its application knew no bounds: Greek heroes from Perseus to Achilles, from Herakles to Oidipous, were interpreted as solar heroes, and even the Trojan War was understood as "a repetition of the daily siege of the east by the solar powers that every evening are robbed of their brightest treasures in the west" (Cox, op. cit.p.166; cf. his work *The Mythology of the Aryan Nations* (1870) for a more detailed statement of his views). The interpretation of Greek mythology in terms of solar symbolism was severely criticised both for the dubious etymologies on which it rested and the very superficial nature or even non-existence of the supposed similarities between the European, Greek and Sanskrit stories (see for example J.P. Mahaffy, *Prolegomena to Ancient History* (1871), Essay II), but it has continued to influence the interpretation of individual legends even up to the present day.[12]

One of the major factors which has led to its general abandonment has been the growing knowledge of the complex nature of mythology achieved through the study of oral tradition in living societies, made known especially by the works of the great anthropologist Sir James Frazer, whose *Golden Bough* (ed. 1, 2 vols., 1890; ed. 3, 12 vols., 1907-15) had a considerable influence on the interpretation of Greek mythology. What Frazer showed was that one could not expect all traditions to have the same origin: some did arise from primitive beliefs about the universe, but others arose from imagination, and others again from the memory of actual events (for Frazer's division of traditions into myth, folktale and legend, and on the definition of these terms see note[13]). Similar conclusions about the composite nature of

---

12. On the work of Max Müller and on solar symbolism in general see further Rose, *HGM* pp.8f.; Dorson, *TMF* esp. pp.78f. For examples of its very recent use in the interpretation of Greek mythology see P.B.S. Andrews, *G&R* 16 (1969) pp.60-6 and M. Guarducci, loc. cit. below n. 46.

13. For Frazer's classification see *ApLoeb* I pp.xxvii-xxxi, where he draws the following distinction: "Myth has its source in reason, legend in memory, and folk-tale in imagination" (op. cit. p.xxxi). It should be noted that this classification has not been accepted by all scholars; some would prefer to define myths by their function in society

mythology were reached by L.R. Farnell, who made a very thorough study of the Greek cults in his *Greek Hero Cults* (1921) and *The Cults of the Greek States* (5 vols., 1896-1909). Farnell published in 1920 a most useful paper entitled "The value and the methods of mythologic study" (in *PBA* for 1919-20 pp.37-51), in which he pointed out the weaknesses of the "comparative" mythologists, suggesting that "we might establish it as a rule of sanity never to interpret a myth as a nature-myth if the human social explanation lies nearer to hand" (op. cit. pp.44f.). Though Farnell writes of the interpretation of myths as "the chief sporting-ground of human unwisdom", his own approach is one of refreshing common sense.

The early 1930's saw the growth of a more positive attitude to the connexion between Greek legendary traditions and the Bronze Age, much of the credit for which must be given to Martin Nilsson. In his book *The Mycenaean Origin of Greek Mythology* (1932) Nilsson demonstrated, by a systematic study of the distribution of Mycenaean remains and the sites of mythological importance, that the origin of the Greek heroic legends must extend back to the Mycenaean period. His conclusion was all the more remarkable at the time, since it was in radical disagreement with the current methods of interpretation on the continent, where there had arisen a school of thought, represented by such eminent scholars as Wilamowitz, E. Bethe and P. Friedländer, whose fundamental belief was that the great mythological cycles of Greece had been created and put together in post-Mycenaean times, in some instances not until the seventh or sixth century B.C. In contrast to the "comparative" mythologists, the adherents of this so-called "historical" school (on the terms "historical" and "comparative" see Nilsson, *MOGM* pp.2-5) concentrated on the development of the

(see, for example, Malinowski, *SCM* p.249) and to subdivide the broad class into different types, such as cult-myth, aetiological myth, allegory etc. (cf. Hooke, *MEM* pp.11-17). But since with ancient Greek mythology we are dealing with that of a past, as opposed to a living, people, and the original functions of the stories are often very hypothetical, it seems worth retaining Frazer's classification, and it has therefore been broadly followed in this book. On the whole subject see further Rose, *HGM* pp.10-14, Halliday, *IEFT* Ch. I (both of whom adopt very similar categories to those of Frazer) and Kirk, *MMF* Ch. I, "Myth, ritual and folktale".

11

stories within the classical period, and attempted to trace how and where the myths and legends were formed.[14] While these scholars did not completely deny that there were some early elements, they believed them to be few and isolated, and regarded the tradition of any historical events as being so distorted that even their true location was forgotten. Thus Wilamowitz maintained that the house of Agamemnon belonged not to Mycenae or mainland Greece at all but to Kyme and Lesbos, and Bethe concluded from his analysis of Homer that the story of the siege at Troy was put together after 700 B.C. and such historical basis as it contained concerned events which had originally taken place in mainland Greece.[15] What Nilsson showed was that such scholars had relied too exclusively on internal analysis of the literary texts, and in putting forward their hypothetical and often elaborate theories had neglected the archaeological evidence.

Today it is widely believed not only that there is an element of historical memory in many of the Greek traditions,[16] but also that the period to which they refer is to be identified with the Mycenaean Age. Since this belief is obviously of direct relevance to the present study, it

14. For example, Friedländer argued that a major part of the Argonautic saga was developed from various Peloponnesian and Thessalian elements by Greek settlers at Miletos, and that the cycle of Herakles' twelve labours was formed and elaborated on Rhodes from a small nucleus of adventures of a Tirynthian hero (see *RhM* 69 (1914) pp.299-317, and *Herak.* (1907) esp. pp.1-38).

15. For these views see Wilamowitz, *GH* esp. p.241, and Bethe, *Homer* I-III (1914-27) esp. III pp.1-25, 57-86.

16. In this book we are primarily concerned with the possibility that the Greek legendary traditions might reflect historical events. This is not to say that this is the only approach currently adopted to their study. One school of psycho-analysts, for example, following in the footsteps of Sigmund Freud, seeks to interpret stories of both Greece and elsewhere as arising from a universal subconscious and reflecting sexual processes and desires: for a discussion of this view, which is open to many grave criticisms, see Michael Grant, *MGR* esp. pp.150-3, 229-32, and (more critically) Dorson, *TMF* pp.80-3. Another approach is to see in either the content or the structure of myths and other traditional stories a subconscious reflection of particular societies or social conditions: on this sociological approach, which has been particularly favoured in France, see Chapouthier's brief discussion in *AEMG* esp. p.264, and compare also Kirk, *MMF* Ch. II on the theories of Lévi-Strauss (though these have only a very limited potential application to Greek mythology).

will be useful to consider in more detail the reasons which have led to its acceptance by scholars. Perhaps the most important reason is the manifest compatibility of these legends, which the Greeks themselves generally believed to be based upon historical fact,[17] with the archaeological discoveries in the Aegean. Homer had told of a war at Troy and of a powerful city at Mycenae; many years ago, sceptics such as Bryant argued that no city ever existed at Troy and that Mycenae could not possibly be "rich in gold". ("There is no reason to think, that Mycenae was ever a place of such wealth and eminence, as Homer makes it. ... all its primitive splendor seems to be intirely fictitious" (*A Dissertation concerning the War of Troy etc.* ed. 1, 1796, p.78; ed. 2, 1799, p.63).) But Schliemann and his successors showed that there was a "strong-walled" city at the reputed site of Ilium, and that Mycenae was a place of major importance in the Late Bronze Age and "rich in gold" beyond all expectation. Furthermore, as Nilsson himself demonstrated in some detail, it is not merely in isolated cases that the traditional fame of a site has been borne out by archaeological discoveries: there is a definite correlation between the sites of mythological importance and the centres of Mycenaean civilisation, and "this close and constant correspondence precludes any thought of casual coincidence" (*MOGM* p.28).

It was obvious that if the legends were to preserve the memory of the Mycenaean Age, there must be some real continuity between that period and classical Greece. At the time that Nilsson wrote, he was aware of a serious objection to his views, namely that it was possible that Greece in the Late Bronze Age was inhabited by a non-Greek people, so that one would have to postulate, as did Sir Arthur Evans, the transfer of the mythology of this people to later invading Greeks (on this see *MOGM* pp.20-2). Nilsson himself met this difficulty with sound arguments, though he lacked an important part of the evidence for disposing of it which has since become available. Ventris'

---

17. The Greeks did not of course all accept their myths and legends as *literally* true: some, as they transmitted the material, consciously criticised and interpreted it with regard both to chronology and to the details of the stories, sometimes rationalising these in the interest of historical probability, sometimes allegorising them for the sake of morality. Grote's discussion entitled "Grecian mythes as understood, felt, and interpreted by the Greeks themselves" (*HGGro* I, Ch. XVI) is here still most valuable.

decipherment of the language of the Linear B documents as Greek has, in the opinion of the vast majority of scholars, provided the clinching argument for the belief, already suspected by Nilsson and others, that the first immigration of Greek-speaking people was to be placed not later than the end of the Middle Helladic period. The proof that the Mycenaeans were Greeks in a real sense of the word[18] makes it much more reasonable to seek elements of continuity in other aspects of culture, including the legendary traditions. A.J.B. Wace was quick to appreciate the significance of this for the study of Greek mythology, and in his Foreword to *Documents in Mycenaean Greek* (1956) he writes: "A fresh examination of the legends of early Greece must also be undertaken to estimate their archaeological and historical value" (*DMG* p. xxviii).

Finally it has now been recognised, thanks to the work of H.M. and N.K. Chadwick and others,[19] that Greek epic poetry belongs to a class of heroic tradition known from other societies, which, though much elaborated by fiction and overlaid with folktale and myth, was "based on actual people and actual events" (so C.M. Bowra in *The Meaning of a Heroic Age* (1957) p.3). Moreover, since Milman Parry's studies in the formulaic nature of the Homeric poems,[20] it has become possible for us to see how the epic could preserve traditions long after the

18. Protests have recently been raised against the unqualified use of the term "Greeks" for Bronze Age inhabitants of Greece (see, for example, McNeal in *Antiquity* 46 (1972) pp.19-28). While fully accepting the need for a more careful distinction between language, race and culture, I regard it as wholly reasonable to speak of Greeks in the later Bronze Age, thereby emphasising the continuity of language between Mycenaean and Classical Greece. McNeal surely goes too far in saying that it is "perfectly gratuitous to assume any necessary connexion" between the Linear B scribes and the society in which they lived (see his p.22). Even if those who could read and write were in the minority (perhaps only a specialised class of scribes), one can see no reason why Greek should have been used unless it was the language of a substantial element in the population. In this respect there is no true parallel between Mycenaean Greek whose documents are confined to Greece and Crete, and Akkadian in the Near East, which began as a language of Babylonia and then became a *lingua franca* of written documents over a much wider area.

19. See esp. H.M. Chadwick, *HA* (1912); H.M. and N.K. Chadwick, *GL* (3 vols., 1932-40); and for more recent work Bowra, *HP* (1952).

20. See *The Making of Homeric Verse: the collected papers of Milman Parry*, ed. Adam Parry, 1971.

14

period to which they had originally belonged. We also have a number of specific examples, admittedly few but nevertheless well authenticated, where information about political geography, material culture and even actual persons and events seems to have been preserved from the Bronze Age. The fact that "the Iliad and Odyssey describe in accurate detail places and objects which never existed in the world after the Mycenaean era" is described by D.L. Page as "one of the most certain and important discoveries ever made in the field of Homeric scholarship" *(HHI* (1959) pp.218f.), and taken with the evidence from Homeric dialect provides convincing proof that the pedigree of Greek epic extends back to the Mycenaean Age (on the whole subject see further Page, *HHI* esp. Chapters IV and VI).

It is then generally believed that the origins of Greek mythology lie in Mycenaean times. But there remains wide disagreement as to *what proportion of the tradition as now preserved* goes back to that period, and how far it is legitimate to make use of this material as a source for Greek prehistory. Some scholars are extremely sceptical about the value of the legends and totally discount them as a source; others make extensive use of them, even where they are uncorroborated by other sources, and rely on them in great detail; others again are eclectic, taking only certain parts of the traditions as valid evidence, and varying in the degree to which they believe that they may be used. It is by no means obvious upon what criteria the choice between these contrasting attitudes ought to be made. One of the aims of the present work is to reconsider what the legends have to contribute to the study of the Mycenaean Age, and if possible to establish some methods by which they might best be used.

The whole field of Greek mythology is clearly too vast to be discussed in detail in a single book, and an attempt to treat it in outline would be bound to have an element of superficiality. One legend has therefore been taken as the main object of our study, and we propose to examine it both in its own development and in its relation to the other sources, and then, in the final Chapter, to apply what is learnt from this to the wider problem of the historical value of Greek legend in general. The story is that of Kadmos, who traditionally came from Phoenicia and founded Thebes, and there are a number of reasons why this seems particular worthy of study. First, not all legends are equally capable of being correlated with archaeological evidence, since many are concerned with the kind of events which could not be expected to leave any trace in the material record (e.g. marriages, sudden deaths, quarrels, combats with animals); but with legends of migration (as also with those of major wars or conquests) it seems more reasonable to look for a relationship between the archaeological and literary sources. Second, since the story of Kadmos is concerned with an arrival from the orient, the history and archaeology of the Near East may be brought to bear on its understanding, and the linguistic evidence is also relevant. Third, it is a story of particular interest for its own sake, since there has been and still is such radical disagreement among scholars about its interpretation. For example, even in very recent years F. Vian has claimed that Kadmos' Phoenician origin is a mere late invention (this view is discussed below in Chapter IV), whereas M.C. Astour has argued that it reflects the fact of a major Semitic immigration into Greece in Mycenaean times (see Chapter VII). But each of these scholars has used only part of the relevant evidence. In the following chapters an attempt is made to examine the evidence *from all sides*, and it is hoped that such an all-round study may have something to contribute not only to the interpretation of this single story, but also to the understanding of Greek legend as a whole.

CHAPTER II

THE LEGEND OF KADMOS: ITS SOURCES, DEVELOPMENT AND INTERPRETATION

The story of Kadmos was a popular one in antiquity and is related or mentioned by a very large number of classical writers. It also occurs as a theme in art, especially on vase-paintings and coins.[21] The references were collected together at the end of the last century by O. Crusius, and the whole story analysed in his article in W. H. Roscher's *Ausführliches Lexikon der griechischen und römischen Mythologie* (II (1890-7) cols. 824-93). K. Latte some years later again reviewed the literary evidence in a briefer, but very thorough, article in *RE* (X. 2 (1919) cols. 1460-72). These two articles remain the most convenient source of references to the tradition, and are extremely valuable as such, but the views which Crusius and Latte put forward about the origins and development of the legend need to be reconsidered in the light of new work on particular aspects of the subject. A more recent treatment of the legend is that of F. Vian in his book *Les origines de Thèbes: Cadmos et les Spartes* (1963), and we shall have occasion to mention his work frequently in the following chapters.[22]

In addition to these fully documented accounts, there are a number of brief summaries of the legend in the various mythological

21. The artistic representations can make only a limited contribution to the study of the development of the legend, as they are comparatively few in number and confined to a rather narrow range of themes: see Crusius in *Roscher* II cols.824-93 passim and Brommer, *VGH* pp.339f.; cf. also n. 22 on Vian. In this Chapter interest will therefore be centred round the literary sources, but the artistic evidence will be mentioned where it is of importance for variant versions.

22. Vian discusses the evidence of vase-painting, gems and coins, as well as the literary sources. His work is confined to the figure of Kadmos himself, and does not include representations of the abduction of Europê, but these have been treated by Bühler in her recent book *Europa* (1968).

handbooks.[23] The main difficulty with any of these is that they are necessarily a conflation of elements attested at very different dates, and, because the material is much simplified, the reader is often left unaware of how much variation and contradiction was present in the traditions. He will indeed derive from these general accounts only a very vague idea of the story in the earlier periods (i.e. the fifth century B.C. or earlier), as all of them make extensive use of elements from later sources. Nevertheless it is essential for the interpretation of the legend to know, as far as is ascertainable, what formed the most early parts of it and what may be only late accretions.

Our starting point must therefore be a study of the legend and its sources: for this purpose it will be convenient first to consider which elements are known to have formed part of the story by the end of the fifth century B.C., and then to outline the principal new features attested after that date. This arrangement will enable us to discuss some of the factors which appear to have led to the accretion of new elements. Only then will the way be clear for an assessment of the legend's value as a potential source for history, and in subsequent chapters detailed consideration will be given to those elements which appear most likely to reflect historical facts, and which have been interpreted by scholars in widely different ways.

There are no continuous accounts of the legend extant from the fifth century or earlier. The story as it was known then has to be pieced together from the fragments of continuous accounts now lost, e.g. those of the logographers Pherekydes and Hellanikos, and from the allusions to different parts of the story relevant to an author's purpose, such as can be found in the epic, early lyric, Herodotos and the tragedians. These assume that the reader or audience has a prior knowledge of the story: our difficulty is that we do not have this prior knowledge, and we cannot simply assume that the versions found in the later continuous accounts, e.g. Ovid, Hyginus and Apollodoros' *Bibliotheca* (which is not earlier than 140 B.C. and may well be a century or two later), are sound evidence for the early traditions.

---

23. Among the summary accounts the following may be specially mentioned: Rose, *HGM* esp.pp.184-6; Graves, *GM* esp. nos. 58 and 59; and Kerényi, *HG* esp. pp.25-33 (the fullest and best documented of the general accounts).

18

Indeed they often differ, as we shall see, from what is known of the earlier versions, and we therefore begin by narrating the story as known from the brief references of the fifth century or earlier without using any details which are attested only in the later accounts.

According to the references found in sources dating from before the end of the fifth century B.C., Kadmos was a Phoenician, coming from either Tyre or Sidon, and was a son of Agenor, and descended from the Argive heroine Io.[24] He was apparently related to a Phoenician princess Europê, commonly regarded as the daughter of Phoinix. Zeus seduced Europê, taking the form of a bull to do so, and carried her off to Crete, where she became the mother of Minos, Sarpedon and Rhadamanthys.[25]

Kadmos meanwhile went in search of Europê, accompanied by various Phoenicians including a kinsman Membliaros and the heroes Thasos and Kilix (whose relationship to Kadmos and Phoinix was variously explained). Membliaros was left by Kadmos to found a settlement on Thera; Thasos settled on the island of Thasos; Kilix was said to have given his name to the Cilicians.[26]

Kadmos himself proceeded to Delphi, where he consulted the oracle, and was told to follow a guiding cow and to found a city where she sank to the ground. He obeyed the oracle, and followed the cow to the future site of Thebes in Boeotia. He then prepared to sacrifice the cow, and went to seek water from a spring, which he found guarded by

24. For Kadmos as son of Agenor see Soph. *O.T.* 268; for the descent from Io see Bakchylid. XIX. 41-8 Snell and compare Eur. *Ph.* 676-82; for the Phoenician origin see the authorities listed below in nn. 48 and 49 (many of whom also call Kadmos the son of Agenor).

25. The story of Europê is already in Homer and Hesiod (see *Il.* XIV. 321f.; Hes. fr.141 M-W), and she is frequently depicted in art of the archaic and later periods riding on the bull: for details see Bühler, *Europa* pp.51-66, esp. pp.51-5 on representations up to end of the fifth century B.C. On Kadmos' relation to Europê see p.24 with n.33.

26. The principal authority is Herodotos (II. 44, IV. 147, VI. 47, VII. 91). For Kadmos' relation to Phoinix, Kilix and Thasos see the genealogies according to Pherekydes and Euripides (Tables 1 and 2, p.26). There is no justification for calling Membliaros "the nephew" of Kadmos (so How and Wells, *Commentary on Herodotus* I pp.438f.; cf. Hammond, *HGHam* ed. 2 p.654): no precise relationship is given by Herodotos, or by the later sources, where he is referred to simply as one of those with Kadmos (Steph. Byz. s.vv. Anaphe, Membliaros and Thera).

a dragon or huge snake belonging to Ares. He slew this creature and sowed its teeth; up sprang armed men, and a fight ensued. Pherekydes related that Kadmos threw stones among the Spartoi or Sown Men and that they all killed one another except five. These five survivors are mentioned in several writers, and their names are given as Echion, Oudaios, Chthonios, Hyperenor and Peloros.[27]

Next Kadmos married Harmonia, the daughter of Ares and Aphrodite, at a splendid wedding attended by the gods, including the Muses and Graces, who brought gifts. Kadmos himself gave his bride a necklace made by Hephaistos, which was later identified with the famous one by which Eriphyle was bribed. The foundation of Thebes is usually imagined as occurring after this wedding, though Pherekydes apparently placed it before the sowing of the dragon's teeth. One other variant should also be mentioned at this point: Hellanikos seems to have adopted rather a different version of the wedding, in which Harmonia was the daughter of Elektryone (or Elektra) in Samothrace, and sister of Dardanos and Eetion. He further says that Kadmos called the Elektran Gates at Thebes after Harmonia's mother.[28]

27. Eur. *Ph.* 638-89 gives the fullest extant account of these events. Other authorities are Aeschylus and Pindar, who mention the Spartoi several times, Pherekydes (*FGrH* I A, 3 frs.22 and 88) and Hellanikos (*FGrH* I A, 4 frs.l and 96), who differ from one another on certain details, but give the same names for the Spartoi, and Mousaios (fr.18 Kinkel *EGF,* who told of the consultation of the Delphic Oracle. Full references will be found in Vian, *Or. Theb.* pp.27-31, with a useful discussion of the vase-paintings (ib. pp.36ff.).For a new vase (Campanian hydria-calpis) showing Kadmos, with a companion, killing the dragon see Vermeule, *KD.*

28. The chief literary authorities for the wedding are Hes. *Theog.* 937, Theogn. 15-18, Pind. *Pyth.* III. 88-95, Fur. *Ph.* 822f.; for Hellanikos' variant account see FGrH I A, 4 fr.23. In art the wedding appears to be depicted on an Attic black-figure vase (ca.500-480 B.C.) now in the Louvre, in which we see Kadmos and Harmonia (both labelled) in a chariot drawn by a lion and a boar, with Apollo accompanying them, playing his lyre (Brommer, *VGH*p.339, A l; Vian, *Or. Theb.*p.36 no.2). A similar scene on a vase now in Göttingen has been interpreted as showing the same incident (Brommer, *VGH* p.339, A 2; Beazley, *Paralipomena* p.185).The detail of the lion and the boar is not paralleled in the literary sources for Kadmos, though it features in the story of Admetos (Vian. *Or. Theb.* pp.120f.). For Kadmos' settlement at Thebes and for a variant account of the origin of Harmonia's necklace see further Pherekyd. *FGrH* I A, 3 frs.22 and 89.

Not much is related about Kadmos' reign at Thebes. Hesiod tells how he begot five children there, four daughters, Ino, Semele, Agaue and Autonoe, and one son Polydoros. Pindar alludes to Kadmos' prosperity and the sufferings which followed upon it through his daughters. Their stories seem to have been well known by the fifth century, and are certainly very violent: Ino was said to have been driven mad by the gods, and to have leapt into the sea with her children. She subsequently became a sea-goddess under the title Ino Leukothea, and her story is mentioned as early as Homer. Semele was loved by Zeus and became the mother of the god Dionysos; but she was killed by the lightning of Zeus when he appeared to her in his glory. Agaue married Echion, one of the original Spartoi, and became the mother of Pentheus. The tragic story of how she and her sisters tore Pentheus to pieces in a Bacchic frenzy is related in Euripides' *Bacchae* and needs no retelling here. Autonoe, the last of Kadmos' daughters, married Aristaios, and became the mother of Aktaion, who was torn to pieces by his own hounds, according to a well-known version, at the will of Artemis whom he had offended.[29]

No legends are told about Kadmos' son Polydoros, who even after the fifth century maintained a very shadowy existence. His chief function seems to have been to provide a link between the house of Kadmos and that of Oidipous. According to what appears to be the traditional genealogy given by Sophokles and by Euripides in the *Phoenissae,* he was the father of Labdakos, who in turn begot Laios, the father of Oidipous. Curiously enough, Euripides in the *Bacchae* says that Kadmos had no male children.[30]

29. For Kadmos' children at Thebes see Hes. *Theog.* 975-8, Pind. *Pyth.* III. 88-99, *Ol.* II. 22-30 (where allusion is made to the fates of Semele, Ino and an unnamed daughter), and Eur. *Ba.* passim; on Ino see also Hom. *Od.* V. 333-5 and Eur. *Med.* 1284-9, and on Kadmos' children in general see Rose, *HGM* pp.149-53, and 185 with further references.

30. See Soph. *O.T.* 267f., Eur. *Ph.* 5-9 and Hdt. V. 59 for the usual genealogy, and contrast Eur. *Ba.* 1305; for Polydoros in the later tradition see Rose, *HGM* p.185 with his n. 17.

Concerning the death of Kadmos there seem to have been three different traditions current by the fifth century, and they are all combined in the end of Euripides' *Bacchae,* when the god Dionysos appears and foretells the future fate of Kadmos and his wife Harmonia. They will (1) be turned into snakes; (2) drive an ox-waggon to a barbarian country, where they will become leaders of the barbarians and invade Greece, sacking many cities till they reach Delphi, where their success will end; and (3) be saved by Ares and translated to the Isles of the Blest. It is difficult to see exactly how Euripides pictured all three of these fates befalling Kadmos.[31]

This completes our survey of the legend of Kadmos as attested by the fifth century B.C., except for one point, the introduction of writing. Various traditions are recorded among ancient writers about the introduction or invention of letters. For example, Stesichoros said that Palamedes invented them, and other writers refer to an invention by different mythical or heroic figures such as Hermes, Linos or Kekrops. Others favoured the view of an introduction (rather than invention) of writing from outside: thus Hekataios of Miletos and various later authorities said that Danaos first introduced writing from Egypt. Herodotos however says that letters were introduced to Greece by certain Gephyraeans who came over with Kadmos, and he uses both the terms Φοινικήϊα and Καδμήϊα γράμματα in this connexion. Later writers say that Kadmos himself introduced letters from Phoenicia or

31. See the discussion by Dodds in his edition of the *Bacchae* pp.235f. Euripides is the only authority from the fifth century to mention the snake transformation or the exile of Kadmos and Harmonia to a barbarian country, but Pindar (*Ol.* II. 78) refers to Kadmos' translation to the Isles of the Blest. It should be noted that Herodotos (V.61) knows of a tradition that Cadmeians withdrew from Thebes to live among the Encheleis, but he places the event in the reign of Laodamas, the son of Eteokles, some seven generations *after* Kadmos; he also refers to an oracle that Illyrians and Encheleis would invade Greece and perish after sacking Delphi (IX. 42f.), but he does not connect these events with Kadmos and Harmonia. Later tradition connected Kadmos and Harmonia themselves with the Encheleis and Illyrians (see later in Ch. II).

even that he invented them.[32]

After the fifth century B.C. much fuller and more detailed versions of the Kadmos story are found, and many features are now attested for the first time. Not all parts of the story are equally developed: there is for example curiously little elaboration of the events of Kadmos' reign at Thebes. New details are particularly marked in the matters of the hero's genealogical relationships, the settlements, cults and inventions associated with him, the story of the foundation of Thebes (including the consultation of the oracle, dragon-killing and the sacrifice of the cow), and the events of his later life after he had departed to the north. We will now examine these aspects of the legend as they are attested in the later sources, and then consider what motives might have given rise to the new features which they contain. This study in turn will throw into relief those parts of the legend which might be of potential value as evidence for historical events and circumstances.

(1) The genealogy and family relationships of Kadmos

It is perhaps not sufficiently realised how much the different sources vary in the matter of Kadmos' family relationships. In the tradition before the end of the fifth century B.C. Kadmos is described as the son of Agenor, and Europê as the daughter of Phoinix; their relationship to each other is not explicitly stated in any extant sources, but since Phoinix is said by several authorities of this date to be son of Agenor, one may reasonably assume that Europê was regarded as

---

32. For Kadmos' association with letters see esp. Hdt. V. 58, Ephor. *FGrH* III A, 70 fr.105, Timon of Phlius fr.61 (58 Wachsmuth), Lind. Temp. Chron. citing Polyzalos of Rhodes, *FGrH* III B, 532 B, Joseph. *Ap.* I. 10, Diod. Sic. III. 67, V. 57, 74 etc. (cf. Zeno of Rhodes, *FGrH* III B, 523 fr.l). A number of ancient views concerning the origin of letters (including their introduction to Greece by Kadmos) are discussed by Pliny (*N.H.* VII. 192), Tacitus, *Ann.* XI. 14, Hyginus (*Fab.* 277) and the scholiast to Dionys. Thrax (ed. Hilgard, *Grammatici Graeci* I iii, p.183). For a good modern discussion of the views of the ancients see Jeffery in *CH* pp.545-7; cf. also her longer article in *Europa. Festschrift E. Grumach* pp.152-66. An early example of the use of Φοινικήια in the sense of letters is to be found in an inscription from Teos, dated by Tod to 470 B.C. (*GHI* no.23); for the occurrence of ποινικαστάς "scribe" and ποινικάζεν "write" on a newly discovered inscription from Crete (dated to ca. 500 B.C.) see Jeffery and Morpurgo-Davies in *Kadmos* 9 (1970) pp. 118-54. See further below n. 190.

Kadmos' *niece*.[33] After the fifth century many writers continue to refer to Kadmos as son of Agenor and to Europê as daughter of Phoinix the son of Agenor, but a large number allude to them as *brother and sister,*

33. For Phoinix as son of Agenor see Hes. fr. 138 M-W; Pherekyd. *FGrH* I A, 3 fr.21; Eur. *Phrixos* fr. 819 Nauck *TGF* (on which see n. 35). The scholia to Eur. *Rhes.* 29 say explicitly that Euripides made Europê the daughter of Phoinix the *son* of Agenor, and this taken with the *Phrixos* fragment would make her Kadmos' niece. It should however be noted that remarks of such scholiasts may not be entirely reliable evidence for what the older writers said: the scholiast to Aesch. *Suppl.* 317 says that Euripides made Phoinix the *brother* of Agenor, the consequence of which would be to make Kadmos and Europê cousins. Such a relationship for them is not otherwise attested, for although Nonnos also makes Phoinix and Agenor brothers, Europê in his genealogy is daughter of Agenor and thus is Kadmos' sister (see Table 4 on p.27).

The position in other fifth century writers is equally obscure: it is not known where Pherekydes put Europê in the family tree, and the dangers of speculating on the point may be illustrated by the fact that Jacoby says that she must have been the daughter of Agenor and thus Kadmos' sister (see his commentary on fr. 21), while Gomme suggests that she was the daughter of Phoinix and therefore Kadmos' niece (*LCL* p.66). Nor can there be any certainty about their relationship in Hellanikos, since although certain scholiasts to the *Iliad* (II.494) mention Kadmos as Europê's brother and later refer to Hellanikos, this reference cannot be taken as reliable evidence for details of Hellanikos' version (see below in Ch. IV). Herodotos does not mention what relation Kadmos is to Europê.

The most reasonable explanation for these obscurities is that no precise blood-relationship between Kadmos and Europê was firmly established in the earliest tradition. It may be mentioned here that the poet Asios of Samos (? 7th to 6th century B.C.), while describing Europê as daughter of Phoinix, gives a genealogy which differs from any of the other known versions by making her granddaughter on her mother's side of Oineus (an Aetolian king) and aunt of Ankaios, king of the Leleges at Samos (fr. 7 Kinkel *EGF* = Paus. VII. 4. 1). Asios' genealogy may be tabulated as follows:

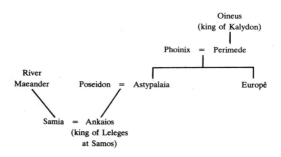

24

sometimes without mentioning the names of their parents, and sometimes making them both children either of Phoinix or — much more commonly — of Agenor.[34] Further variants occur with regard to other members of Kadmos' family, as may be seen most conveniently in the genealogical Tables (pp. 26-8). The following are especially notable:

(a) *Kadmos' mother.* The only authority to mention the name of Kadmos' mother before the end of the fifth century is Pherekydes, who names her as Argiope (see Table 1). After the fifth century the mother of Kadmos, and also of Europê, is normally named as Telephassa — alternatively as Telephae or Telephe — (see for example Apollodoros' genealogy in Table 3); but Argiope also appears occasionally, either as mother of both Kadmos and Europê (so Hyginus, see *Fab.* 6 and 178), or of Kadmos alone (see the genealogy given by Schol. ad Eur. *Ph.* 5 in Table 6). A very late variant found in a number of Byzantine writers makes Kadmos' mother Tyro, the eponymous heroine of Tyre (see the genealogy according to Eustathios in Table 5, and cf. Bühler, *Europa* p.9).

(b) *Kadmos' brothers.* In the earlier tradition there were two principal variants concerning Kadmos' relation to the heroes Phoinix, Kilix and Thasos: in Pherekydes, Phoinix was Kadmos' half-brother, Kilix was Phoinix's son, and Thasos was Phoinix's grandson (see Table 1). In Euripides on the other hand, if we can trust the evidence of the

It is of interest to note that Astypalê (sic) occurs as sister of Europê in the eclectic genealogy given by the scholiast to Eur. *Ph.* 5 (see Table 6 on p.28). But no indication is given in the fragment of Asios that his Europê was related to Kadmos: nothing is told about her except her genealogy, which seems to be a local Samian variant (see Latte in *RE* X. 2 col. 1462).

34. Apollodoros (III.1.1) reports the two principal variants, that Kadmos and Europê were both children of Agenor, or that Europê was the daughter of Phoinix. For Kadmos and Europê as both children of Phoinix see Konon *FGrH* I A, 26 fr. 1, *Narr.* XXXII and XXXVII, and Schol. ad Hom. *Il.* II 494. Further details concerning the ancient variants are given by Frazer in *ApLoeb* I p.296 n. 2 and p.298 n. 1.

25

TABLE 1: *Kadmos' genealogy according to PHEREKYDES*
(FGrH I A, 3 frs.21, 86, 87)

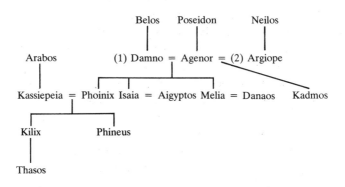

TABLE 2: *Kadmos' genealogy according to EURIPIDES*
(Phrixos fr. 819 Nauck *TGF*, on which see note 35)

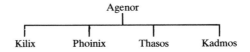

TABLE 3: *Kadmos' genealogy according to APOLLODOROS*
(Bibl. II. 1. 3f., III.1.1)

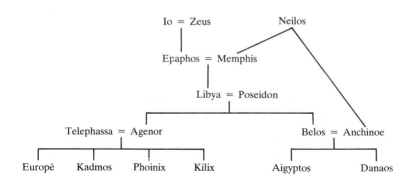

TABLE 4: *Kadmos' genealogy according to NONNOS*
(Dionysiaka II. 679-98, III. 266-319)

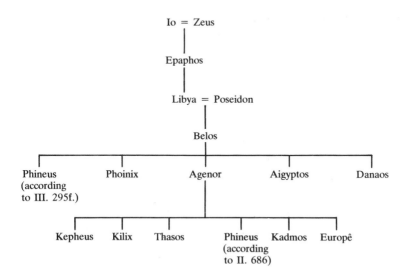

27

TABLE 5: *Kadmos' genealogy according to EUSTATHIOS (ad Dion. Per. 899, 912)*

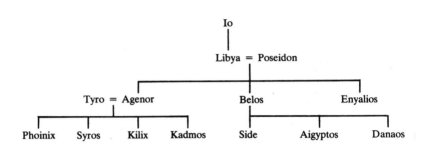

TABLE 6: *Kadmos' genealogy according to SCHOLIAST on EURIPIDES Phoenissae 5*

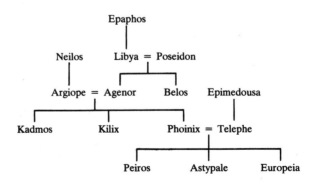

Phrixos,[35] Kadmos, Phoinix, Kilix and Thasos all appear to have been brothers (see Table 2). After the fifth century these four are still normally regarded as brothers, but additional heroes with oriental connexions also appear in the family. Kepheus and Phineus, for instance, whom Euripides made the children of Belos (fr. 881 Nauck *TGF* = Apollod. II.1.4), appear in Nonnos as children of Agenor and Kadmos' brothers (see Table 4). Similarly Eustathios includes among Kadmos' brothers Syros, eponymous hero of Syria (see Table 5).

(c) *Kadmos and Danaos.* Here once more the later tradition contrasts with that found in sources up to the fifth century B.C. Before the end of that century, though Kadmos and Danaos are separately attested as descendants of Io, the only authority to mention a specific relationship between them is Pherekydes, who makes Danaos and his brother Aigyptos the husbands of Kadmos' half-sisters (see Table 1). After the fifth century B.C. Kadmos and Danaos (and also Aigyptos) are regarded as cousins, their fathers Agenor and Belos being brothers (see Table 3, the genealogy according to Apollodoros). There are however other variants, for example that found in Nonnos' account of the story where Danaos and Aigyptos appear as uncles of Kadmos (see Table 4).

(2) **The search for Europê and the various settlements attributed to Kadmos**

In sources after the fifth century B.C. many more details are given about Kadmos' search for Europê, and he or his Phoenicians are accredited with further settlements in various parts of the Aegean.

(a) *Samothrace.* Hellanikos' version of a Samothracian parentage for Harmonia (see above p.20) probably presupposes a visit of

---

35. The *Phrixos* fragment (819 Nauck *TGF*) is preserved partly by Tzetzes and partly by the scholia to Eur. *Ph.*; and the beginning of it is also quoted by Aristophanes (*Ran.* 1225f.). But in spite of this the fragment presents one crucial difficulty: in the first two lines it refers to Kadmos as the son of Agenor, while in lines 7-9 it says that Agenor had *three* sons, Kilix, Phoinix and Thasos. Possibly the text is corrupt: Schneidewin emended *Thasos* to *Kadmos*; possibly the sense is incomplete and Euripides was going on to explain that Kilix, Phoinix and Thasos were sons by another wife or something similar. There can be no doubt that Euripides made Kadmos the son of Agenor, as this is both included in the part quoted by Aristophanes and attested in other plays.

Kadmos to Samothrace. In the later attested traditions we are told a great deal about a visit of Kadmos to this island: he was imagined as having been initiated into the mystery cult here (Diod. V. 48); and even as having met Harmonia at the festival and carried her off (Demagoras *FHG* IV p.378 fr.1). His mother Telephae was said to have accompanied him in his search for Europê, and some said that she died in Samothrace (Mnaseas *FHG* III p.154 fr.28; for alternative views see below under (b) Thrace). Ephoros gave a circumstantial account of Kadmos' visit to Samothrace, and mentioned a festival there in which ritual search was made for the abducted bride Harmonia (*FGrH* II A, 70 fr.120). Kadmos himself was identified with Kadmilos, one of the "Kabeiroi" or mystery gods of Samothrace.[36]

(b) *Thrace.* Another area in the north of Greece believed to have been visited by Kadmos is Thrace, where according to Apollodoros his mother Telephassa died (Apollod. III. 1 and 4; for yet another version, that she died in Thasos, see Steph. Byz. s.v. Thasos). The local historian Hegesippos of Mekyberna in his *Palleniaka* tells how Kadmos came to Thrace seeking Europê, but found not the daughter of Phoinix but another lady of the same name, after whom the whole northern part of the mainland was called *(FGrH* III B, 391 fr. 3). Other writers associate Kadmos with the mines of Mt. Pangaion (see below p.32); the mythographer Konon gives an interesting account of a visit of Kadmos to Chalcidice (on which see below p.41).

(c) *Other places.* Other visits attributed to Kadmos or his followers may be more briefly mentioned: a visit to Rhodes is attested by Diodoros and the *Lindian Temple Chronicle* (see below p.32); Strabo briefly reports that there were once Arabs (Ἄραβες) in Euboea who had come over with Kadmos (X.1. 8); and the Etymologicum Magnum (s.v. Taphioi) refers to Taphian pirates who were originally some of

36. See the obscure reference in Lykophron, *Al.* 219f. and Nonnos, *D.* IV. 85-90; on Kadmos in Samothrace see further Vian, *Or. Theb.* pp. 64-8 and Latte in *RE* X. 2, cols. 1468f. For the sake of convenience I have here followed the common practice of referring to the mystery gods of Samothrace as Kabeiroi. This is in accordance with the usage of ancient authorities such as Herodotos, but it should be noted that the title has not been confirmed in the inscriptions from Samothrace, and this has led to the suggestion that the Samothracians themselves may have avoided the term Kabeiroi (see Hemberg's discussion, *Kab.* pp.73-81).

the Phoenicians sent out with Kadmos. The island of Anaphe was said to have been called Membliaros after Kadmos' companion of that name who was the founder of Thera (Stephen of Byzantium, s.vv. Anaphe, Thera and Membliaros). It is interesting to see that Hyginus (*Fab.* 178) says that Kadmos' brother Phoinix went to Africa and that the Carthaginians ("Poeni") are called after him. Phoinix fitted ill into the scheme whereby Agenor told his sons to leave Phoenicia and not return until they had found their sister, with the result that they settled in the places called after their name. Hyginus or his source seems to have found a happy solution to the problem!

(3) The dragon-killing and foundation of Thebes

Very much more detailed accounts are now found of the events associated with the foundation of Thebes. What purports to be a versified reply of the Delphic Oracle is preserved in the scholia to Euripides' *Phoenissae* (line 638). From this and from other sources we learn of such details as the name (Pelagon) of the man from whose herd the guiding cow came, and of a peculiar moon-shaped marking on her (see Apollod. III. 4. 1; Hyg. *Fab.* 178; Paus. IX. 12. 1); we are also told of the very route she took to Thebes (Ov. *Met.* III. 19; Nonn. *D.* IV. 319-347), and are even given the information that the town Mykalessos was so called because the cow lowed (ἐμυκήσατο) there (Paus. IX. 19. 4).

Full details are also given of how Kadmos killed the dragon: the earlier logographers had differed as to whether Kadmos had used a sword or a stone for this (see Hellanik. *FGrH* I A, 4 fr. 96; Pherek. *FGrH* I A, 3 fr. 88); Nonnos makes the hero use both sword and stone, while Ovid gives him stone, javelin and spear.[37] In addition, we may note that while the early literary sources are silent about any companions of Kadmos at this point, they regularly feature in the later accounts, and some of the scholiasts actually supply names for certain of them (see Schol. on *Dion. Per.* 391 and Tzetzes *ad Lykophr.* 1206). The later poets also make Kadmos plough the land before sowing the

---

37. See their lurid and detailed accounts of the combat: Nonn. *D.* IV. 356-417 and Ov. *Met.* III. 50-94. In some of the vase-paintings before the end of the 5th century B.C. Kadmos is armed with a pair of spears (Vian, *Or. Theb.* p.46).

dragon's teeth, a detail found in the Argonautic saga and essential to the story there (for the ploughing see Ov. *Met.* III. 104f., Nonn. *D.* IV. 424-6; also Stat. *Theb.* IV. 434-42). Other late writers (e.g. Apollod. III. 4. 2) record the detail that for killing the dragon Kadmos had to undergo servitude to Ares for a period of eight years.[38]

(4) Cults and inventions associated with Kadmos

In the fifth century B.C. certain cults were said to have been introduced by Phoenicians associated with Kadmos, though not by Kadmos personally (see Hdt. II. 44 on Thasian Herakles, and cf. also id. V. 61 on the Gephyraeans and the rites of Demeter Achaia at Athens). Later sources associate Kadmos himself with the building of altars or a temple to Athene and Poseidon on Thera (Schol. b and f on Pi. *Pyth.* IV. 10, Schol. f referring to Theophrastos); with the founding of a temple to Poseidon at Rhodes; and with the dedication there to Athene Lindia of a tripod inscribed in Phoenician letters (Diod. V. 58; for the tripod see also the *Lindian Temple Chronicle* col. 3 = *FGrH* III B, 532 fr.1 B-C). Kadmos' wife Harmonia is further said in a tradition reported by Pausanias (IX. 16. 3) to have dedicated images made from the figureheads of Kadmos' ships to Aphrodite at Thebes under the three titles of Ourania, Pandemos and Apostrophia.[39]

In addition to religious cults, Kadmos was credited with the invention or introduction of various arts. Besides writing, which was already associated with his name in the fifth century sources (see above p.22), he was said to have invented the mining and working of gold in Thrace (Plin. *N.H.* VII. 197; cf. Clem. Al. *Strom.* I. 16), and to have discovered bronze-working at Thebes (Hyg. *Fab.* 274) and stone-quarrying either in Thebes or Phoenicia (Plin. *N.H.* VII. 195) or at Mount Pangaion in Thrace (Clem. Al. *Strom.* I. 16). Certain aqueducts at Thebes were also said to have been first built by him

38. The elements of oracle and animal guide, dragon-killing, and servitude to Ares are discussed at length by Vian in *Or. Theb.* Chs. III-V, pp.76-118. His discussion is useful for its full documentation, though some of his conclusions are very speculative.

39. The cult of Aphrodite Ourania is independently attested at Kythera, where Herodotos (I. 105) says that it was of Phoenician origin; on this and the evidence of cults in general see further Ch. IV pp.80-2.

(ps.-Dikaiarchos, *FHG* II p.258, fr.59 sect.12), and in one tradition the first introduction of the lyre was attributed to him (Nikomachos of Gerasa, *Exc.* 1, p.266 Jan).

(5) Kadmos' adventures after he left Thebes

In the fifth century B.C. there already existed a tradition that Kadmos and Harmonia retired from Thebes after their reign there, but the end of Euripides' *Bacchae*, our source for this information, does not in its present state tell us where they were believed to have gone (cf. above p.22). Later sources say that Kadmos and Harmonia withdrew to Illyria, and they associate them with a variety of places over a large area (see Map 2) stretching from Epeiros in the south to the river Naron in the north (north of modern Dubrovnik in Yugoslavia). In Epeiros Kadmos and Harmonia were said to have arrived in the company of one Epeiros, daughter of the Sown Man Echion, who brought with her the dismembered remains of Pentheus. Parthenius (32. 4) who reports this information derived the name Epeiros from this woman, and mentions the spot where she was believed to have been buried. Kadmos and Harmonia themselves were imagined as having proceeded further north to live in Illyria among the Encheleis (see, for example, Ap. Rh. IV. 516-21; Apollod. III. 5. 4). Apollodoros tells us that they assisted the Encheleis against the Illyrians, that Kadmos became their king, and in his old age begot a son Illyrios. This son is also mentioned by Stephen of Byzantium (s.v. Illyria) who however places Illyria in north-east Greece near Mt. Pangaion! Kadmos was further believed to have founded two towns in Illyria; one was Lychnidos, situated on Lake Lychnida (the modern Lake Ochrid); the other was Bouthoe (Budua, near Rhizonium, on the coast north of Epidamnos), which was said to have received its name from the swiftness of the oxen which drew Kadmos' chariot there.[40]

---

40. For the foundation of Lychnidos see Christodoros (a writer of the late 5th century A.D.) in Anth. Pal. VII. 697; for Bouthoe see Philo of Byblos, *FGrH* III C, 790 fr. 32. Certain other late writers, Choiroboskos of the 4th to 5th centuries A.D. and Theognostos of the 9th century A.D., mention a son of Kadmos named Rhizon, eponymous hero of the area (for references to Rhizon see Crusius in *Roscher* II col. 852).

The transformation of Kadmos and Harmonia into snakes was also placed in Illyria, and various monuments and objects associated with the pair are reported in different areas. Stephen of Byzantium attests that their tombs (τάφοι) were shown near the rivers Aoos and Drilon (s.v. Dyrrhachion, referring to Eratosthenes); Apollonios of Rhodes (IV. 516) speaks of their τύμβον as being on the Ἰλλυρικοῖο μελαμβαθέος ποταμοῖο (possibly intending the river Drilon, possibly the Gulf of Rhizonium - see Vian, *Or. Theb.* p.126); Dionysios the Periegete (390-7) refers to the ἐρικυδέα τύμβον of Kadmos and Harmonia somewhere in this area, and pseudo-Skylax (24) mentions a ἱερόν to them near the river Rhizon. In the same context both these writers refer to two rocks associated with Kadmos and Harmonia, and Dionysios tells us that they stand on the spot where Kadmos and Harmonia were turned into snakes, and that if danger threatens the area the rocks miraculously move close together (for a discussion of these passages see Müller, ap. Skyl. 24, *GGM* I, pp.30f.). Nonnos describes how Kadmos and Harmonia were turned into stone snakes, and locates this event somewhere on the Illyrian coast (see *D.* IV. 418-20, XLIV. 115-8, XLVI. 364-7). Other writers refer to a θεμείλιον (foundation; Gow: "abode") of Kadmos and Harmonia in the area of the rivers Drilon and Naron (Nicander, *Ther.* 607), and to a μνημεῖον at a celebrated spot (now unidentifiable) named Kylikes (Phylarchos *FGrH* II A, 81 fr.39). Such allusions well illustrate Strabo's remark (VII. 7. 8) that the scenes of the stories about Kadmos and Harmonia in this part of Greece were still pointed out in his day.

How are the many differences between the earlier and later versions of the story to be accounted for? Undoubtedly the absence of some elements in sources dating from the fifth century B.C. or earlier results from the comparative paucity of the sources themselves, and from the fact that writers like Herodotos tend to assume that the story is already known to their readers. In other words, some of the details which are not attested until the later sources may nevertheless be very old, and we cannot rule out the possibility that they might preserve a memory handed down from the Mycenaean period. At the same time, common sense tells us that a good many elements in the story attested only in later sources are in fact later accretions and inventions, and the longer the gap is between any supposed historical events lying behind the legend and the first attestation of a detail, the greater are the chances that the detail has arisen from a cause which has nothing to do with historical tradition. Many details of this kind may be readily recognised as soon as the processes by which they appear to have been introduced into the story are understood, and it is to these processes that we now turn our attention.

Two main factors can be seen at work in the elaboration of the legend. The first of these is the **imaginative treatment of the story:** as Nilsson has written, "the artistic vein of the Greeks seized the myths and reshaped them freely" *(Cults, Myths, Oracles, and Politics in Ancient Greece* (1951) p.11). The role of imagination in the reshaping of the myths is most obviously seen in those literary genres where the story is adapted to the writer's artistic purpose, namely in drama and in narrative poetry. Thus the Greek tragedians not only choose the versions of the stories which best suit their purpose, but on occasion even seem to invent with some freedom. In the story of Kadmos we may note that Euripides in one play (*Ph.* 6f.) follows the traditional version going back to Hesiod that Kadmos left a son called Polydoros, while in another play (*Ba.* 1305), where it makes the situation more poignant, he says that he had no male children (cf. p.21 above). It is sometimes assumed that where the tragedians are giving versions not found before they must be drawing on lost epic sources, but the possibility of their originality in plot and detail of events should not be underestimated (cf. H.C. Baldry's discussion in "The dramatization of the Theban legend", *G&R* 3 (1956) pp.24-37).

This imaginative treatment is even more striking in the narrative poems of Roman writers like Ovid and Statius, and in the late epic of Nonnos. These authors give full and detailed accounts of such events in our story as the killing of the dragon and the sowing of its teeth, in which they appear to be sometimes conflating older variant versions, for example as to the weapon used by the hero, sometimes borrowing details from other sagas, such as the motif of ploughing the land before sowing the teeth, and sometimes inventing on their own initiative, as is obviously true in many of the details of their descriptions (on the dragon-fight cf. above p.32 with n. 38).

A less obvious aspect of imaginative treatment is the filling up of gaps in the tradition through a desire to give as full an account as possible of the story. This motive may be detected not only in the poetic versions but also in the work of the early prose writers, the logographers, who were evidently eager to fill up the gaps left by Homer and the epic, and to supply readers with the names of mythological characters and other details not given in the earlier versions.[41] In our legend we find that the logographers Pherekydes and Hellanikos are the first authors to give names for the Sown Men (Spartoi) who sprang up from the dragon's teeth instinct above p.20 with n. 27). This process by which it was attempted to fill out all the details of a story continues into late antiquity, and is particularly noticeable in the mythographers, lexicographers, Byzantine chroniclers, and scholiasts. Thus late scholia are the first sources for the detail of the names of Kadmos' companions killed by the dragon (cf. above p.31). This motive is aptly described by Burn as "the instinct of the tidy Greek mind to clear up all the puzzles and to leave no frayed edges hanging, and above all to know what relation everybody was to everybody else, and everybody's genealogy back to Adam" (MPG p.18). Certain genealogical details were undoubtedly created by the imagination in order to link different heroes with one another, and it is interesting in comparing the various genealogies given for Kadmos to see how the scholiast to Euripides' Phoenissae manages to combine in one family tree several variants in the tradition concerning the parentage of Kadmos and Europê (see Table 6, where both Argiope and Telephe appear; see also n. 33 on the genealogy given by Asios of Samos). Thus imagination would appear to have played an important part in the filling out of details in our story, though it must be stressed that it is often far from certain exactly which details arise solely from the invention of the poets and prose writers and which they may have acquired from earlier traditions now lost.

41. For this aspect of the work of the logographers see esp. Forsdyke, GBH pp.143, 164-6; cf. also Bury, AGH pp.18f., on the interpolation of links in pedigrees by Pherekydes, and Pearson, EIH p.161, on Hellanikos.

The second main factor at work in the development of the story is the **application of reason to the traditions**, which resulted in ethnographical speculation and other similar processes. The Greeks of the fifth century and later were interested in the origins of peoples and their relationship to one another, as can be seen time and again in the writings of Herodotos (cf. Gomme's discussion, *LCL* pp.241f.). Ethnographical speculation sometimes took the form of the placing of the eponymous heroes of different races in a genealogical relationship with one another, and in the legend of Kadmos this process must have been at work not only in late writers such as Eustathios or his source, who includes the eponymous heroes of Syria, Tyre and Sidon in the family tree of Kadmos (see Table 5), but also as early as the fifth century B.C. when there is attested a relationship between Kadmos and the various eponymous heroes of Cilicia, Phoenicia and Thasos. Such ethnographical theorising by which the eponymous ancestors of different peoples are placed in a genealogical relatioship with one another is not limited to the Greeks, and the family tree of Kadmos in its later form, such as that found in Apollodoros (see Table 3), may aptly be compared with Genesis Chapter X, where the eponymous ancestors of many peoples including the Egyptians, Canaanites, Elamites, Assyrians and Aramaeans are placed in a family relationship and made descendants of three sons of Noah.

Historical or ethnographical speculation may also account for other elements in the story of Kadmos, such as association of the hero with certain cults like that of Aphrodite Ourania, first connected with him in late sources, but already known as Phoenician in the fifth century B.C. (see above p.32 with n. 39). It could also account for the increase in the number of places said to have been visited by Kadmos and his companions in the later sources (cf. the versions of visits to Thrace, Rhodes and Anaphe cited above pp.30f.), and for such details as the association of Phoinix with the Carthaginians, and of Kadmos with the Taphian pirates and with Ἄραβες in Euboea (on these see above p.30). Speculation on the etymology of place-names and the occurrence of homonyms may also have influenced the development of the legend, as is witnessed perhaps by Kadmos' association with Mykalessos, Epeiros and Bouthoe (see above pp.31, 33) and possibly also by the tradition (discussed below pp.48f.) connecting him with

Egyptian Thebes.[42]

A further motive which may prompt the introduction of new elements into a tradition is local antiquarianism, by which the origins of local monuments and of the names of places and objects are explained. This process can be seen at work in Kadmos' association with local aqueducts at Thebes (see above p.32), in the explanation of the name of the Elektran Gates there by reference to Harmonia's mother Elektra (see p.20) or to a sister of Kadmos otherwise unknown named Elektra (see Pausanias IX. 8. 4), as well as in the versions of the legend which linked Kadmos with various objects and monuments in Illyria (see above p.34).

A similar process is that of religious syncretism, whereby the god or hero of one area is identified with a similar one belonging to a different place. This can be observed in Kadmos' identification with the god Kadmilos in Samothrace (see above p.30) and possibly also in the identification of Harmonia with a local goddess of the mysteries there (cf. above p.30 and Latte, *RE* X. 2 col. 1468). Another example is the confusion of Europê and Astarte at Sidon (for which see Lucian, *Syr. D.* 4). It has also been conjectured that the elaborate Illyrian episode may be due, at least in part, to the identification of Kadmos with a local snake god there (see R.L. Beaumont in *JHS* 56 (1936) p.196).

These two main factors of imagination and reason overlap, and sometimes both are at work in a single process acting upon the tradition, as is seen most strikingly in the **rationalisation** of the old

---

42. It must be noted however that ethnographical and historical speculation of this sort is one of the more difficult processes to detect, since often the possibility is open to interpret individual parts of the tradition either as basically historical or as arising from ancient theorising. Thus some of the elements mentioned above could be historical even though proof for this is lacking (see esp. Ch. VIII on possible Phoenician settlement on certain islands and n. 183 on the tradition of an Egyptian origin for Kadmos).

stories in the interests of historical verisimilitude. This process goes back at least to the fifth century B.C., when many Greeks could no longer take all the old stories at their face value, but when they still believed in them as substantially true historically. One of the oldest attested rationalising versions is to be found in the writing of Herodotos in the early chapters of his *Histories* (I. 1-5), when he discusses the causes of the Persian Wars and gives a rationalising version of the rapes of both Io and Europê, attributing these to Persian and Phoenician sources. On Europê, he says that certain Greeks, who would have been Cretans, put in at Tyre and carried off the king's daughter. This was done, according to the Persian account, in reprisal for the kidnapping of Io from Argos by Phoenician sailors. Whether or not Herodotos himself believed these versions, he puts them forward with the appearance of serious intent, and they certainly show that such rationalising interpretations of the myths were known in the fifth century B.C.

Rationalisation becomes increasingly common in the later sources, beginning with mythographers such as the notorious Palaiphatos, who lived in the fourth century B.C., and Euhemeros of similar date, who has given his name to Euhemerism, the rationalising interpretation of myth whereby the gods are interpreted as men. It is worth considering these rationalising versions at some length, since they are both interesting for their own sake and important for the study of possible historical elements in the tradition.

The rape of Europê by Zeus in bull form naturally called for some new interpretation (we have already seen how in the version given by Herodotos the girl was carried off by Cretans). Palaiphatos (Περὶ Ἀπίστων XV) asks how a maiden could be expected to mount the back of a wild bull, or how a bull could swim all the way from Phoenicia to Crete. Zeus, he says, would have found a better means of transport! The truth is that a man from Knossos named Tauros carried off the king's daughter while fighting at Tyre. Such a version of the rape is found not only in the writings of the sceptical Palaiphatos; later historians provide similar rationalising accounts with every appearance of seriousness. Thus the historian Arrian of the later second century A.D. says that king Tauros of Crete took Tyre in a naval battle and carried of Europê (*FGrH* II B, 156 fr. 58), and

various Byzantine writers give a similar version.[43] A human character named Tauros, it is interesting to note, reappears in rationalisations of the Minotaur story (see Plutarch, *Life of Theseus* XIX). It would surely be a grave error to take such accounts as these at their face value, and to postulate an Achaean king of Crete (whether named Tauros or not) who raided Tyre; yet writers can still be found who favour such interpretations of the legend (see R. Graves, *GMI* (1955) p.197, and J. Zafiropulo, *HGAB* (1964) pp. 24-7, 91f. on which cf. below p.193).

Another element which came in for rationalisation was the killing of the dragon and the sowing of its teeth. Palaiphatos' account here is very instructive: according to his version (Περὶ ᾿Απίστων III) Kadmos left Phoenicia after a quarrel with his brother Phoinix over the kingship. At Thebes he fought a battle with a man named Drakon and his followers. Drakon possessed some tusks (ὀδόντας) of ivory which Kadmos seized when he killed him. But Drakon's companions stole the tusks and ran away, becoming scattered over a large area; they then collected together and attacked the Thebans and the people said: "Τοιαῦτα κακὰ ἡμᾶς ὁ Κάδμος εἰργάσατο Δράκοντα ἀποκτείνας· ἐκ γὰρ τῶν ἐκείνου ὀδόντων πολλοὶ καὶ ἀγαθοὶ ἄνδρες γενόμενοι σπαρτοὶ καταγωνιάζονται ἡμᾶς". From this true event, Palaiphatos tells us, the myth of Kadmos was invented: "τούτου τοῦ πράγματος ἀληθινοῦ γενομένου ὁ μῦθος προσανεπλάσθη". One notices here the dependence of the "explanation" on punning phrases in the Greek - ἐκ τῶν ἐκείνου ὀδόντων "from his teeth" or "because of his tusks", ἄνδρες... σπαρτοί "sown" or "scattered" men, δράκοντα "a dragon" or the proper name Drakon. Much use is made of similar ambiguities in other rationalistic versions. Thus the historian Androtion of the fourth century B.C. says that the Spartoi of Thebes were so called because they were a mixed and scattered race who gathered together to follow Kadmos from Phoenicia (*FGrH* III B, 324 fr. 60), and Drakon appears as a human being and the father of

---

43. See Bühler, *Europa* p.35, referring to Ioan. Malalas, Ioan. Antioch., Georg. Hamart., Kedrenos and Eustathios. A different rationalisation, also found in very late writers, was to interpret *Tauros* as a figurehead, name, or some other part of a ship: see Bühler, *Europa* p.36, and cf. the obscure reference in Lykophron, *Al.* 1299.

Harmonia in the version of Derkylos, a writer of unknown date *(FGrH III B, 305 fr.6)*.

A more subtle rationalisation of the legend is to be found in the Διηγήσεις of Konon, a mythographer writing in the Augustan age. According to his account *(FGrH I A, 26 fr.1, Narr.* XXXII and XXXVII), which may rightly be termed "pseudo-historical", Kadmos was a powerful Phoenician living in Egyptian Thebes, which at that time was under Phoenician rule. He was sent out ostensibly to look for his sister Europê, but in fact to win the continent of Europe. He was accompanied on the expedition by an Egyptian named Proteus who left Egypt in fear of the King Bousiris. Together they visited Thasos and Thrace, and Proteus settled in Pallene, winning the friendship of the local king, marrying a local heroine, and eventually becoming king himself. Kadmos went on to Boeotia, where he fortified Thebes and defeated the local inhabitants by the use of ambushes and strange new weapons, the helmet and shield, previously unknown to the Greeks. The Boeotians in their terror said that the ground had sent up armed men. This according to Konon is the "ἀληθὴς λόγος"; all the rest is "μῦθος καὶ γοητεία ἀκοῆς". It is interesting here to see the political motivation for Kadmos' expedition (cf. Palaiphatos' version p.40 above), the explanation of how newcomers succeeded in overcoming the local inhabitants, and the combination of a Phoenician and Egyptian origin for Kadmos. A more frivolous version of the story is that of Euhemeros, who said that Kadmos was the king's cook at Sidon and ran off with a flute girl from the court named Harmonia *(FGrH I A, 63 fr. 1)*!

One other rationalistic version must also be recounted, since it is remarkable for its attempt to explain the myth that Kadmos was the grandfather of the god Dionysos. This is an account of Kadmos given by Diodoros of Sicily (I. 23), who attributed it to certain Egyptian priests. In this version Kadmos was a citizen of Egyptian Thebes, whose daughter Semele was violated by an unknown person. She gave birth to a son, who had a striking resemblance to the representations of the god Osiris. To avoid disgrace to his daughter, Kadmos gave out that his grandson was the god Osiris and paid sacrifice to him. Later the story was taken back to Greece by Orpheus, and it became accepted that Dionysos was the son of Kadmos' daughter Semele at Boeotian

Thebes. The religious syncretism by which Dionysos is identified with Osiris is noticeable in this version, and is characteristic of this whole section of Diodoros' work (I. 10-29), where he gives what purports to be an Egyptian account of the early history of mankind in which the Greek gods are identified with Egyptian counterparts, and numerous Greek heroes are said to have been originally Egyptian.[44]

Rationalisation would then seem to have affected the story of Kadmos to a considerable extent, and ludicrous though some of these rationalising versions are, they are instructive as showing firstly the ancient expectation that historical truth lay behind the myths if properly interpreted (compare Thucydides' attitude to the traditions in his "Archaeologia"), and secondly the need to distinguish different types of material in the traditions and not to look for historical fact in details which may well be due only to the ancient application of reason and imagination to what is in origin either myth or folktale (on these terms see above Chapter I p.10 with n. 13).

It will be useful therefore, if we are to isolate possible historical elements in the story, to consider briefly which elements are most likely to have originated in folktale and myth. Folktale elements are generally recognisable by the universality of their themes, which may occur in several different cultures (a most useful aid in the identification of these is S. Thompson's *A Motif-index of Folk-literature*). In our story, the motifs which would appear most obviously to belong to folktale are those of the animal-guide leading to the site of a city (see Thompson, *MIFL* under Class B 150, esp. B 155 to 155.4, and below n.165), the slaying of the dragon, which is paralleled in many different cultures (see Thompson, *MIFL*, Class B 11.11 and cf. also Class A 531), and the throwing of stones among Kadmos' armed adversaries, the Spartoi.[45]

Mythical elements are not always so easily distinguished, apart

44. On this part of Diodoros see Burton, *DSC* esp. pp.101-3 and p.106 (on syncretism). She is however wrong to say that "according to Greek tradition, Cadmus had no connexion whatever with Egypt" (*DSC* p.101): see Ch. III pp.47f. with n. 51.

45. For parallels see Mary Grant, *The Myths of Hyginus* pp. 42 and 46 on *Fab.* 22 and 28; cf. also Halliday, *IEFT* p.53, where it is concluded that this element is a "*märchen* incident".

from aetiological myth, which is recognisable by its explanatory function. They are generally identifiable by the divine origin of the characters in the story, a matter on which there is not always agreement among scholars, though Farnell has established some useful principles for distinguishing heroes of divine and human origin (see his discussion in *GHC* Chapter II). In the story of Kadmos a number of elements already found in the tradition by the fifth century B.C. are best interpreted as religious myth. These are (a) the rape of Europê by Zeus in bull form, which may perhaps be a version of the ἱερὸς γάμος or union of a god with an earth- or fertility-goddess (so Farnell, *GHC* pp.47f.); (b) the birth of the god Dionysos to Kadmos' daughter Semele, where Dionysos, a palpably divine character, enters into the story (Kadmos' daughter Semele has herself often been interpreted as an earth-goddess: see for example Dodds' edition of the *Bacchae* (ed. 2, 1960) pp.63f.); (c) the transformation of Kadmos' daughter Ino Leukothea into a sea-goddess (Ino Leukothea is already a goddess in Homer, and her divine origin would seem to be confirmed by the evidence of her widespread cult: see Farnell, *GHC* pp.35-47); and (d) the metamorphosis of Kadmos and Harmonia into snakes, where we are dealing with clearly supernatural events, most plausibly interpreted as expressing the belief that the pair attained immortality (cf. Rose, *HGM* p.186).

What elements then in our story might *prima facie* appear to have originated in memory of the past, or, in other words, belong to the category of legend in the strict sense of the term? The most important would seem to be those connected with Kadmos' origin in the East, namely the idea that the founder of Boeotian Thebes came from Phoenicia, that he and his Phoenician companions founded various settlements on their way to Greece, and that Kadmos introduced writing to Greece. A further element for which a historical basis would seem possible is the withdrawal of the Theban royal pair to Illyria. The elements just listed have neither the universality of folktale nor any clear religious function;[46] they are connected with real places, Thebes,

46. Kadmos' wanderings in the Aegean in search of Europê have sometimes been interpreted as religious myth. Thus in the 19th century Cox proposed that Europê was "simply the broad-spreading flush of dawn, which is first seen in Phoinikia, or purple

Phoenicia and Illyria; we may therefore tentatively assign them to the category of legend and consider the possibility of a historical basis for them.[47] Out of these elements the Illyrian episode has recently been discussed at some length by Vian *(Or. Theb.* pp.124-33), who concludes that it may possibly rest on a "substrat historique", though there is not sufficient archaeological and other evidence to identify this with precision. (He thinks tentatively of a migration from Thebes to Illyria.) We shall here concentrate our attention on the *oriental* elements in the story, and for this purpose it will be necessary to examine more closely the ancient evidence for the belief in Kadmos' Phoenician origin, and then to consider the various ways in which this part of the tradition has been interpreted by modern scholars.

region of the morning", and he took Kadmos' journey to Greece as "the weary search of the sun through the livelong day for his early lost sister or bride" (*MAN* I p.438). But such theories were based upon the general belief, now discredited, that all Greek mythology had a solar origin, and on etymologies of doubtful worth (e.g. Φοινίχη as "land of the sunrise"). Others have understood Europê as originally a moon-goddess (so Frazer in *GB* Vol. IV (ed. 3, 1911) p.73; cf. also ib. p.88); but although there is some very slight evidence for lunar elements in late versions (e.g. the references to a moon-shaped marking on Kadmos' guiding cow) it is extremely doubtful if these can be used as evidence for the original role of Kadmos and Europê (see further Cook, *Zeus* I pp. 524-6, 538-41, arguing for the belief that Europê was originally an earth-goddess, who later became associated with the moon after she was identified with Astarte at Sidon). It is curious to see how a solar interpretation is still to be found in the very recent work of Guarducci, *EpG* I (1967) pp. 44f., where Kadmos is described as "un antico dio solare venerato sulla rocca di Tebe".

47. It must be emphasised that it is only *prima facie* that these elements belong to the category of legend: as we have seen earlier in Ch. II, the story of Kadmos was much elaborated and reinterpreted over a period of time by the Greeks themselves, and it has already been suggested that the traditions of certain of Kadmos' settlements in the islands could have arisen from ancient ethnographical speculation (see above p.37). But examples of such speculation are especially difficult to identify (cf. n. 42), and we cannot rule out the possibility of a historical origin for elements of this kind. Conversely Kadmos' association with writing, which we have here listed as *prima facie* having a possible historical basis (see further Ch. VIII) might in fact be only the result of intelligent speculation (cf. Ch. IV p.83). In the same way certain other arts associated with Kadmos such as mining (for which see further below Ch. VIII with nn. 195, 197, 202) could conceivably belong to more than one of these categories.

CHAPTER III

THE PHOENICIAN ORIGIN OF KADMOS IN THE ANCIENT TRADITION AND IN MODERN SCHOLARSHIP

There are abundant references to the origin of Kadmos in Greek literature from the fifth century B.C. onwards, and the belief is very widely attested that he came to Greece from the East. The normal view appears to be that Kadmos came from Phoenicia (Φοινίκη); this is the first country to be mentioned explicitly as his place of origin, and the one attested in many sources. A most important early witness to this belief is Herodotos, who mentions the Phoenician origin several times and believes that Kadmos originated in Tyre. He clearly knows a developed form of the story, and ascribes settlements at Thera and Thasos to Kadmos and his Phoenicians, and the introduction to Greece of the alphabet (Φοινικήια or Καδμήια γράμματα) to certain Gephyraeans, who were originally Phoenicians who had come over with Kadmos. The evidence of Euripides is also important. He mentions the Phoenician origin of Kadmos in three of his plays, and makes much of it in the *Phoenissae*. He also refers to the Phoenician origin of Europê several times. Apart from these two writers, the fifth century logographer Hellanikos of Lesbos may have told of the origin of Kadmos and Europê in Phoenicia.[48]

After the fifth century, references become very frequent. Kadmos himself is often said to have introduced letters from Phoenicia, or even to have invented them (see above p. 22 with n. 32). Knowledge of a Phoenician connexion for him is shown by a large number of authors including various historians — Ephoros and Androtion in the fourth

---

48. For the Phoenician origin in the 5th century B.C. see Hdt. II. 49, IV. 147, V. 57ff., and cf. also I. 2, II. 44, IV. 45; Eur. *Ph.* 5f., 638ff. and passim, *Ba.* 170-2, 1025, *Phrixos* fr. 819 Nauck *TGF* (on Kadmos); id. *Cret.* fr. 472 Nauck *TGF, Phrixos* fr. 820 Nauck *TGF, Hyps.* fr. 1 iii 20f. Bond (on Europê); *FGrH* I A, 4 fr. 51, on which see Ch. IV p.71.

45

century B.C., Hegesippos of Mekyberna probably in the same period, Diodoros of Sicily in the first century B.C., Josephus the Jewish historian in the first century A.D. and Arrian in the second century A.D.; by geographers such as Strabo, by the great traveller Pausanias in the second century A.D., by mythographers as early as Palaiphatos and Euhemeros in the fourth to third centuries B.C., as well as the later Konon, Apollodoros, Hyginus and the Vatican Mythographers; and by writers of all types of literature, including Isokrates, Timon of Phlius, Nicander, Ovid, Martial, the Elder Pliny, Tacitus, Plutarch, Lucian, Achilles Tatius, Clement of Alexandria, Oppian, Dictys Cretensis, Diogenes Laertios, Eusebios, Nonnos, and also by various Byzantine chroniclers, lexicographers and scholiasts, among them Ioannes Malalas, Stephen of Byzantium and the Etymologicum Magnum.[49]

One cannot be certain exactly what territory these authors intended by Phoenicia, but the fact that several of them mention Tyre or Sidon as the home-town of Kadmos or Europê or call them "Tyrian" or "Sidonian" seems to indicate that they understood Phoenicia to mean the coastal territory associated with the historical Phoenicians whose chief cities were Tyre and Sidon rather than as having a much wider significance (on the ancient usage of the name Phoenicia see further Ch. V with notes 83 and 84). The connexion with Tyre is attested by Herodotos, Euripides, Arrian, Palaiphatos

49. For the Phoenician origin in the sources after the 5th century see Ephor. *FGrH* II A, 70 fr 105; Androt. *FGrH* III B, 324 fr. 60; Hegesipp. Mek. *FGrH* III B, 391 fr.3; Diod. Sic. III. 67, IV. 2, V. 57, 58, 74; Jos. *Ap.* I. 10; Arr. *An.* II. 16. 1, *FGrH* II B, 156 fr.58 (cf. fr.64); Str. IX. 2.3; Ps.-Skymn. 661f.; Paus. IX. 5. 1, IX. 12. 2; Palaiph. III Festa; Euhem. *FGrH* I A, 63 fr. 1; Konon *FGrH* I A, 26 fr.1, Narr. XXXVII; Apollod. III. 1; Hyg. *Fab.* 178; Myth. Vat. I. 149, II. 77 Bode *SRML*; Isokr. X. 68; Aristot. fr. 501 Rose; Timon of Phlius fr. 61 (58 Wachsmuth); Polyzalos of Rhodes in Lind. Temp. Chron. *FGrH* III B, 521 B. 3; Nicander *Ther.* 608; Ov. *Met.* II. 840ff.; Martial VI. 11. 7; Plin. *N.H.* VII. 192, 195, 197; Tac. *Ann.* XI. 14; Plut. *Sull.* 17, *De Exilio* 17. 607b; Lucian *Syr. D.* 4; Ach. Tat. II. 2, cf. I. 1; Clem. Al. *Strom.* I. 16; Oppian *Cyn.* IV. 291; Dict. Cret. *Epist.* 1, *Prologus* 1; Diog. Laert. I. 22; Euseb. *Chron.* p. 46 Helm, *Praep. Ev.* X. 4. 4, X. 5. 1 Mras; Nonn. *D.* I. 45ff., III. 320-4, IV. 231 etc.; Hesych. s.v. *Phoinikiois grammasi;* Ioan. Mal. *Chron.* 2, p.30 Dind.; St. Byz. s.v. Membliaros, cf. s.v. Onkaiai; Suda s.v. Kadmos, citing an epigram of Zenodotos; Et. M. s.v. Taphioi, cf. s.v. Hellotia; Schol. Aesch. *Sept.* 486; and Schol. Dion. Thrac. p.183 Hilgard.

Oppian, Pausanias, Nonnos and Ioannes Malalas; with Sidon by Euripides, Isokrates, Euhemeros, Nicander, Lucian, Hyginus, Nonnos and scholiasts to the *Iliad* (II. 494) referring to Hellanikos. The distinction in the literary sources between Tyre and Sidon as Kadmos' home-town should not be pressed, since often both Sidonian and Tyrian seem to be used loosely as synonymous with Phoenician, as can be seen most clearly in Ovid's use of the terms in his narrative of the story of Kadmos and Europê.[50]

Phoenicia was not, however, the only oriental country associated with Kadmos. He was connected with Egypt in the genealogy of Pherekydes (see Table 1 above p.26), and from about 300 B.C. a rival tradition or belief is attested, that Kadmos came originally from Egypt, though it should be noted that many of the authorities for this believe that Kadmos was a foreigner in Egypt rather than an Egyptian by nationality. The first explicit mention of Egypt as the country from which Kadmos set off is found in the fragments of Hekataios of Abdera (or Teos), who himself visited Egypt and wrote in the time of Ptolemy I a history of the country. In a fragment of this history preserved by Photios and Diodoros of Sicily *(FGrH* III A, 264 fr.6), he says that Kadmos, together with Danaos, was a leader of the foreigners who were expelled from Egypt at the same time as Moses and the Jews. Other authorities for an Egyptian connexion are Diodoros of Sicily himself, who in his highly rationalised account makes Kadmos a citizen of Egyptian Thebes; Konon, who says that Kadmos was a Phoenician whose native city was Egyptian Thebes, the Phoenicians at that time having their capital in Egypt; Eusebios (third to fourth centuries A.D.), who makes Kadmos migrate from Egyptian Thebes to

---

50. For the Tyrian connexion see Hdt. I. 2, II. 49, IV. 45; Eur. *Ph.* 639, *Hyps.* fr. 1 iii 20 Bond; Arr. *FGrH* II B, 156 fr. 58; Palaiph. XV Festa; Oppian *Cyn.* IV. 291; Paus. V. 25. 12; Nonn. *D.* III. 323, IV. 303; Ioan. Mal. *Chron.* 2, p.30 Dind.; cf. also Propertius III. 13. 7; Martial VI. 11. 7. For the Sidonian connexion see Eur. *Ba.* 171, 1025, *Phrixos* fr. 819 Nauck *TGF;* Isokr. X. 68; Euhem. *FGrH* I A, 63 fr. 1; Nicander *Ther.* 608; Lucian *Syr. D.* 4; Hyg. *Fab.* 178; Nonn. *D.* I. 46, III. 324; cf. also Ach. Tat. I. 1. Ovid tells the story in *Met.* II. 839ff.; see esp. II. 840, 845; III 35, 129 for his use of the terms Tyrian and Sidonian. Similar loose use of Tyrius and Sidonius has been noted also in Virgil and Statius: see Austin's commentary on *Aen.* IV. 75. Eusebios makes Kadmos reign at both Tyre and Sidon, having migrated to Phoenicia from Egypt (*Chron.* p.46 Helm).

Phoenicia; the universal historian Charax (of uncertain date); Nonnos (fifth century A.D.), who makes Kadmos a Phoenician who has lived in Egypt, his father Agenor having founded Egyptian Thebes; the scholia to Lykophron compiled by the brothers Tzetzes in the twelfth century A.D.; and the scholia to Euripides' *Phoenissae*. In addition, Hyginus says that Kadmos took letters from Egypt to Greece, and Stephen of Byzantium records it as the opinion of certain scholars that Kadmos named the town Bouthoe (which he founded in Illyria) after Bouto in Egypt. Finally, Pausanias, who himself followed the view of a Phoenician origin for Kadmos, refers to the alternative school of thought, saying that those who say that Kadmos was an Egyptian and not a Phoenician are contradicted by the fact that he sacrificed the guiding cow to the goddess Athene under the Phoenician name of Onga (Onka) and not under the Egyptian name of Sais.[51]

It is clear from the literary authorities mentioned that there was a widespread belief that Kadmos came to Greece from the East, whether from Egypt or Phoenicia. In addition to these more direct references there are other indications of the extent of the tradition: (1) Various coins from Tyre and Sidon dating from about 125/6 B.C. to the second or third centuries A.D. depict Kadmos or Europê;[52] Achilles Tatius (II. 2) tells how the story of Kadmos was related at a festival of Dionysos at Tyre; Ioannes Malalas *(Chron. 2. pp.30f. Dindorf)* describes a festival at Tyre named κακὴ ὀψινή which commemorated the abduction of Europê from there one evening. These pieces of evidence would seem to suggest that the idea of a Phoenician origin for Kadmos was fostered at Tyre (on Kadmos at Tyre see further Crusius in *Roscher*II cols.870-2, and Latte in *RE*X. 2 cols.1470-1). (2) Kadmos is associated directly or indirectly with various cults in Greece believed by the ancient authors who discuss

51. For an Egyptian connexion see Diod. Sic. I. 23; Konon *FGrH* I A, 26 fr. 1, *Narr.* XXXII and XXXVII; Euseb. *Chron.* p.46 Helm (ann. Abraham 562), *Praep. Ev.* II. 1. 24f. Mras; Charax *FGrH* II A, 103 fr. 14; Nonn. *D.* IV 265ff.; Tz *adLyk.* 1206; Schol. Eur. *Ph.* 638; Hyg. *Fab.* 277; St. Byz. s.v. Bouthoe; Paus. IX. 12. 2.

52. The coins depict Europê and the bull, Kadmos slaying the dragon, joining hands with Harmonia, giving a papyrus scroll to the Greeks, and, almost certainly, setting off by ship on his voyage to Greece: see Hill, *CGCP,* Index II (Coin Types) s.v. Europa and Kadmos; cf. also Vian, *Or. Theb.* pp.43f. with pl. X; Willetts, *CCF*p. 153; Jidejian, *Tyre* p.101 with figs. 94-8.

them to be Phoenician, for instance, that of Athene Onka at Thebes, that of Aphrodite Ourania also at Thebes and that of Tyrian Herakles at Thasos (these and other cults associated with Kadmos will be discussed below in Chapter IV pp.80-2). (3) In sources dating from the fifth century B.C. onwards Kadmos is said to be descended from Epaphos, born to Io in Egypt, to be brother (or less commonly son) of Phoinix, the eponymous hero of the Phoenicians, and to be related to various heroes with oriental connexions (see above pp.23-9 with the genealogical Tables, and p.36). Such genealogies imply the belief that the peoples typified by the eponymous heroes are related, and the placing of Kadmos in relationship with them would seem to presuppose a recognition of his oriental connexions.

There are however two pieces of genealogical evidence which might appear to be in opposition to the general picture of an oriental origin for Kadmos. The first is the *very* late reference in Photios' lexicon and the Suda to Kadmos as son of Ogygos (a legendary king of Thebes), which is a variant not found elsewhere: but even this would not preclude an oriental connexion, and in any case the reference is one which can have little claim to represent a genuine ancient tradition.[53] The second is the fact that Kadmos was normally believed

53. In Photios and the Suda (s.v. Ὠγύγια κακά) Kadmos is mentioned as son of Ogygos, and in a separate entry (s.v. Ὠγύγιον) it is suggested that the adjective Ὠγύγιος, meaning "ancient", might be derived from the fact that Ogygos was the first king of Thebes - a reference to a belief (for which see Varro R.R. III. 1-3) seemingly in conflict with the traditional foundations of the city by either Kadmos or Amphion and Zethos. It would however be highly dangerous to take these passages together as evidence for an ancient rival tradition that Kadmos was originally Greek, since (1) there is no explicit attempt to make Kadmos Greek, and although Ogygos may have been originally a Boeotian hero, the traditions about him vary enormously: he is also said to be Attic, he was connected with Lycia, and even in certain sources made an early king or founder of Egyptian Thebes (see Wörner in Roscher III cols. 684-94; Miller in RE XVII cols. 2076-8); and (2) the idea of Kadmos as son of Ogygos first appears in the *ninth century A.D.*: it would seem probable that the association of these heroes, rather than reflecting an old belief that Kadmos was a Greek, resulted from a desire to reconcile two unrelated traditions about early Thebes. (Crusius in Roscher II cols. 843-4 attempts to emend the text of Pherekydes (FGrH I A, 3 fr.21) to include Ogygos in the genealogy of Kadmos given there; but his arguments are unconvincing, and in any case the effect of accepting his suggestion would be to bring Ogygos into an oriental genealogy rather than to make Kadmos Greek.)

to be a descendant of Io. Since Io is traditionally an Argive heroine, might it be argued that Kadmos, by virtue of his descent from her, was thought to be in any sense Greek? In answer to this we can only say that no ancient author ever claims that Kadmos was a Greek or denies that he was a foreigner; on the contrary he is cited, along with Danaos and Pelops, as typical of the "βάρβαροι", foreigners, who came to Greece and made themselves rulers of cities there (see the hostile references in Isokrates, X. 68 and XII. 80, and Plato, *Menexenos* 245c-d). If we are to press the details of Kadmos' genealogy (which is probably an unwise procedure), we should find that Kadmos had Greek blood in him through his great-great-grandmother Io, Egyptian blood through his great-grandmother Memphis, Libyan blood through his grandmother Libya, Phoenician blood through his mother Telephassa, not to mention divine blood through Zeus and Poseidon! (See the genealogy according to Apollodoros given in Table 3, p.27.)

Let us then sum up the conclusions that can be drawn about the ancient beliefs concerning Kadmos' origin. Before the fifth century B.C. there is no explicit reference to it. From the fifth century onwards he is thought by all the authors who refer to his origin to be oriental, coming to Greece either from Phoenicia, where he is associated with Tyre and Sidon, or from Egypt, where however he is often regarded as a foreigner. Although comparatively early sources trace his descent from Io, at the same time these authors also give him Phoenician or Egyptian ancestors, and the late reference to Kadmos as the son of Ogygos cannot be taken as implying the existence of any real doubt that he was an oriental. We may then conclude that the tradition of Kadmos' eastern origin is very well attested in the sources from the fifth century B.C. onwards, and the striking point about the ancient evidence is the lack of any rival tradition that Kadmos was a Greek.

We come now to consider what modern scholars have made of this part of the legend. In general his supposed origin in Phoenicia has roused much more scholarly interest and controversy than his Egyptian connexion, which has been largely ignored, or else dismissed as a later accretion, possibly influenced by the desire to link the founder of Boeotian Thebes with Egyptian Thebes.[54] The Phoenician origin too has often been thought to be merely the result of learned theory, or else due to invention or misunderstanding, but at the same time there have always been scholars who have maintained the genuineness of the tradition. Opinions have naturally changed over the years with the discovery of new evidence, particularly the archaeological evidence, and it is important in assessing the arguments of scholars to bear in mind what other sources of knowledge were available to them besides the literary references.

Whereas up to the early part of the nineteenth century the tradition of Kadmos' Phoenician origin was commonly accepted as having a historical basis,[55] since that time the growth of a more sceptical outlook (cf. above Ch. I pp. 2f.) has led many scholars to deny that the legend reflects the fact of a settlement in Greece from Phoenicia, whether Phoenicia is defined in a strict or loose sense.[56] A

54. Cf. Vian, *Or. Theb.* pp.32-5, Latte, *RE* X.2, col. 1471, von Geisau, *Der kleine Pauly* III (1969) col. 41. A number of scholars have sought to combine the traditions of Phoenician and Egyptian origins in historical reconstructions: see, for example, later in Ch. III on L.B. Holland, W. Dörpfeld and J. Bérard. For a very recent scholar who takes up the Egyptian origin, postulating an Egyptian settlement at Thebes, see Spyropoulos in *AAA* 5 (1972) pp.16-27, and cf. Ch. VIII, n. 186.

55. The belief that the legend of Kadmos reflects a historical settlement in Boeotia may be found in numerous scholars before the mid-nineteenth century, including Banier, *MFA* esp. Vol. III (1740) pp.391ff.; Gillies, *HAG* (1786) p.6; Mitford, *HGMit* I (ed. 2, 1789) pp.20, 31, 89; and Heeren, *SPAG* (1829) p.65. A striking dissentient was Jacob Bryant (for whom cf. above Ch. I), who writes, characteristically: "I cannot be induced to think, that Cadmus was ... a Phenician. Indeed I am persuaded, that no such person existed" (*NSAM* II (ed. 3, 1807) pp.428f.; cf. also the preface to Vol. I p.xxxv). Bryant's attitude is here very much the same as it was to the question of history in the Homeric poems; he conflates into a whole all the details about Kadmos regardless of their source and date of attestation, and then shows that no one person could have done so many things.

56. Phoenicia as strictly defined is only the narrow strip of the Levantine coast from about Arvad in the north to Mt. Carmel in the south, including in its territory the cities of Tyre and Sidon (see Map 3), and this appears to be the sense in which the term is used by many of the classical writers who connect Kadmos with Φοινίκη (cf. above p.46 and see further Ch. V with nn. 83 and 84). Modern usage of the term varies: older scholars generally use it in this strict sense, but more recent writers often employ "Phoenician" loosely to include not only the historical Phoenician seafarers of the Iron Age, but also their Canaanite and other West Semitic precursors, who occupied this and a much larger area in the second millennium B.C. Thus the term has quite often been applied to the culture of Ras Shamra in North Syria (on this see Ch. VI with n. 132).

comprehensive list of such scholars would be very long indeed, but it seems worthwhile to single out the most important contributions to this view of the question. We take as our starting point the work of K.O. MÜLLER, who, as early as 1820, seriously called in question the genuineness of Kadmos' Phoenician origin. Müller, who has been looked upon as the founder of the so-called "historical" school of mythology (see Nilsson, *MOGM* p.8 and cf. above p.11), argued that the story of Kadmos' origin in Phoenicia, like that of Danaos and Kekrops in Egypt, had no basis in historical fact. Kadmos was in his view originally the god of a Theban tribe, and the idea of his being a Phoenician arose when later invading tribes (the Boeotians) misunderstood the purely Greek proper name Phoinix as an ethnic meaning "the Phoenician" *(Orchomenos und die Minyer* (1820) pp.113-22). Müller's arguments had a long-lasting influence, and Kadmos' Phoenician origin was similarly dismissed as being due to a mistake or invention by many scholars, including T. KEIGHTLEY, who attributed "the fable of his Sidonian origin" to the Phoenicians themselves *(The Mythology of Ancient Greece and Italy* (1831) pp.293-4), A.W. VERRALL, who suggested in his edition of Aeschylus' *Seven Against Thebes* (1887, p.xviii n. 3) that the Phoenician origin may have been the "deliberate fabrication of quasi-historic antiquarians", by J. TOEPFFER in *Attische Genealogie* (1889, pp.294f.), and by F. STUDNICZKA, who confidently maintained that the identification of the Kadmeioi with the Phoenicians was "eine von den haltlosesten Hypothesen der ältesten naiven Geschichtsconstruction der Hellenen" *(Kyrene. Eine altgriechische Göttin* (1890) p.56).

Another distinguished member of the "historical" school to reject Kadmos' Phoenician origin was E. BETHE, famous for his theory that the legend of the Trojan War had its origin in events originally located in mainland Greece and only later transferred to Asia Minor (cf. above p.12). Bethe argued that Kadmos, Europê and Phoinix were all originally Boeotian heroes *(Thebanischer Heldenlieder* (1891) p.20), and in this he was followed by O. CRUSIUS in his article in Roscher's lexicon *(Roscher* II (1890-97) esp. cols. 880-6). Other scholars equally denied that the Phoenician origin was historical, and offered different and more elaborate explanations of how the tradition arose.

Thus E. MEYER in his monumental *Geschichte des Alterthums* (Vol. II (ed. 1, 1893) pp.147-53) maintained that Kadmos was merely an invention of genealogical poets as the eponym of the Kadmeia, while Europê was originally a Boeotian earth-goddess and Phoinix a Cretan god, who later became identified with the invented eponymous hero of the Phoenicians. According to his complicated hypothesis, first Europê was made the daughter of Phoinix in Crete, then "die genealogische Poesie" made Kadmos brother of Phoinix and uncle of Europê, and thus he became a migrant from Phoenicia. Later still Kadmos was made the brother of Europê, and all Phoenician settlements in the Aegean whether real or imaginary were ascribed to him and his contemporaries. Meyer strongly emphasised his belief that the story of Kadmos was "das Erzeugnis eines literarischen Processes, nicht historische Ueberlieferung", and that one thing could be certain: "eine phoenikische Ansiedlung in Boeotien weder aus der Europa-, noch aus der Kadmossage gefolgert werden darf" (substantially the same conclusions were expressed in the later edition of this work; see Vol. II. 1 (1928) pp.254f. with note 3 there).

Writing about the same time as Meyer, K.J. BELOCH also attacked the idea of Phoenician settlement in Boeotia as the historical basis of the Kadmos story, asserting: "Phoenikische Ansiedlungen aber haben am aegaeischen Meere niemals bestanden". Kadmos, Europê, Phoinix and Minos were for him all "good Greek gods", and the idea that they were Phoenician arose because "der echtgriechische Sonnenheros Phoenix (der 'blutrote') hat es sich gefallen lassen müssen, zum Semiten gestempelt zu werden, und mit ihm sein Bruder Kadmos" *(Griechische Geschichte* I (ed. 1, 1893) pp.75f., 167f.; see also his article "Die Phoeniker am aegaeischen Meer" in *RhM* n.f. 49 (1894) pp.111-32). It is of interest here to note the influence of the old solar interpretation of Greek legend (on which see above Ch. I, pp.9f. and n.46).

Beloch, like Meyer and the earlier scholars whose work we have been discussing, believed in a very extensive reshaping of Greek legend in the historical period. When they were writing, Mycenaean archaeology was in its infancy, and it is worth remembering that even in the 1890's it was still a very live issue whether or not the Phoenicians were the originators of the Mycenaean culture.[57] With the great archaeological interest that Schliemann's discoveries engendered and the subsequent excavations carried out by various scholars in all parts of Greece, archaeological arguments began to play a more prominent part in the controversy concerning Kadmos and the Phoenicians, and were often used to support the conclusions of literary analysis and mythological theory. Thus the excavators of Thera denied the historicity of a Phoenician settlement on Thera, attributed by Herodotos and others to a kinsman of Kadmos, largely on the grounds that Phoenician remains were absent from the archaeological discoveries there (see *Thera* I (1899) ed. HILLER VON GAERTRINGEN p.142 and *Thera* II (1903) ed. H. DRAGENDORFF p.235). The Greek excavations at Thebes which followed in the years 1906-29 naturally roused great interest, and after only a few preliminary reports had been published scholars were concluding that the absence of Phoenician objects confirmed their suspicions about the literary evidence (see for example R. DUSSAUD in *Les civilisations préhelléniques* (1910) pp.250f.). A.D. KERAMOPOULLOS, the excavator of Thebes, after several seasons' work there also concluded that Kadmos' Phoenician origin could not have been based on historical fact, since Phoenician remains were entirely lacking at Thebes and the city seemed to have followed the normal Mycenaean development (*AD* 3 (1917) pp.5, 62f.). His conclusions have been much quoted by later scholars.

Meanwhile the study of the literary tradition continued. L. MALTEN re-examined the legends of Thera, and concluded that Kadmos' presence there was the result of the speculation of a noble Spartan family of the sixth century B.C.: "Dei theräische Kadmos entstammt also der Spekulation eines Adelsgeschlechtes, das in 6. Jahrhundert aus Sparta in Thera einzog und nun in seinem und Spartas Interesse eine Vorgeschichte der Insel konstruierte. Ein ethnographischer Wert wohnt demnach den Kadmosleuten auf Thera nicht inne" *(Kyrene (Philologische Untersuchungen* 20, 1911) p.184).

Shortly after this, the Phoenician element in the early literary

---

57. For the view that Mycenaean civilisation was Phoenician see esp. Helbig, *SQM* (1896), and for criticisms see Myres, *CR* 10 (1896) pp.350-7. See further the work of Reinach cited below in n. 68.

tradition about Kadmos was subjected to a close scrutiny by the historian A.W. GOMME in an article entitled "The legend of Cadmus and the logographi" *(JHS* 33 (1913) pp.53-72 and 223-45). This article is perhaps the most important contribution to the subject made by any modern scholar, and though written over sixty years ago still remains the most thorough assessment of the early literary evidence that has been attempted. In it Gomme examines the chronological development of the story of Kadmos from the literary sources, and suggests that the idea of a Phoenician Kadmos may have originated as a learned theory of the logographers, presumably in Asia Minor. Gomme's arguments are important and will be discussed in detail in Chapter IV, where the conclusions which he has drawn from the evidence will be reconsidered.

K. LATTE's article on Kadmos in Pauly-Wissowa appeared soon after Gomme's article and embodied his conclusions. Latte however stressed his belief that Kadmos' genealogy belonged to S.W. Asia Minor, in particular to Caria, Samos and Miletos, and he argued that the idea of Kadmos' Phoenician origin arose at Miletos, where the whole saga was developed and received its canonical form. This was an old theory maintained by many German scholars, including Wilamowitz, E. Schwartz and P. Friedländer, to whose work Latte refers *(RE* X. 2 (1919) cols. 1462f.; see further below n.78).

The case against Kadmos' Phoenician origin must have seemed overwhelming: in 1921 L.R. FARNELL was able to write that "the days are past when we believed in Kadmos the Phoenician" *(GHC* p.44). Yet in some ways Farnell's statement seems to be the high-water mark of scepticism, and since that date few scholars can be found who make such categorical denials of a historical foundation for the legends of Phoenicians as did the early German scholars.[58]

---

58. This is not to suggest that since the appearance of Farnell's *GHC* in 1921 no scholars can be found who reject the possibility of a historical basis for the tradition of Kadmos' Phoenician origin. A sceptical attitude continued to appear in Germany, where the conclusions of Latte in *RE* and of Wilamowitz in various works (e.g. *Pindaros* p.33) had a strong influence: see particularly Schober in *RE(T)* (1934) col. 1454; Ziehen, ib. col. 1526; and Philippson, *DGL* I.2 (1951) p.511. Cf. further n. 63 below on scholars who have been influenced by Gomme and Vian.

Recently however the literary evidence for the story of Kadmos has been discussed by F. VIAN in his book *Les origines de Thèbes*(1963), where he rejects any historical foundation for the Phoenician origin. Vian's attitude (to which we shall return in the next Chapter) is on the whole exceptional; the general tendency in recent years has been to accept some ultimate historical basis for the idea of a Phoenician Kadmos; the disagreement which occurs is about what historical facts gave rise to the tradition.

It may be helpful to divide the scholars who accept some historical basis for the Phoenician origin into two groups: (1) those who accept that there was a foreign or non-Greek element at Thebes, but do not believe that these foreigners came from the eastern Mediterranean; and (2) those who believe that there were once settlements in Greece, or at least at Thebes, of people who came from the eastern Mediterranean and might be described (whether accurately or loosely) as Phoenician.

(1) Scholars in this first group often understand Phoenicia in the tradition to have meant originally something quite different from what the classical Greeks or present-day writers intend by the term. In the early decades of this century when Minoan Knossos was being excavated and scholars were attempting to evaluate the place of Minoan civilisation in the prehistory of Greece, it was suggested that the word Phoenician originally meant "red-man" or "redskin", and that it was applied to various peoples of red-brown complexion whom the early Greeks met. Hence it was proposed that "Phoenician" might have once meant "Minoan", and that the story of Kadmos coming from Phoenicia to Thebes was a memory of Minoan settlement there. A notable exponent of this interpretation was H.R. HALL, who as early as 1909 in an article on the discoveries in Crete wrote: "No doubt the whole Kadmos series of legends, connected with Thebes in Boeotia, has nothing whatever to do with the Semites: the Kadmeian Φοίνικες, the 'Red Men', were Aegeans, probably Cretan colonists like the Minyae. We way dismiss from history these Phoenicians at Thebes, where their position has always seemed slightly absurd" *(Proc. Soc. Bibl. Arch.* 31 (1909) p.282; cf. also his later works *The Ancient History of the Near East* (ed. 3, 1916) p.60, and *The Civilization of Greece in the Bronze Age*(1928) p.269). The idea met

with widespread approval, and was adopted by Sir John MYRES both in an early discussion of excavations at Thebes (see *YWCS* for 1911, p.27) and in the first edition of the *Cambridge Ancient History*, where he wrote of " 'those who came with Cadmus' whose original Cretan ancestry had been displaced by the belief in a Phoenician origin" *(CAH* Vol. III (1925) p.634; cf. also his book *Who Were the Greeks?* (1930) esp. pp.197, 199-201, 321f.). Support was also given by A.R. BURN in *Minoans, Philistines, and Greeks* (1930; see esp. p.77), and he still maintained this interpretation in the *Oxford Classical Dictionary* (ed. 1, 1949) s.v. Phoenicians, where he described the prehistoric remains at Thebes as Minoan and concluded: "'Phoenician' in Greek myths, then, usually = Minoan Cretan".[59]

Other scholars favoured the idea of a loose meaning for the term without stressing the Cretan element. Thus it has been understood to have once included the inhabitants of Caria and the rest of coastal Asia Minor, the Levant and sometimes even Libya (see C. AUTRAN, *Phéniciens* (1920) pp.54f., 81 and passim; A.H. KRAPPE in *Am. Journ. Sem. Lang. and Lit.* 57 (1940) p.243). The idea is appropriately expressed in R. WEILL's question: "Qu'est-ce que ce Kadmos 'Phénicien', mais si nettement créto-égéo-asianique?" (*Syria* 2 (1921) p.121); it would be hard to find a vaguer definition of Phoenician than this! An alternative suggestion was that Phoenicia originally meant Illyria, that Kadmos was an Illyrian hero and that there was an early Illyrian migration to Boeotia (see G. BONFANTE in *CPh* 36 (1941) pp.1-20 and the other writers mentioned by Vian, *Or. Theb.* p.132 n. 6). Recently M.B. SAKELLARIOU has put forward a similar but more complicated hypothesis, suggesting that Kadmos may have been in origin "une figure pélasgique" and that there was a migration of Pelasgian tribes from Illyria to Thebes. He tentatively proposes that, if "Φοίνικες" originally meant Pelasgians — a view which he seems to favour, Kadmos' connexion with "Φοινίκη" went back to Illyria (*La migration grecque en Ionie* (1958) pp.369-75).

Of these several hypotheses, the most important is undoubtedly

---

59. In the revised edition of the *OCD* (1970) s.v. Phoenicians Burn writes more cautiously: "The name 'Phoinix' ('Red') ... may first have been applied to any copper-skinned Mediterraneans".

that which interprets "Phoenician" in the Kadmos story as meaning "Minoan"; it will be discussed at length in Chapter V, where a fuller account will be given of the way in which this theory developed, with detailed references to the work of scholars who have supported it. The alternative suggestions which have been mentioned here will be criticised more briefly in notes 84 and 119 below.

(2) We now consider the views of the second group of scholars, those who postulate a settlement or dynasty from the eastern Mediterranean as the historical basis of the legend of Kadmos. Throughout the nineteenth century, in spite of the arguments of the sceptics, there continued to be some who accepted the traditions of Phoenician settlement in Greece as true, and F. LENORMANT in particular argued against K.O. Müller's views and in support of a Phoenician settlement in Boeotia as the reality behind the legend of Kadmos (see his lengthy discussion in *Les premières civilisations* II (1874) pp.313-437). Others who accepted the presence of Phoenicians in Boeotia included C. THIRLWALL (*A History of Greece* I (1835) pp.68f., 74, 76), J. KENRICK (*Phoenicia* (1855) pp.97-101) and M. DUNCKER (*History of Greece* I (English edition, 1883) pp.71-4). At the beginning of the twentieth century the Phoenician cause found a new champion in V. BÉRARD, who became famous for his hypothesis put forward in *Les Phéniciens et l'Odyssée* (1902-3) that the story of Odysseus' wanderings as told by Homer was based on tales of actual Phoenician voyages in the western Mediterranean. Bérard believed that there was a Phoenician colony at Thebes, and adduced arguments from its geographical situation in support of his view. He also accepted a Semitic derivation for the names of Kadmos and Europê, as had previously been argued by F.C. MOVERS and H. LEWY,[60] and interpreted the story of Kadmos'

60. See Movers, *Die Phönizier* I (1841) pp.516f. (on Kadmos), and Lewy, *SFG* (1895) pp.214 (on Kadmos), 139 (on Europê). The idea that Kadmos' name might be connected with the Semitic root *qdm*, meaning "the east", did not originate with Movers as sometimes stated (e.g. Vian, *Or. Theb.* p.52), but is earlier mentioned by various writers: see, for example, Keightley, *MAGI* (1831) p.294; Mitford, *HGMit* I (ed. 2, 1789) p.89; Sharpe, *DUOP* (1751) p.96; it can be traced right back to Samuel Bochart in the 17th century (*Chan.* (1646) pp.486f.). The proposed oriental etymology for Europê is also very old: see, for example, Ukert, *GGR* I.2 (1816) pp.211f. with references to earlier literature.

search for Europê as a myth about the morning and evening star (op. cit. I pp.224ff.). Bérard's arguments do not seem to have convinced many, though T.G. TUCKER accepted the presence of a Phoenician settlement at Thebes (in the introduction to his edition of Aeschylus' *Seven Against Thebes* (1908) p.xiii), and Gilbert MURRAY was among those who accepted a Semitic derivation for Kadmos' name (*The Rise of the Greek Epic* (1907) p.33). Many of Bérard's geographical arguments were criticised by A.W. Gomme (in *BSA* 18 (1911-12) pp.189-210), who seems to have been led on from his studies of the geographical position and topography of Thebes to investigate the question of whether Kadmos was originally a Phoenician in the tradition (see above, p.55).

Bérard's theories took little account of the new Mycenaean evidence, but an attempt to relate this to Greek legend was made in 1928 when L.B. HOLLAND published an article entitled "The Danaoi" (*HSPh* 39 (1928) pp.59-92). Holland suggested that the legends of foreigners, such as Danaos, Kadmos and Pelops, who became rulers in Greece in the period before the Trojan War, were a memory of Greek-speaking invaders from Phoenicia and Egypt. He proposed that one branch of Greek-speaking Northerners had invaded mainland Greece ca. 1900 B.C., while another group of the same race had crossed to the Troad and made their way southwards to Phoenicia and Egypt, from where they took to the sea and so reached Greece in the sixteenth and fifteenth centuries. Holland, it should be noted, thought that "Phoenicia" and "Egypt" in the tradition were virtually synonymous, since in his belief Phoenicia at the relevant time was "simply one section of the Egyptian sea-coast" (op. cit. p.80).

The idea of invaders (or an immigrant dynasty) from Egypt and Phoenicia in the sixteenth or fifteenth century has been put forward by a number of scholars since Holland. One of these was W. DÖRPFELD, the distinguished excavator of Troy, who maintained the belief that the Greek legends were literally true, and proposed that Kadmos came to Greece from Egypt at the time of the Hyksos expulsion (sixteenth century B.C.). Dörpfeld held that Kadmos was an Arab, that the Hyksos themselves were "Arabische Volkstämme" and that the Phoenicians originally came from Arabia. His work on the Phoenicians, which was published in *Alt-Olympia* (1935), was unfortunately vitiated not only by his extreme literalism but also by his outdated views on the character of the Mycenaean civilisation. Even in the 1930's he maintained the old hypothesis, put forward when Schliemann's discoveries were first made, that Mycenaean culture was Phoenician (cf. n.57), and he stoutly argued that Mycenaean and Orientalising Greek art were but "old" and "new" Phoenician art (see esp. *Alt-Olympia* I pp.290-5, 320f., 349-76; II pp.401-44).

Meanwhile new evidence was becoming available from the Near East. Excavations at Ras Shamra in North Syria revealed ancient Ugarit, a Canaanite city in contact with the Mycenaean world, and a number of scholars sought to find a link between its inhabitants, who have often loosely been termed Phoenicians, and those of the Kadmos legend. Among the most striking of the Ugaritic discoveries were the literary texts, and R. DUSSAUD was the first to note a similarity between one of the myths related in these and the story of Europê (see *RHR* 105 (1932) esp. pp.252-4; cf. C.F.A. Schaeffer's brief discussion in *The Cuneiform Texts of Ras Shamra-Ugarit* (1939) pp.60f., where he writes that the story of Europê "indeed originated on the Phoenician coast"). Though Dussaud had earlier been inclined to deny a historical basis for the Kadmos legend (see above p.54), he now proposed that it might preserve the memory of Mycenaean Greeks who had settled in Syria and Phoenicia and later returned to Greece (see *Syria* 12 (1931) p.394; *Les découvertes de Ras Shamra (Ugarit) et l'Ancien Testament* (ed. 2, 1941) pp.29f.; *L'art phénicien du II* millénaire* (1949) p.16, note 2). Dussaud particularly insists that the migrants from the East would have been Greeks not Semites, writing that Kadmos "n'est pas un Phénicien, mais un héros de la Grèce propre. Pour avoir vécu en Phénicie, il en recevra l'épithète de phénicien, mais cela n'empêche pas qu'il ne soit originaire de Thèbes. Lorsque la pénétration des Égéens et des peuples d'Asie Mineure, cessant d'être pacifique, amène la réaction des orientaux et oblige Cadmos à rentrer dans sa patrie, il y apporte l'alphabet ... " (*Les découvertes de Ras Shamra etc.* pp.29f.). The evidence from Ras Shamra is clearly relevant to our study of the legend of Kadmos, and its contribution will be assessed below in Chapters VI and VII.

The Ugaritic discoveries naturally prompted other conjectures. G. THOMSON (*Studies in Ancient Greek Society I: The Prehistoric*

Aegean (1949) pp.376f., cf. p.124) and more recently his colleague R.F. WILLETTS (*Cretan Cults and Festivals* (1962) pp.156-8) proposed that the Kadmeioi were a Semitic tribe that migrated first from Phoenicia to Crete, taking with them the story of Europê, and then from Crete to Thebes. I. VELIKOVSKY was even bolder, and in a series of rash conjectures identified Kadmos with a historical king of Ugarit, by the name of Niqmed, a contemporary of the Egyptian pharaoh Akhenaten, whom he dated to the ninth century B.C. and identified with the Greek hero Oidipous! Kadmos, according to Velikovsky's theory, was driven from Ugarit by Assyrian invaders, and fled to Greece, taking with him a cross between the cuneiform and Hebrew alphabets, a wife called Sphinx and the story of Oidipus/Akhenaten *(Oedipus and Akhnaton* (1960) p.190, referring to his earlier work *Ages in Chaos* I (1953) pp.219ff., where however there is no mention of Kadmos by name).

But the possibility of a link between the Greek legends of foreign conquerors and the expulsion of the Hyksos was not neglected. J. BÉRARD, the son of Victor Bérard, in an article entitled "Les Hyksôs et la légende d'Io" (*Syria* 29 (1952) pp.1-43) suggested that the story of Io's wandering to Egypt and of the return of her descendants five generations later might be a reflection of the foreign Hyksos rule in Egypt and of their expulsion in about 1580 B.C. Bérard identified Epaphos, Io's son, with the Hyksos king Apopi, and rather more tentatively Kadmos with another Hyksos king Khamdi.

There appeared shortly after this Robert GRAVES' book *The Greek Myths* (1955), in which many attempts are made to link Greek legend and Near Eastern history. Graves asserts that 'Zeus's rape of Europe ... records an early Hellenic occupation of Crete" and also possibly "commemorates a raid on Phoenicia by Hellenes from Crete" (op. cit. Vol. I p.197); that "the dispersal of Agenor's sons seems to record the westward flight of Canaanite tribes early in the second millennium B.C., under pressure from Aryan and Semitic invaders" (ib. p.196); and that "the Cadmeians came from Asia Minor, probably on the collapse of the Hittite Empire" (ib. p.38). It is difficult to reconcile these confidently stated conjectures with one another, and hard to take them seriously when no historical or archaeological evidence is cited in their support.

Over the last few years several scholars have connected the Kadmos legend with Phoenician activity in the Aegean, though not all have placed this as early as the second millennium B.C. J. FONTENROSE in *Python* (1959, pp.307 and 467) maintains that the Phoenician origin of the legend is "visible on its face", and that the story of the dragon-killing was probably brought direct from Sidon and Tyre to Boeotia "in the period when Phoenician traders came to the Greek peninsula". (He does not say when this was!) The orientalist D. BARAMKI in *Phoenicia and the Phoenicians* (1961, pp.11 and 59) accepts the presence of Phoenician trading stations at Thebes, Thera, Thasos, Kythera and Corinth, and apparently dates these to the early Iron Age. A similar date appears to be followed by Nina JIDEJIAN in her recent book *Tyre through the Ages* (1969, pp.34-7, 62), though she is vague about the chronology in this context and actually dates the Phoenician exploitation of Thasos as late as "some time during the Persian period" (i.e. between 550 and 330 B.C.).

A more widely accepted view favours the Late Bronze Age as the historical period to which the legend of Kadmos' Phoenician origin refers. G. HUXLEY in *Crete and the Luwians* (1961, pp.16f., 36f.) suggests that Kadmos was an immigrant from the Levant at the beginning of the Late Helladic period, that Europê's connexion with Phoenicia has a historical basis and that the legend of Danaos may well be the memory of the establishment of a new dynasty from Egypt at Mycenae about 1550 B.C. The suggestion that the rise of the Late Helladic civilisation was to be explained by the arrival of new leaders from the East and that the legends of Kadmos and Danaos preserved the memory of such events (as the story of Europê might similarly preserve the memory of a new dynasty from Syria in MM III Crete) had already been proposed by F.H. STUBBINGS both in lectures at Cambridge and in a communication to the Mycenaean Seminar in London (extracts from a summary of this paper, which was read on 23 February 1955, are quoted by L.R. Palmer in *TPhS* for 1958 pp.94f.). Some of these ideas have now been incorporated in Stubbings' chapters of the revised edition of the *Cambridge Ancient History.*[61]

61. *CAH* ed. 2, fasc. 4 (1962) p.74 = ed. 3 Vol. I Part 1 (1970), Ch. VI p.244; fasc. 18 (1963) pp.11-14 = Vol. II (not yet published), Ch. XIV.

Other scholars also have recently maintained a belief in some kind of oriental settlement at Thebes in Mycenaean times as providing a historical basis for the legend of Kadmos' Phoenician origin. J. ZAFIROPULO adopts an extremely literalist approach to Greek legends in his *Histoire de la Grèce à l'âge de bronze* (1964). He interprets the rape of Europê as a raid on Phoenicia by the first Achaean king of Crete in 1360 B.C., and takes the story of Kadmos' search for her almost at its face value. Zafiropulo's method of interpretation will be discussed below in Chapter IX. M.C. ASTOUR in *Hellenosemitica* (1965) follows a different method, comparing the various themes or motifs in the legend of Kadmos with similar ones from Near Eastern mythology. Astour concludes that so many themes are West Semitic in origin that they must have been brought to Mycenaean Greece by a West Semitic tribe. He supports this conclusion with proposed Semitic etymologies for numerous personal and place names connected with the legend of Kadmos and related stories. This comparative method of study and its contribution to the interpretation of the legend will be examined in Chapter VII. Both Astour and Zafiropulo wrote before the important discovery of a number of oriental seals at Thebes, and were only able to include reference to them in later editions of their books.[62] These finds have prompted a number of new conjectures and suggestions to do with the legend of Kadmos' coming from Phoenicia to Thebes, and these will be discussed in Chapter VI (esp. pp.133f.).

We are now in a position to summarise the conclusions of modern scholarship about the Phoenician origin of Kadmos. This is no easy task. For whereas among ancient authorities we found a general consensus of opinion (see p.50), no such agreement exists among scholars of the nineteenth and twentieth centuries. Two radically opposed views are to be distinguished: first, that the idea of Kadmos as a Phoenician is not an old tradition at all, but due to misunderstanding, invention, or learned theory; and second, that the idea had its origin in historical fact. But there is wide diversity of opinion among scholars

62. Zafiropulo, *Mead and Wine* (Eng. trans. of *HGAB* by Peter Green, 1966) pp.14-16; Astour, *HS* ed. 2 (1967) pp.391f.

who hold each of these views. Those who hold the first vary widely in their explanations of how the legend arose, while those who seek a basis for the tradition in actual events differ radically in their reconstructions of the historical facts. There are differences of opinion as to the *nature* of any incursion that the legend records — invasion, immigration, arrival of new leaders in small numbers, trading venture, or colonisation; as to its *date* — beginning of the Late Helladic period (Hyksos period), Late Mycenaean period, or early Iron Age (period of main Phoenician seafaring); and as to its *source* — Crete, Illyria, Phoenicia proper, Egypt, or elsewhere in the eastern Mediterranean.

While a separate criticism of each of the interpretations mentioned lies beyond the scope of this work, it is hoped that the course of our discussion in the following Chapters will lead us to re-examine at least the more important hypotheses put forward by scholars who believe in some historical basis for the legend. But first we must turn our attention to a crucial question: was Kadmos originally a Phoenician in the tradition? If his Phoenician origin were proved to be only a later invention, then all the attempts to find a historical basis for this part of the legend would be but lost labour.

CHAPTER IV

HOW ANCIENT IS THE PHOENICIAN ELEMENT IN THE LEGEND OF KADMOS?

The case against the antiquity of the tradition of Kadmos' Phoenician origin has been argued most fully by A.W. Gomme. In this Chapter it is proposed to consider afresh the arguments which he put forward sixty years ago, as well as those of F. Vian, who has much more recently denied a historical basis for this part of the legend.[63]

Gomme's argument falls into two parts. The essence of the first is this: when the literary sources for the legend of Kadmos are examined, it will be found that the earliest of them are completely silent about his having been a Phoenician (see *LCL* esp. pp. 54-60, 70-2). Homer mentions Kadmos only once, quite incidentally, as the father of Ino Leukothea *(Od.* V. 333-5). The passage does not associate the hero with any particular area in Greece, but there are a number of places in the *Iliad* and *Odyssey* which mention Καδμεῖοι or Καδμείωνες at Thebes, and while this cannot be taken as proof that Kadmos himself was associated with Thebes, it does make it seem quite likely. The *Theogony* of Hesiod, the fragments of the Epic Cycle, Pindar and Aeschylus all associate Kadmos exclusively with Thebes. As for Europê, in whose search Kadmos was said to have left Phoenicia and come to Greece, in Homer (*Il.* XIV. 321), the Hesiodic fragments (fr. 141 M-W) and the epic poet Asios of Samos (fr. 7 Kinkel *EGF*), she is

---

63. On these two scholars cf. Ch. III above. Vian's conclusions have been accepted by some scholars (e.g. Burton, *DSC* p.101 n. 4), but they have also met with criticism (see, for example, Bruneau in *REG* 78 (1965) p.382). Gomme's powerful influence is still much felt, as can be seen from the way in which his conclusions are fully accepted in such recent works as Vermeule, *KD* (1972) pp.182f., 186, and Muhly, *HAP* (1970), where it is stated that "the Phoenician elements in the story of Cadmus, especially his connections with Europa, are all late developments which go back no earlier than the fifth century B.C." (*HAP* p.40). I am grateful to Professor M.S.F. Hood for referring me to Muhly's article, which will be cited frequently below.

the daughter of Phoinix, but this does not necessarily imply that these authors thought that she was Phoenician. None of these poets refers to any connexion between Kadmos and Europê or to the motif of his search for her, and similarly the allusions to the treatment of the Europê story by other early poets (Eumelos, Stesichoros and Simonides) make no reference to the oriental origin. The elements of the Kadmos story which seem to interest the early poets are the marriage to Harmonia at Thebes, Kadmos' offspring there, his sowing of the dragon's teeth and the springing up of the Spartoi, the Sown Men. Gomme therefore concludes that before the fifth century B.C. there is no clear evidence that Kadmos or Europê were thought of as Phoenician, and that in none of the sources before that date is mention made either of Kadmos' search for Europê, an element in the story with which his Phoenician origin is closely connected, or of any relationship between the two of them.

Gomme's second main argument against accepting the antiquity and authenticity of the tradition is as follows: the authors who first attest a connexion between Kadmos and Europê and their origin in Phoenicia are the logographers and Herodotos, who, Gomme argues, did not simply relate epic traditions in prose form, as was once supposed by Busolt and others, but systematised and rationalised them, and even "corrected" them in the light of their own theories and researches. Hekataios of Miletos and Herodotos in particular were impressed with the antiquity of oriental civilisations. They had both visited Egypt, and were inclined to see it as the source of Greek institutions and religious beliefs. Hekataios, for instance, attributed the introduction of letters to Danaos from Egypt *(FGrH*I A,1 fr.20), in contrast to an earlier attested tradition that the alphabet was invented by the Greek Palamedes, while Herodotos derived the names of nearly all the Greek gods from Egypt (II. 50-1), and preferred the tale of the Egyptian priests that Helen stayed in Egypt to the Greek tradition that she went to Troy. He also believed in an Egyptian origin for the phallic rites of Dionysos (II. 49), and gives us his reasons for this, which are illuminating and worth summarising: the rites are the same in Egypt and in Greece; since this cannot be due to coincidence and one cannot think that the Egyptians got them from the Greeks, it follows that the Greek rite must be derived from Egypt. Here Herodotos is clearly giving us his own deductions. Similarly, he uses the results of his own enquiries to deduce that the Gephyraeans did not come from Eretria as they themselves believed, but were originally Phoenicians who came over with Kadmos (V. 57-61). From these and other examples (for details see *LCL* esp. pp.228-40) Gomme argues that Herodotos and his immediate predecessors were not above altering the tradition in the light of their own conjectures, and that the whole idea of Kadmos as a Phoenician may have originated in some such learned theory. He does not commit himself to saying which of the logographers might have been the originator of it, but he thinks it possible that "the Phoenician theory" may have originated in Ionia and have reached mainland Greece at about the end of the first quarter of the fifth century (*LCL* p.66).

Let us now examine Gomme's arguments in detail, beginning with the absence of Kadmos' "Phoinikertum" from the early tradition. The argument is not without force, but it must be remembered that it is a negative one, an *argumentum ex silentio,* and as such open to the objection that none of the early sources states that Kadmos is *not* a Phoenician. One might well argue that if they knew of Kadmos as a Phoenician, they may have had good reasons for not mentioning the fact: Pindar as a patriotic Theban may have preferred not to recall that the traditional founder of his city was of foreign origin. Then the early references to Kadmos are brief and incidental to the story being related, as for example the *Odyssey* passage and the references in the Epic Cycle, and one cannot expect them to mention the origin of a hero unless it suits their purpose to do so. Furthermore, the early epic sources which mention Kadmos or Europê, apart from the *Iliad, Odyssey* and *Theogony,* are fragmentary, and nobody can be sure what was in the missing parts. A good example of this is the Hesiodic description of the rape of Europê. When Gomme wrote his article, the only evidence for Hesiod's version was a résumé in the scholia to the *Iliad* (XII. 292), and even then, since the scholiast referred to both Hesiod and Bakchylides as his authorities, one could not tell how much of the story was due to each author. Since Gomme wrote, a fragment of Hesiod's *Catalogue of Women* has come to light on papyrus telling the story of Zeus and Europê (K 1 Merkelbach, frs. 141, 143 M-W, Ox. Pap. 1358 fr.1) . In it we see that Hesiod called her the daughter of

Φοινιϰος ἀγαυοῦ and that Zeus carried her across the ἁλμυρὸν ὕδωρ before his union with her. The papyrus is fragmentary and the beginning of the story missing, but the point is that if we had only one or two lines immediately preceding the present fragment (oŕ indeed even the whole of the first line) we might well know from where Hesiod thought Zeus carried off Europê. It could be argued that there are other places from which Zeus might have carried her across the sea, but since Phoenicia is her home in the later tradition we certainly cannot preclude that the Hesiodic *Catalogue* contained a version in which Europê was carried off from Phoenicia.

In this connexion it is worth reconsidering what Homer and Hesiod meant by calling Europê the daughter of Phoinix. As scholars from K.O. Müller onwards have been at pains to point out, the name "Phoinix" need not have an ethnical connotation, as is illustrated by the existence in the *Iliad* of Achilles' friend Phoinix, for whom no Phoenician connexion is apparent.[64] But we must not lose sight of the fact that "Phoinix" *can* mean Phoenician, and often does. Homer uses both Φοῖνιξ and the feminine Φοίνισσα in the sense of "Phoenician" (*Od.* XIV. 288, XV. 417), as well as the plural Φοίνιϰες which occurs several times. In another fragment of the *Catalogue of Women* (fr. 139 M-W), Phoinix appears as the father of Adonis, whose oriental origin surely cannot be questioned, while in other fragments (frs. 138 and

64. Little attempt was made in ancient times to connect Phoinix the tutor of Achilles with Phoenicia. Some very tenuous links may be noted here, though it must be admitted that even their cumulative weight is very slight indeed: (a) the Homeric references (*Il.* IX. 448, X. 266, II. 500, cf. Strabo IX. 2. 12-17), if taken all together, connect him with Boeotia and specifically with Tanagra, which is associated with Phoenicians by Herodotos (V. 57; cf. the end of Ch. V with n. 117). How and Wells, following Toepffer, even suggest that this may be the origin of Herodotos' idea that the Gephyreans of Tanagra were Phoenicians, but this seems to be highly speculative. (b) A late tradition (Schol. Dion. Thrac. p.32 Hilgard; cf. Tzetzes, *H.* XII. 68) ascribes to him the invention of letters, though this might have arisen from confusion with Phoinix the brother or near-relative of Kadmos. (c) There is a curious similarity, long ago pointed out by Biblical commentators and recently re-emphasised by Astour (*HS* pp.144f.), between the story of Phoinix (*Il.* IX. 445-56) and that of Reuben (Gen. XXXV. 22; XLIX. 4). But the Genesis account is only a brief fragment of uncertain interpretation, and it would in any case be a mistake to attach too much weight to this type of evidence, as will become apparent in the discussion of oriental parallels in motif (see Ch. VII).

137 M-W) Phoinix is not only son of Agenor and father of Phineus, but also husband of Kassiepeia, who is said to be the daughter of Arabos, and therefore oriental. There has been debate whether these other heroes named Phoinix are identical with Phoinix, the father of Europê (see Vian, *Or. Theb.* p.57 with n.2), but the important point is that since the Hesiodic poems know at least one oriental hero called Phoinix, one must not base too much on the fact that Europê in the extant fragments is not explicitly made Phoenician. Indeed, since no scholiast or mythographer ever hints at the possibility that Hesiod placed the home of Europê, "daughter of Phoinix", elsewhere, it may well seem a likely inference that the Hesiodic *Catalogue* knew of her Phoenician origin (so too Vian, *Or. Theb.* pp. 57, 69).

Gomme's further point was that no literary authority before the fifth century B.C. states that Kadmos and Europê were even related. This is true, but once again it could be argued that there is no reason why the kinship of the two should be mentioned in any of the works which have survived from that period, and that such fragmentary references as we possess certainly do not preclude it. Indeed, it seems possible that Stesichoros, who lived in the late seventh and early sixth centuries B.C., may have regarded Kadmos and Europê as being related, since he is known to have told the story of the sowing of the dragon's teeth at Thebes in a poem about Europê. This information is preserved by the scholiast to Euripides' *Phoenissae* 670, who discusses whether Kadmos sowed the teeth at the advice of Athene or Ares, and says "but Stesichoros in his *Europeia* says that Athene sowed them" (fr. 15 Bergk = 21 Edmonds). Although Kadmos is not mentioned by name, the context here and the wide attestation in later literature of Kadmos' connexion with the sowing make it probable that Kadmos played at least a subordinate part in Stesichoros' version of the story, rather than that he was not associated with the sowing at all (cf. also Vian, *Or. Theb.* p.26). This reference does not of course prove that Kadmos and Europê must have been regarded as related by Stesichoros, but at least it warns us of the danger of drawing too many conclusions from the silences of the early tradition.

The second main argument put forward by Gomme is that the idea of Kadmos as a Phoenician occurs first in the logographers, and "if it can be shown that writers of the fifth century, Herodotus and the logographi, were less interested in local tradition than in learned theory, especially when the latter is based on researches in foreign countries, we do then get some probability for the view that a statement found in them, but in no earlier writer, may be theory and not tradition" (*LCL* p.223). Gomme then demonstrates very successfully, as can be seen from the examples quoted above (p.66f.), that Hekataios and Herodotos were interested in learned theory and in correcting tradition from the results of their researches abroad. But before taking the further step of supposing, as Gomme does, that the legend of Kadmos reflects such a learned theory, we need to investigate more closely which of the logographers say that Kadmos was a Phoenician, and to consider whether we can be certain that they are the first Greek writers to do so.

It is difficult to date any of the logographers with certainty, but it is recognised that Hekataios of Miletos was the earliest, and was active about 500 B.C. Akousilaos of Argos and Pherekydes of Athens are generally thought to be contemporaries, younger than Hekataios and writing in the first half of the fifth century, while Hellanikos of Lesbos was probably writing later still, in the last quarter of the fifth century (Jacoby in *RE* VIII (1913) col. 109, and elsewhere; Lesky, *HGL* p. 330). No fragment of Hekataios is preserved which mentions either Kadmos or Europê, and though he must have discussed Thebes in his *Periegesis* there is, as Gomme admits, no evidence that he knew the "Phoenician theory". Akousilaos does not mention Kadmos in the extant fragments, and refers to Europê only once in a passage which casts no light on our problem (*FGrH* I A, 2 fr. 29).

This means that the only logographers *known* to have mentioned Kadmos are Pherekydes and Hellanikos. Pherekydes clearly knew the story of the search for Europê, and described the killing of the dragon, the sowing of its teeth and Kadmos' wedding to Harmonia, when he gave her a necklace that Zeus had originally given to Europê (*FGrH* I A, 3 frs. 22, 87, 88 and 89). What is more, he gives us a detailed genealogy for Kadmos, the earliest one surviving (*FGrH* frs. 21 and 86; cf. fr. 87; see Table 1 above, p.26), in which Kadmos is the son of Argiope, daughter of the Nile and second wife of Agenor, who is father of Phoinix and grandfather of Kilix by his first marriage. Two points stand out in this genealogy: first the striking differences between it and those attested in the later sources (discussed above, pp.25-9) and second the *Egyptian* connexion. This is seen in the way that he is made son of Agenor by a daughter of the Nile, just as Apollodoros and other writers expressed the view that Danaos and Aigyptos came from Egypt, by making their mother daughter of the Nile (cf. Table 3 above, p.27). Pherekydes then seems to be the earliest logographer to make Kadmos an oriental, and although Phoenician connexions are certainly present (Phoinix is Kadmos' half-brother), the Egyptian ones seem to be at least equally prominent.

Hellanikos also appears to have told the story at length, and several fragments of his account survive (*FGrH* I A, 4 frs. 1, 23, 51 and 96). Unfortunately many of the details of what Hellanikos wrote are not certain; the longest fragment on Kadmos (fr. 51) is a passage in Schol. A D on Hom. *Il.* II. 494, which relates the story in detail and then says "ἱστορεῖ Ἑλλάνικος ἐν Βοιωτιακοῖς καὶ Ἀπολλόδωρος ἐν τῷ γ". A substantial part of the narrative is verbatim the same as our text of Apollodoros, which leaves it doubtful how much might have been derived from Hellanikos. Vian has a good discussion of this problem (see *Or. Theb.* pp.21-5), though he is concerned only with that part of the story which dealt with Kadmos' foundation of Thebes. His conclusion (*Or. Theb.* p.25 and n.3) is that, while some scholars, including Latte and Jacoby, were mistaken in thinking that nothing at all in the scholion could be ascribed to Hellanikos, Gomme went to the other extreme and exaggerated Hellanikos' importance as a source for the scholiast's account. As far as the Phoenician origin is concerned, we can only conclude that while Hellanikos may or may not have included it as part of his story of Kadmos, it is most unlikely that he could have put forward any rival theory.

The only other author whose views on Kadmos need to be discussed here is Herodotos himself, who was an older contemporary of Hellanikos. Herodotos in the *Histories* takes it for granted that Kadmos is a Phoenician, and the story of Europê is alluded to as if it was presumed to be familiar to his readers. Europê is the daughter of the king of Tyre, and Kadmos' relation to her is not explicitly stated, but he leaves Tyre in search of her and makes his way to Thebes (for references see n.48 to Ch. III). This part of the story is fully developed, and we can be certain in agreeing with Gomme that if Kadmos'

Phoenician origin is a theory, it was well established by the time Herodotos wrote his *Histories*.

Let us now return to Gomme's point that if *our first sources* for a Phoenician Kadmos are more interested in learned theory than tradition there is some probability in the view that this Phoenician origin is theory and not tradition (see p.70 above). It is clear that Herodotos himself did not originate the theory, and if Pherekydes is earlier than Hellanikos (which seems a justifiable assumption), he is then the earliest logographer to mention an oriental Kadmos. But Gomme's comments on the characteristics of the logographers are largely applicable only to the Ionian writers. Pherekydes of Athens (and Akousilaos) were less interested in rationalisation or learned theory, as the following quotation from Jacoby will illustrate: "Nor is it surprising ... in how different a spirit (compared with the Milesian Hekataios) these first 'historians' from Greece proper dealt with their subject-matter: there is no trace in their remains of the scientific spirit which provoked, and the rationalism which pervaded the 'historical' work of the Milesian, while Pherekydes had an even stronger liking than Akusilaos for what we must term fairy-tales, which apparently were preserved by oral tradition.[65] Gomme himself says that Pherekydes was not so impressed with barbarian antiquity (*LCL* p. 243), though he stresses Pherekydes' independence of the epic — or rather the fact that he is the first authority for many details, such as the names and motives of characters, not related in it (cf. Forsdyke, *GBH* p.143). Thus the first logographer in our extant sources to mention an oriental origin for Kadmos seems not to be one of the Ionians, whose treatment of tradition Gomme discusses so aptly, but Pherekydes, and though we cannot claim that he followed the epic blindly, we do know

65. Gomme, writing in 1913, accepted the identification of Pherekydes of Athens with Pherekydes of Leros (*LCL* p.66), but Jacoby has shown that these are two distinct writers: see "The first Athenian prose-writer" in *Mnemosyne* 13 (1947) pp.13-64, reprinted in *AGGFJ* (ed. Bloch) pp.100-43, from p.142 of which the quotation in our text was taken. On Pherekydes see also Lesky, *HGL* pp.221f.

that certain details of the genealogy of Kadmos that he gives were in the epic. Hesiod in the *Catalogue of Women* (fr. 138 M-W) makes Phoinix the son of Agenor and husband of Kassiepeia and father of Phineus, which is exactly what we find in Pherekydes (see Table 1 above, p.26). We may conclude therefore that while Herodotos and Hellanikos may be at times more interested in learned theory than tradition, the first logographer known to suggest an eastern origin for Kadmos, i.e. Pherekydes, is not such a writer.

One further point remains to be discussed in connexion with the suggestion that Kadmos' Phoenician origin may derive from a theory of the logographers. The poet Bakchylides of Keos, who wrote in the first half of the fifth century B. C. (see Lesky, *HGL* p.202) and was therefore approximately contemporary with Pherekydes, also knew of an oriental connexion for Kadmos. In Ode XIX, one of the first written by Bakchylides for Athens and probably datable to before 474 B.C. (A. Severyns, *Bacchylide* (1933) pp.65f.), Bakchylides refers to Io going to the banks of the Nile and giving birth to Epaphos, who became ruler of the Egyptians and ancestor of the house of Agenor from which Kadmos sprang:

> ἐπεὶ παρ' ἀνθεμώ[δεα
> Νεῖλον ἀφίκετ' οἰ[στρο...
> Ἰὼ φέρουσα παῖδ[α ...
> Ἔπαφον· ἔνθα νι[ν ...
> λινοστόλων πρύτ[ανιν ...
> ὑπερόχῳ βρύοντ[α ...
> μεγίσταν τε θνα[τ ...
> ὅθεν καὶ Ἀγανορί[δας
> ἐν ἑπταπύλοισ[ι Θήβαις
> Κάδμος Σεμέλ[αν φύτευσεν
>   (XIX. 39-48 Snell).

Bakchylides therefore as well as Pherekydes connected Kadmos with Egypt, and this passage must be considered side by side with the contemporary passages of Pindar, which do not mention a foreign origin. Bakchylides also seems to know of the Phoenician origin of Europê: in Ode XVII. 53f., she is called "νύμ[φ]α Φοίνισσα", where the epithet can hardly have anything other than an ethnic sense.[66] It might well be supposed that Bakchylides' work as an epinician writer would incline him to accepting tradition rather than altering and "improving" it; he is certainly not normally characterised as a theoriser and rationaliser and can have no axe to grind in making Kadmos (and probably Europê) oriental in these passages. If the eastern origin of Kadmos is only the invention of the logographers, it is surprising to find what appears to be an expression of it in Bakchylides, who is after all contemporary with the first logographer known to mention it.

Let us now sum up the position so far reached: first, our earliest sources (Homer, Hesiod and the early epic) do not state that Kadmos came from the East, but the references are brief and many of the sources fragmentary, so that there may have been reasons for the omission of any mention of the fact, or its absence may be fortuitous. Similarly Europê's eastern origin is not specifically mentioned in the earliest sources, but the same counter-arguments apply here, and it is quite possible that the Hesiodic *Catalogue* did in fact make her Phoenician. We must agree with Gomme that Kadmos and Europê may not have been originally related, as is suggested by the fluctuation in the later tradition about their precise blood-relationship (cf. pp.23-5 with n.33) as well as by the silence of the earliest sources, which however may not be quite so complete as Gomme argued (cf. above p.69 on Stesichoros). But it must here be stressed that the antiquity of Kadmos' Phoenician origin in the tradition is not necessarily dependent on the antiquity of his relationship to Europê, and his search for her may well be an elaboration of the original motif

---

66. Compare the Homeric γυνὴ Φοίνισσα in *Od.* XV. 417. Jebb translates Φοίνισσα in Bakch. XVII. 54 as a patronymic, but this usage of the word is not otherwise attested, and is unlikely in view of the frequent occurrence of Φοίνισσα in an ethnic sense (see Liddell and Scott s.v. Φοῖνιξ). No doubt Jebb was influenced by the fact that earlier in the same poem, Europê was spoken of as Φοίνικος κόρα; but the formal parallelism itself strongly suggests that Φοίνισσα is an ethnic: in lines 29-36, where Theseus is the speaker, he says: εἰ καί σε (Minos) ... τέκεν... Φοίνικος .. κόρα (to Zeus), ἀλλὰ κἀμὲ Πιτθέος θυγάτηρ ... τέκεν (to Poseidon); and later in lines 53-60 Minos replies: εἴπερ με νύμ[φ]α Φοίνισσα ... τέκεν (to Zeus), ..., εἰ δὲ καὶ σὲ (Theseus) Τροιζηνία ... φύτευσεν Αἴθρα (to Poseidon), ...

of the rape by Zeus.

Secondly, certain logographers, notably Hekataios and Hellanikos, seem to have been given to learned theory, as was also Herodotos, but these are not the earliest extant authors to make Kadmos and Europê Phoenician. Pherekydes writing before Hellanikos, and in all probability before Herodotos (who, as Gomme admits, cannot have originated the theory), connects Kadmos with Egypt and Phoenicia and knows of his search for Europê, while Bakchylides whom nobody would expect to be prone to learned theory makes Kadmos descended from Egyptian-born Epaphos. It is perfectly possible that some other Ionian logographer conceived of the "Phoenician theory", such as the shadowy Kadmos of Miletos, whose very existence is disputed, or one of the writers of the history of Persia, such as Dionysios of Miletos (about whom exceedingly little is known) or Charon of Lampsakos, but this is the purest conjecture. We have no reason to believe that these writers even mentioned Kadmos or that they exhibited the same characteristics as Herodotos and Hekataios. We may conclude that, while Gomme has put up a good case for regarding Kadmos' "Phoinikertum" as a learned theory, a close examination of his arguments has revealed some considerations which make his case seem less plausible, and certainly the possibility must remain open that the Phoenician origin of Kadmos already formed part of the tradition before the logographers.[67]

We must now turn our attention to the views of a more recent scholar, who has maintained substantially the same opinions as

67. It is relevant here to compare the situation with another story of a foreign ruler in Greece, namely that of Danaos, for whom an origin in Egypt is attested by many classical writers. In the last century the more sceptical German scholars dismissed this tradition as a comparatively late invention (see K.O. Müller, *OM* p.113; Meyer, *GAMey* II (ed. 1, 1893) p.70 and elsewhere). As with Kadmos, the hero's foreign origin does not occur in Homer (indeed there is no mention of an individual Danaos, though the ethnic Danaoi appears frequently); but it is at least likely to be older than the logographers, since it appears in a fragment of a lost epic named the *Danais* (fr. 1 Kinkel *EGF*), which refers to the daughters of Danaos arming themselves by the river Nile:

"καὶ τότ᾽ ἄρ᾽ ὡπλίζοντο θοῶς Δαναοῖο θύγατρες
πρόσθεν ἐυρρεῖος ποταμοῦ Νείλοιο ἄνακτος."

See further nn. 69 and 208.

Gomme with regard to the genuineness of the tradition of Kadmos' Phoenician origin, but who has put forward additional reasons for not accepting it. F. Vian in *Les origines de Thèbes* (1963) re-examines the legend of Kadmos to see if the episode of the Spartoi or Sown Men might reflect the existence in prehistoric Greece of a specialised warrior class, of which he believes he has already found evidence in the myth of the battle of the gods and giants. We are here concerned not with his far-reaching conclusions that the story of Kadmos preserves traces of an Indo-European tripartite society, and that the Spartoi represent the warrior class who provided expiatory victims, but with his discussion of the Phoenician element in the legend, which, he concludes, is nothing more than a "mirage",[68] and was invented at Miletos some time between about 650 and 550 B.C.

What new evidence then does Vian adduce for rejecting the Phoenician origin as genuine? His arguments are stated mainly in his second chapter (*Or. Theb.* pp.51-69), and five main reasons may be distinguished, besides the silence of the earliest literary sources which we have already discussed.

(1) Vian draws attention to the vase-paintings, and stresses the fact that in these Kadmos is never dressed as an Asiatic, even in the fourth century B.C. This is true, but one must be careful about the implications drawn from this fact. Although certain figures, notably Medeia, the Amazons and Thracians are often portrayed in a distinctive Asiatic dress, there is no uniform rule about artistic representations of heroes believed to be foreign. Thus Andromeda, Pelops, Priam and the Trojans are all shown sometimes in Greek dress

---

68. The term "mirage" as applied to the Phoenicians is not new; it was used repeatedly by Rhys Carpenter (see *HVA* (1933) pp.41, 42, 52, 53; also *AJPh* 56 (1935) p.13), and can be traced back to the 19th century controversies over the origins of Mycenaean culture and the debt of Greece to the East, when S. Reinach published his celebrated study "le mirage oriental" (*L'Anthropologie* 4 (1893) pp.539-78 and pp.699-732). In this article Reinach discusses both the older "mirage arien", by which India was taken to be the cradle of civilisation, and the "mirage sémitique", by which early civilisation was understood as synonymous with Babylon and Egypt and an exaggerated importance was attached to the role of the Phoenicians as its intermediaries to the West.

and sometimes in oriental.[69] With the representations of Kadmos, the vase-painters seem to be primarily interested in the killing of the dragon, an episode for which his Phoenician origin is not particularly relevant. In any case we know from the literary sources that belief in the Phoenician origin was very well established by the fourth century, and the fact that no vase-painting survives from this period showing Kadmos dressed as an oriental might more appropriately be used as evidence for the freedom with which the vase-painters represented their myths than as an argument to support the view that the "sémitisation" of Kadmos was still incomplete.[70] The evidence of the

69. For representations of Andromeda, showing both types of dress, see Phillips in *AJA* 72 (1968) pp.1-23 (with pls. 1-20); for Pelops see Weizsäcker in *Roscher* III s.v. Oinomaos (cols. 764-84), and cf. also Arias and Hirmer, *HGVP* pls. 212-3 (neck-amphora near the Meidias Painter, with Pelops in Greek dress); for Priam see, among others, Trendall and Webster, *IGD* p.56, no. III. 1. 21 (oriental dress), Arias and Hirmer, *HGVP* pls. 125, 139 (Greek dress). The dress of the Danaids is also relevant here: though Aeschylus in his *Supplices* (lines 234-7) stresses that they wear foreign dress, they are apparently shown on vase-paintings in Greek dress (for a list of relevant representations see Brommer, *VGH* p.364; cf. Beazley, *EVP* pp.146f., favouring the view that by the time of the vase-paintings in question the identification of the water-carriers in Hades with the daughters of Danaos had already been accomplished).

70. It is interesting to note that Europê, who is intimately connected with Kadmos from the 5th century B.C. onwards (if not earlier), is depicted in oriental costume on an Apulian red-figure vase now in New York (see Bieber, *HGRT* p.77, fig. 283; Trendall and Webster, *IGD* pp.52-4, no. III. 1. 17). But too much significance cannot be attached to this, as the scene on the vase is apparently set in Caria or Lycia, where according to a scantily attested tradition Europê migrated later in her life with her son Sarpedon (see Aesch. fr.99 Nauck *TGF* = 50 Weir Smyth; cf. Hdt. IV. 45, where she migrates from Phoenicia to Crete, and then from Crete to Lycia). More important, an early relief vase-fragment, now in Paris, shows Europê on the bull wearing a long patterned dress and what has been identified as an Assyrian bracelet (Lambrino, *CVA* Paris, Bibl. Nat. fasc. 2 p.72 and pl. 94.2, where however the illustration of the bracelet is unfortunately too small for any detail to be seen). Europê wears slippers with pointed up-turned toes, which have close oriental analogies (see, for example, Madhloom, *The Chronology of Neo-Assyrian Art* (1970) pp.69f. with pls. XXXVI. 2 and 3, XLIX. 5, LVI. 2; normally Europê is represented as bare-footed). This relief fragment is perhaps the earliest representation of Europê known, dating to the middle or end of the 7th century B.C. (see Schefold, *MLGA* pl. 11b; Bühler, *Europa* p.51), and may be of Boeotian manufacture (de Ridder, in *Mélanges Perrot* pp.297-301; Bühler, loc. cit.). If this really is an oriental Europê, then both date and possible provenance make it of the utmost importance for the question of the earliest evidence for a tradition of her Phoenician origin.

vases should not be ignored, but too much weight must not be attached to it.[71]

(2) Vian argues that Kadmos' companions "portent des noms grecs ou sont de simples éponymes". This is a piece of evidence which must be regarded with even greater caution than the last: if the fact that the names of Kadmos' companions are Greek is to be used to support the view that Kadmos was originally Greek in the tradition and not foreign, then one must be very sure that these companions are an integral part of the story and not later embroidery. But most of the companions listed by Vian (Or. Theb. p.54 n.6) are mentioned only in very late sources, like Stephen of Byzantium (? sixth century A.D.), the source for his supposition that Karchedon and Itanos were companions, or Tzetzes (twelfth century A.D.) and the scholiast to Dionysios the Periegete, whom he uses as evidence for Deioleon (Deileon) and Seriphos (Eriphos) as companions. Some of them are not even securely attested as companions at all: for example Phalanthos, who was said to have led a Phoenician colony to Rhodes (Ergias, FGrH III B, 513 1), was not connected with Kadmos, and it is merely persuasive speculation to assert that his Phoenicians "sont manifestement les anciens compagnons de Cadmos" (Or. Theb. p.61). It is surely illogical to use such late and unreliable sources as evidence for the original nationality of Kadmos in the tradition. In fact, the earliest sources do not name any companions, and the names of those which do occur by the fifth century B.C. (Membiaros, and the eponyms Phoinix, Kilix and Thasos) are of very doubtful derivation. Where the etymologies of proper names are so uncertain, they cannot be regarded as reliable evidence. Vian himself recognises this (see Or. Theb. pp.52, 156f.) with reference to Kadmos' own name, for which both Semitic and Indo-European derivations have been proposed,[72]

71. I am grateful to Professor A.D. Trendall for discussing the evidence of the vase-paintings with me in 1966.

72. The etymology of the name Kadmos is obscure. Vian mentions (Or. Theb. pp.156f.) only two of the theories which have been proposed, namely (1) a derivation from Greek κέκασμαι meaning "excel", also "be equipped" (this is favoured by many scholars, including Boisacq and Frisk); and (2) a connexion with an Armenian root kazm- meaning "equipment", "ornament" (so Dumézil in JA 215 (1929) pp.253f.; it may be mentioned that Dumézil himself, though he noted the Armenian parallels, favoured an origin for the word in (non-IE) Georgian, where the root kazm- appears

but fails to apply the same reasoning throughout his work. One cannot therefore feel that the evidence of the names of Kadmos' companions adds any weight to Vian's case.[73]

with similar meanings). Others have postulated a connexion with Greek κόσμος or κατάδαμ- (see the discussion of Crusius in *Roscher* II col. 882; also Studniczka, *Kyrene* (1890) pp.56f.; Friedländer, *Herak.* (1907) p.61). The meaning "equipment" gives good sense for the common noun κάδμος in Cretan, attested in Hesychios: κάδμος· δόου. λόφος. ἀσπίς. Κρῆτες, but it is by no means certain that the proper name Κάδμος has the same origin. The main shortcoming in Vian's discussion is his failure to consider the alternative derivation from the Semitic. Here the obvious root with which to connect the name is *qdm* meaning "in front", and hence "of old" and "the east" (cf. Hebrew *qeḏem*, "east", and the related terms *qāḏîm*, "east", *qaḏmōnî*, "Easterners", and the proper name *Qaḏmî'ēl*). This derivation is accepted by many older scholars (see n.60), and has recently had the support of Fontenrose, *Python* (1959) p.307 n. 60, Huxley, *CL* (1961) p.53 n. 17.13, Astour, *HS* (1965) pp. 152f., 221-3, and Muhly, *HAP* (1970) p. 38. Phonetically there are no difficulties, and the proposed meaning "Easterner" is appropriate for both the proper name Kadmos and the ethnic Kadmeioi (the same Semitic root would also provide an etymology for Kadmilos, the name of one of the Kabeiroi). In view of these facts, the Semitic derivation would seem at least as plausible as the IE alternatives, and it certainly cannot be dismissed, as is done by Vian, without consideration. See further below Ch. VII with n. 157.

73. It is noticeable that Vian nowhere discusses the derivation of Europê's name, though this heroine is associated with Kadmos at least as early as the "companions" whose names he uses as evidence for Kadmos' Greekness. Here again scholarly opinion is divided between an IE and a Semitic etymology.

(a) *Indo-European.* Three main proposals have been put forward: (i) Escher adopts a derivation from Greek εὐρύς, "broad" and the root ὀπ-, "eye", "face" (see *RE* VI (1909) col. 1287). (ii) Aly suggests that the name is a feminine form of the adjective εὐρωπός, "dark", and derived from εὐρώς, "dank decay" and ὤψ, "face" (*Glotta 5* (1914) pp.63-74), (iii) Vürtheim proposes a derivation from εὖ, "well" and ῥώψ, "willow" (see his paper cited by Nilsson, *MMR* (ed. 2, 1950) p.532, n. 93).

(b) *Semitic.* Those who adopt a Semitic etymology derive the word from the root *'rb*, meaning "to enter", "to set" (of the sun), hence Hebrew *'ereḇ'*, "evening", "west", and the related forms in Akkadian, Assyrian and Arabic: see the discussion in Rawlinson, *HHer* II (ed. 4, 1880) p.83, and the writers cited above p.58 with n. 60; further references are given by Berger in *RE* VI col. 1298 and Frisk, *GEW* I p.593.

Both the Indo-European and Semitic etymologies are rather speculative, and present either phonetic or semantic problems as explanations of the personal name and geographical term Europe. With regard to the Semitic derivation, Astour makes a valiant attempt to overcome the difficulties in both consonants and vowels *(HS* pp.129-31), but cannot be regarded as eliminating them. We are forced therefore to agree with Frisk's conclusion (loc. cit.) that the origin of the name is "unerklärt". See further n. 155 to Ch. VII on the evidence of Hesychios.

(3) Vian draws on the evidence of cults, and adduces a similar argument to the last, namely that those which Kadmos traditionally founded on the way to Greece are either Greek or pre-Greek, the implication being that one might expect them to be oriental. Two major objections must here be made to the argument: first, the evidence of cults is bound to be very ambiguous, since their origins are so often obscure, and much depends on what is meant by the term "Greek". Even if a cult goes back to the Mycenaean period, it may still be of foreign origin (see, for instance, W.K.C. Guthrie in *CAH* ed. 2, fasc. 2 (1961) p.28, on Dionysos). The cults connected with Kadmos are no exception to this ambiguity, and in almost all of them either a foreign or a Greek origin could be maintained. Thus the cult of Aphrodite Ourania, Pandemos and Apostrophia at Thebes (see above p.32) has been interpreted as reflecting both a triple Indo-European divinity of sovereignty, the people and war (Vian, *Or. Theb.* pp. 143-7), and three attributes of the Semitic goddess Ishtar (Astour, *HS* p.160, adopting the earlier conjecture of V. Bérard). Such interpretations about origins are bound to be highly speculative where one has only the literary evidence to go on, and even where there is also archaeological and epigraphical evidence scholars are often divided. Thus the cult of Thasian Herakles, said by Herodotos to have been founded by Phoenicians sailing in search of Europê (II. 44), has been interpreted both as a foreign introduction and as a purely Greek development.[74] Similarly there has been much disagreement about the origin of the Kabeiroi, the mystery gods attested by Greek authors in a number of places including Samothrace, where they were associated

---

74. This cult is an unusual one, since Herakles was worshipped as both god and hero in Thasos: there is archaeological evidence for sacrifice made to him both in a bothros, as a hero, and at a high altar, as a god, and incriptions confirm the existence of a double cult known also from literary sources. M. Launey, one of the excavators of Thasos, has maintained that the cult of Thasian Herakles is foreign, and has argued that there was a Phoenician settlement on the island ca. 1500 B.C., but other authorities are inclined to accept the double cult as purely Greek, and to be highly sceptical about the proposed Phoenician phase (see Launey, *ET* I (1944) pp.189ff. and *contra* Nock in *AJA* 52 (1948) pp.299f., and Pouilloux, *ET* III (1954) pp.352f. The evidence from Thasos is discussed further below in Ch. VIII.

with Kadmos.[75]

Secondly, Vian fails to note one very important aspect of the cults associated with Kadmos, namely that so many of them were thought to be foreign by the Greeks who attest them. Thus Herodotos believed in an oriental origin for the cult of Aphrodite under the title of Ourania (I. 105 and 131); he similarly thought that Thasian Herakles was from Tyre (II. 44), that the worship of Demeter Achaia, introduced by the Gephyraeans who came with Kadmos, was Phoenician (see V. 61 and 57) and he connected Kadmos indirectly with certain rites of Dionysos which he believed were introduced from Egypt (II. 49). Likewise, Athene Onka (Onga), to whom Kadmos was believed to have sacrificed his guiding cow, was said by Pausanias to be Phoenician (IX. 12. 2) and the same belief is also found in Stephen of Byzantium (s.v. Onkaiai), the Scholia to Aeschylus' *Seven Against Thebes* 149 and the Scholia to Euripides' *Phoenissae* 1062. Finally Diodoros of Sicily attests that the priests of Poseidon on Rhodes, whose cult Kadmos was believed to have founded, were said to be of Phoenician descent (V. 58). The statements made by the ancients about these cults may well be only the result of syncretism and conjecture, and they certainly

---

75. Many older scholars believed that the Kabeiroi were Phoenician in origin (cf. below n. 151), but more recent scholars have been inclined to interpret them as Phrygian (cf. Guthrie's comment in *OCD* (ed. 2, 1970) s.v. Cabiri, "non-Hellenic deities, probably Phrygian"; see further the discussions of Kern in *RE* X.2 cols. 1399-1450 and Hemberg, *Kab.*). Controversy has particularly centred round the name Kabeiroi, which has been connected with the Semitic root *kbr*(cf. Arabic *kabir,* Hebrew *kabbîr* "great"). This etymology, which goes back to Scaliger and which has recently been adopted by Astour (*HS* p.155), is attractive in that it corresponds well to the common designation of these gods as "Μεγάλοι Θεοί"; but it is open to the objection that at Samothrace, where the mystery gods are most clearly connected with "Phoenician" Kadmos in the literary sources and where one would *prima facie* expect strongest evidence for the use of the supposedly Phoenician term, the title Kabeiroi has not been found on any of the inscriptions so far excavated (cf. above n. 36). It must also be admitted that it would be possible for the name Kabeiroi to be Semitic without the cult itself also being so (for this view see Reinach, *RA* 32 (1898) pp.56-61, and Hemberg, *Kab.* pp.28, 13 *l*; for a compendium of alternative suggestions on the origin of the name Kabeiroi see ib. pp.318-25). It may be noted that although cults of the Kabeiroi are attested in Boeotia both at Anthedon on the coast and near Thebes, they are not linked in any of the literary authorities with Kadmos.

cannot be used by themselves as valid evidence for the origins of the cults in question. Nevertheless, they do bear additional witness to the extent of the tradition of Kadmos' Phoenician origin, and, since we have no evidence to prove them wrong, make any argument based on cults about the *Greekness* of Kadmos very weak indeed.[76]

(4) Vian finds it significant that Cyprus is missing from Kadmos' traditional ports of call, since this is on the route from Phoenicia to Greece. But this also would seem a very weak argument for more than one reason. First, while Cyprus is on *a* route from Phoenicia to Greece, that route is not the only one, and ships did not always call in there (see the accounts of two of S. Paul's voyages in *Acts* 21. 1-3, and 27. 3-7, in neither of which does the ship put in at Cyprus). Secondly, Vian is applying false standards of realism to the traditions. We are not dealing with a realistic account of an actual voyage to Greece, but the search of a hero for a girl carried off by a god in the form of a bull. Even in the later historicising sources, there is no connected account of the voyage mentioning all the supposed ports of call, but different authors mention different places, and if they were all put on a map a most indirect route to Greece would be achieved (see Map 1).

(5) Vian argues that "un seul trait exotique fait exception", namely the introduction to Greece of the Phoenician alphabet, and that this was anachronistically attributed to Kadmos at Miletos. Here two points must be borne in mind: first it is possible that the letters originally associated with Kadmos were some form of Bronze Age script, e.g. cuneiform or Linear B, even though, as we shall see below (pp.174-9), the Φοινικήια associated with Kadmos are most plausibly interpreted as the classical Greek alphabet; secondly, and more important, even if we are right in thinking that the introduction of the Phoenician alphabet has been ascribed to Kadmos anachronistically, this is not an argument against the antiquity of the tradition of the hero's Phoenician origin. Vian believes that the alphabet became associated with Kadmos because Miletos wanted the glory of having given letters to Greece and Kadmos had "nombreuses attaches en

76. For the weakness of Vian's argument from cults see further the remarks of Huxley in *JHS* 85 (1965) p.220.

Ionie" (*Or. Theb.* p. 55). But Kadmos' whole connexion with Ionia and Miletos has been much exaggerated (see below with notes 77 and 78); and there is moreover good evidence that several prominent Milesian writers preferred the version that Danaos introduced letters to Greece from Egypt (see Hekataios of Miletos, Anaximander of Miletos and Dionysios of Miletos, cited by the Scholia to Dionys. Thrax p.183 Hilgard = *FGrH* I A, l fr.20). It is a matter of speculation why Kadmos came to be associated with the introduction of letters, but the most likely reason is that the Phoenician origin of their own alphabet was known to at least some Greeks, and that *Kadmos was already famous as a Phoenician.* If this is so then Kadmos' association with the Φοινικήια is rather additional evidence for belief in a Phoenician origin for him.

The five arguments just discussed are the main additional reasons adduced by Vian for believing that the Phoenican origin of Kadmos is an invention. We must conclude that all of them are weak and inconclusive, and some of them verge on being illusory. It remains to mention that there is exceedingly little to associate Kadmos specifically with Miletos or to support the contention that it was here that the hero was given a Phoenician origin.[77] Vian in this matter has been influenced not by Gomme's suggestion about the logographers but by the views of the older German scholars (cf. above Chapter III

---

77. Vian himself admits (*Or. Theb.* p.58) that the only direct memory Kadmos has left at Miletos is his "jeune homonyme" Kadmos of Miletos. But one simply cannot use the existence of this figure (be he a historical Ionian logographer, as some believe, or a mythical invention, as Vian maintains) as evidence for the Milesians' having fabricated the Phoenician origin of Kadmos. It is true that older scholars such as Wilamowitz and Latte have adduced other arguments for believing that the story of Kadmos originated in this area, e.g. the occurrence of the place-name Kadmos in Caria and the fact that Priene was once called Kadme and its inhabitants Kadmeioi; but links of this kind between Caria and Thebes are much more plausibly explained by the fact that Thebans were among the colonists of this area at the time of the Ionian migration (see Hdt. I. 146; Paus. VII. 2. 10; Strab. XIV. 1. 3 and 12) than by the idea that Kadmos belonged originally to Asia Minor (see further Fimmen, *BBFZ*, esp. p.534; Nilsson, *MOGM* p.127, and cf. Vian's own comment, *Or. Theb.* p. 59). For the views of the older scholars see further n. 78.

p.57), whose dogmatic arguments are far from satisfactory.[78]

The fundamental basis for dismissing the Phoenician origin as a late invention must therefore remain the absence of any mention of the tradition in the earliest sources; but once one admits, as Vian himself does, that the oriental connexion is already present in Bakchylides, and probably even in the Hesiodic Catalogues, then one must ask how much earlier we can reasonably expect it to be attested. (Bakchylides is after all contemporary with Pindar and Aeschylus, included by Vian in his list of "les premiers textes" which associate Kadmos exclusively with Thebes: see *Or. Theb.* p.54.) It is curious that Vian should reject the possibility of a historical basis for the Phoenician element in the

78. The supposed connexion of Kadmos with Asia Minor and in particular with Caria and Miletos was especially stressed by Wilamowitz who expressed his conviction that a critical examination of the saga of Kadmos and his daughters would show "dass sie nicht nach Boeotien gehören, sondern nach Asien, Kadmos speciell nach Milet" (*HU*(1884) p.139); similarly Friedländer maintained that "die Kadmossage wurzelt in Milet" (*Herak.* (1907) p.6), and similar views were adopted by Latte (see *RE* X.2 (1919) esp. cols. 1461-3). Even very recently Grumach has spoken with approval of the idea that "Kadmos und Φοινίκη ursprünglich nach Karien gehören und anscheinend erst spät nach Phönizien übertragen worden sind" (*Kadmos* 4 (1965) p. 45 n. 3, referring to Latte and Vian).

Three main arguments have been adduced: (1) that Kadmos' whole genealogy belongs to the Miletos area; (2) that there is a place-name Kadmos in Caria and that the people of Priene were once called Kadmeioi; (3) that the name Φοινίκη originally meant Caria. But these are far from convincing: (1) the elaborate genealogical relationships of Kadmos are poor evidence for his place of origin, since many of the heroes for whom a special Milesian connexion is claimed are in fact associated with other areas as well. Thus Kadmos' daughter Ino Leukothea, whom Wilamowitz particularly connects with Ionia, had a widespread cult in Boeotia, Megara, Thessaly and many others areas (see Eitrem in *RE* XII. 2 cols. 2293-6), and similarly the hero Phoinix, whom Latte mentions as pointing clearly to S.W. Asia Minor, is connected with other parts including Phoenicia, mainland Greece and Crete (see Türk in *Roscher* III cols. 2401-9). It must be emphasised that the legend of Kadmos itself contains no reference to Miletos, nor is there any hint in classical writers that it played any part in the development of the story. (2) The occurrence of the names Kadmos, Kadme etc. in and near Miletos is well explained by the fact that the Ionian migration had included a substantial contingent from Thebes (see n. 77); Strabo specifically says (XIV. 1. 12) that Priene is called Kadme by some because Philotas who founded it was a Boeotian. (3) There is no adequate evidence to show that Φοινίκη originally meant Caria: see the full discussion below in n. 84.

story, while accepting one for numerous other details attested only much later (see, for example, *Or. Theb.* p.175, where he makes use of Ovid; ib. p.114, when a detail first attested in Apollodoros is taken as authentic; ib. pp.143ff., where he uses information found only in Pausanias for reconstructing a primitive Indo-European cult). One cannot help suspecting that in maintaining that the Phoenician element is a late accretion to the legend Vian is at least partly influenced by the fact that the Phoenician origin of Kadmos is of considerable inconvenience to his theory of early Indo-European elements in the myth. Indeed, his whole presentation of the evidence lacks the clarity and objectivity of Gomme's, and his arguments are often persuasively phrased (e.g. "il est nécessaire ... de *conjurer un mirage* phénicien sans cesse renaissant" (*Or. Theb.* p.51, our italics) or "il faudrait, pour qu'on pût envisager un rapprochement (sc. du nom de Cadmos) avec le sémitique, que l'origine orientale de Cadmos fût assurée ou du moins vraisemblable: *or il n'en est rien* " (ib. p.52, our italics). In this last statement he prejudges the issue before he has even discussed it).

There are other difficulties too in Vian's basic approach to the problem. He assumes that there is a clear-cut division between the element of *myth* in Kadmos' "life", viz. the adventures at Thebes, and the element of legend, viz. the Phoenician origin and the Illyrian sequel. He thinks that it is valid to ask whether the legend is an elaboration of the myth or the myth inserted secondarily in the legend, and concludes, as we have seen, that the former is the case. But this is an oversimplification of the position: there are elements of myth in the Phoenician episode (e.g. the rape of Europê), and elements of legend (e.g. the foundation of a city) in the Theban phase. It is largely meaningless to ask which came first, legend or myth, and even if we regard the "mythical" element, killing of the dragon and associated events, as the older, this does not make the Phoenician origin a "mirage". It may also be added that it is irrelevant to the question of the authenticity of the Phoenician connexion whether the story of Kadmos' foundation is older, or that of Amphion and Zethos.[79]

79. Vian seems to assume that the way is open for a Phoenician Kadmos only if the story of the foundation of Thebes by Amphion and Zethos is the original one and not

Let us now return to the question posed at the end of the last Chapter: was Kadmos originally a Phoenician in the tradition? Gomme, Vian and other scholars have alleged a number of reasons in favour of regarding the idea of a Phoenician origin as an invention of about the sixth century B.C. Of these the strongest seems to be their argument from the silence of the early literary sources (Homer, Hesiod etc.) about Kadmos' "Phoinikertum", supported by the absence of any indication that the vase-painters of the fifth and fourth centuries B.C. regarded Kadmos as a foreigner; but our examination of the early sources has shown that the silence is both less complete and less significant than has sometimes been supposed. The additional arguments put forward by Vian, when examined closely, appear to be very weak and of no great consequence, while the supposed role of Miletos in the formation of the Kadmos legend seems to have been greatly overestimated. Neither Gomme nor Vian has any discussion of the relevant archaeological evidence beyond brief mention of the fact that nothing Phoenician has been found at Thebes; but even this argument needs to be reconsidered in the light of fresh discoveries.

We must then ask whether we have sufficient warrant for inferring that Kadmos was not originally a Phoenican in the tradition, especially in view of the exceedingly well attested and unchallenged belief in an oriental origin found in writers from the fifth century B.C. onwards (cf. above Chapter III pp.45-50). The silence of the earliest sources could be accounted for by a variety of reasons, and it must be remembered that the volume of relevant literature is extremely small. It is therefore safest to conclude that the case for believing that Kadmos' "Phoinikertum" originated as late as the sixth century B.C. (or thereabouts) has not been proved, and the possibility must remain open that it is of greater antiquity, and so conceivably has a basis in historical fact.

that by Kadmos. He then argues that the foundation by Amphion and Zethos is secondary (*Or. Theb.* pp.51, 69-75). But the fact is that the way is equally open for a Phoenician Kadmos (if not more open) if the tradition of his foundation is the original one and that of Amphion and Zethos a later addition. (On these rival foundation stories compare also Nilsson, *MOGM* pp.124-6).

CHAPTER V

KADMOS, MINOAN CRETE, AND THE MEANING OF ΦΟΙΝΙΞ

The various reconstructions of the historical events believed to lie behind the story of Kadmos have one point in common: they assume that the tradition of his Phoenician origin has as its historical nucleus the arrival at Thebes of new people from overseas. They differ however as to the source of the newcomers, the date at which they were believed to have come, and the nature of their enterprise (see the discussion above in Chapter III, pp.57-64). One of the major causes of the greatly differing interpretations that are possible is the dubious origin of the terms Φοινίκη and Φοίνικες, and a number of scholars have attempted to show that they once meant something other than "Phoenicia" and "Phoenicians" (cf. above, pp.56f.).

We shall in this Chapter give our attention to what is in many ways the most remarkable of these conjectures, the one which gained most approval when it was first made and which has influenced the interpretation of the legend of Kadmos ever since. It is the suggestion that Φοινίκη originally meant Crete, and that by Φοίνικες in the tradition Minoan Cretans were once intended. The germ of the idea goes back to A. Fick, who proposed that the term Φοῖνιξ in Greek originally had no ethnic connotation but might have been used for all the peoples of red-brown complexion whom the early Greeks met, and only later have become restricted to the Semites (*VO* (1905) pp.123f.). The same idea occurred also to Sir Arthur Evans, who asserted more dogmatically that "the epithet Φοῖνιξ itself ... has nothing to do with the Phoenicians", and suggested that it was originally applied to the old Aegean race which included the Minoans, whose red skin-colouring had been vividly illustrated by the recent discovery of the Cup-bearer fresco (see *SM* I (1909) pp.56, 80 with n. 5, where he refers to Fick but makes it clear that the idea had occurred to himself independently; cf. also *PM* I (1921) p.9). The hypothesis was adopted and elaborated by H.R. Hall, A.R. Burn and Sir John Myres, all of whom used it to support their interpretation of the archaeological evidence, and it has favourably impressed a good many other scholars.[80]

Hall, Burn and Myres all relate the legend of Kadmos to a colonisation of Boeotia by Minoan Crete, in the context of a general Cretan colonisation or even invasion of the Greek mainland. They differ somewhat as to the date to which they refer the events believed to be reflected in the legend. Hall and Burn associate the coming of Kadmos with the earliest period of intensive Minoanisation of the mainland, about 1600-1500 B.C. Thus Hall, after stressing the Minoan character of the discoveries at Mycenae in the Shaft Graves and at Kakovatos, Vapheio, Tiryns and Orchomenos, writes as follows: "It may be asked: why should these Cretan monuments and relics not argue, not Cretan invaders and colonizers at all, but merely the peaceful adoption of the creations of the more civilized Cretans by the native Greek princes? Here legend speaks, and tells us with no uncertain voice that the bringers of civilization to Greece came from across the sea." He then proceeds to identify with these Minoan "bringers of civilization" not only the "Phoenicians" who came with Kadmos, but also the Cyclopes from Lycia, legendary builders of the walls of Tiryns, Io and Epaphos from Egypt, and the Minyae, the similarity of whose name to tnat of Minos he takes as indicating "a real

80. The work of Hall, Burn and Myres is discussed in detail below. Apart from Sir Arthur Evans, others who have favoured the theory that the "Phoenicians" of legend might have included Cretans are Burrows, *DC* (1907) pp.141f.; Powell, *PhE* (1911) p. 53, also p.44; Wace in *CAH* I (ed. 1, 1923) p.178; Glotz, *AegC* (1925) pp.60f; Carpenter, *AJPh* 56 (1935) pp.7, 9; Dunbabin, *GEN* (1957) p.35; Jackson Knight, *MMHom* (1968) pp.47, 138; cf. also Bury, *HGBur* (ed. 3, 1951) p.77, where the sentence "We have seen how the Cretan Cadmus and Europa were transferred to Phoenicia in the legend" apparently refers to a passage on p.40 of the 2nd edition (1913) but now omitted! Recent allusions to the theory are made by Beattie in *CH* (1962) p.323, Coldstream, *BICS* 16 (1969) p.1, Huxley, *Kythera* (1972) p.36. It may be observed that Nilsson referred to the suggestion as a "sagacious hypothesis", but was himself unable to accept it for archaeological reasons, and preferred to regard Kadmos as a foreigner without being specific about his origin (see *MOGM* p. 126 with n. 50; and for criticisms, Astour, *HS* p. 151). It is of interest to note that long before the discoveries at Knossos the idea of a Cretan settlement at Thebes was put forward by Welcker, *UKK* (1824).

connexion". He writes: "Both 'Egypt' and 'Phoenicia', as well as Karia, may well have substituted in legend for the civilized people of Crete, who were not of Hellenic race, but seemed in many respects Orientals to the later Greeks, as did the Lycians and Carians" (*AHNE* ed. 3 (1916) pp.59f. with nn.). Similarly in a later book Hall refers to the "Cretan colonists whom both archaeology and tradition tell us were the founders of the great civilization on the mainland" (*CGBA* (1928) p.11; cf. p.269).

Burn argues on very similar lines, though he does not refer to Hall: after discussing the archaeological evidence for Minoan settlement on the Greek mainland and arguing that the change in culture was too sudden and profound to be due merely to peaceful penetration, he suggests that the Greek legends about the civilising influence of foreigners have to be understood in the setting of this Cretan colonisation. He writes: "Rather curiously, the eponymous hero Danaos was said in historic times to have come not from Crete, but from Egypt, and Kadmos of Boiotia not from Crete but from Phoenicia; ... Phoenicia and Egypt have been substituted by later Greeks who knew those countries as homes of ancient civilization, while that of Crete had passed and left hardly even its name behind" (*MPG* (1930) p.77).

The reconstruction and dating of Myres are slightly different, but his basic arguments are the same. As early as 1911, in a comment on Keramopoullos' excavation of two chamber tombs at Thebes, Myres had suggested that the movements of Kadmos might be brought "into relation with a dispersal of Cretan personages" after the fall of Knossos (*YWCS* for 1911 p.27). In his later work he argues for a Minoan "exploitation" of the mainland beginning about 1800 B.C., suggesting that this movement was "a deliberate Minoan reinforcement of the 'palace' régime, already established at Thebes" (*WWG* (1930) pp. 346f.). For Myres the Cadmeians of legend were not the builders of the palace and tombs but simply reoccupants (ib. p.322).

In considering these interpretations, as indeed any attempts to interpret legend in terms of history, there are two main questions to be borne in mind. First, is the historical reconstruction consistent with the literary evidence, that is with the legends and traditions themselves? It must be admitted that there may have been much distortion and alteration to the legendary stories between the Bronze Age and their first attestation in classical literature and art; but one can at least take into account the type of tradition that is under review and its development in historical times, so far as this can be traced, and avoid seizing upon one aspect or version without considering its place in the whole. And second, does the proposed interpretation receive any confirmation from the evidence, where available, of archaeology and the various other sources (on which see above pp.3-6)? We must not forget that here too we are bound to be dealing mainly with plausibilities and probabilities rather than facts, since even archaeology can rarely provide firm *proof* of a historical event; but these independent sources of information are particularly important where, as in our present instance, such events as migration and city-foundation are being considered. We shall return below (in Chapter IX) to the problem which faces the prehistorian in correlating these different types of evidence, but for the purpose of our discussion here we may take it as axiomatic that no interpretation can be regarded as plausible unless it is reasonably consistent both with the legends themselves and with the evidence derived from archaeology and other sources.

With regard to the legendary evidence there is one obvious difficulty in the way of the theory of a Cretan Kadmos: in none of our sources is it ever stated that Kadmos came from Crete; throughout antiquity his home-country is said to be Phoenicia or Egypt (see above pp. 45-50). Nowhere is he given Cretan ancestry; where his descent is described, it is from Argive Io or, in one very late source, from Ogygos, for whom Attic, Boeotian and Egyptian connexions may be cited but none with Crete (see above p.49 and n.53). The only substantial connexion[81] between Kadmos and Crete to be found in our sources is

81. Vibius Sequester (? 5th century A.D. or later) says in *De Flum.* 13f. that Harmonia (sic) forgot Kadmos near the river Lethaios (near Gortyn in S. Crete); but the reference may well be an error for Europê, who is associated in other sources with this area (see Solinus 11. 9; cf. also Willetts, *CCF* pp.152f. on coins from Gortyn), and it would certainly be overrash to use such a late, isolated and obscure passage either as evidence that Crete was *Kadmos'* first stop on the way to Greece (so Lenormant, *LPC* II

through Europê, mother of Minos, though she also, it must not be forgotten, traditionally came from Phoenicia. But it would be rash to seize upon this solitary piece of evidence and ignore the rest of Kadmos' genealogical connexions: if Europê was his sister or niece in the traditions, Kilix, Phoinix and Thasos were his brothers or kinsmen, and he is related to a number of other heroes associated with the orient (see above pp. 19, 28f.).

The same basic difficulty lies in the way of the interpretation of the other legends mentioned by Hall and Burn in support of a Cretan conquest of Greece. In none of them are the heroes in question ever described as having come from Crete: Danaos is always said to have come from Egypt, never Crete (see especially Aesch. *Supplices* 1-18 and passim, Herodotos II. 91, and Apollodoros II. 1. 4), while the Cyclopes equally have no Cretan connexion, and that of the Minyae consists solely in the resemblance of their name to that of Minos, a similarity which it is difficult to regard as more than fortuitous, especially in view of the difference of quantity in the vowels (Mĭnyae beside Mīnos).

We are asked then to believe that in each case Crete, the original home of the heroes, has been replaced by some other country, because these countries were regarded as homes of ancient civilisation while memory of the early civilisation of Crete had almost entirely passed away. But this hypothesis exaggerates both the role of the heroes in question as bringers of civilisation and the lack of reference to Crete in the traditions. On the one hand the Greeks had a complex view of the origins of their civilisation: they believed that Kadmos and Danaos were only two of many heroes, some native and others of foreign origin, who had invented or introduced such arts as writing, irrigation and bronze-working.[82] And on the other hand Crete can scarcely be said to have passed away without leaving its mark on myth and legend. If tales of Minos' thalassocracy in the islands, of his divine kingship and

(1874) p.317) or to support the view of a Neolithic settlement in Crete from the south (see Hall, *Proc. Soc. Bibl. Arch.* 31 (1909) p.147)!

82. For a selection of ancient views as to who invented which civilising art see Hyg. *Fab.* 274 or Pliny, *N.H.* VII. 191-205, where native heroes such as Aiakos and Erichthonios appear in company with Kadmos, Danaos and the Cyclopes. The subject is discussed at length by Kleingünther (see Bibliography).

law-giving, if the story of Theseus and the Minotaur, of Minos and Daidalos in Sicily, if the mention of one hundred Cretan cities in the *Iliad* and of ninety in the *Odyssey* have any relation at all to historical fact, then surely they must relate to early Cretan civilisation. Are we then to conclude that the absence in our sources of any mention of a Cretan origin for the heroes referred to by Hall and Myres itself makes their thesis untenable? As far as Kadmos is concerned, one loop-hole remains: the obscurity of the term "Phoenician". If this could be shown to have meant originally *Cretan*, or to have included *Cretan* among its meanings, then the conjectures of Hall, Burn and Myres would merit serious consideration at least with regard to a possible Minoan settlement at Thebes.

It must be admitted that at first sight there seems to be no trace of such a meaning in Greek literature. The name Φοινίκη is regularly used to denote the coastal strip which includes Tyre and Sidon; it is defined by Ptolemy (V. 14. 3 Müller) as stretching from the river Eleutheros, near Arados (Arvad) in the north to the river Chorseos, south of Mt. Carmel, in the south (see Map 3), and while certain references[83] suggest an extension along the coast beyond both these limits, there is no good evidence to support a very wide meaning. It seems clear that Egypt in the south and Cilicia in the north were beyond the limits of Φοινίκη as generally understood by the Greek writers.[84] Φοινίκη then was the name given by the Greeks to the

83. Certain passages of Herodotos (III. 91, IV. 38) suggest that the term *Phoinike* may have been extended to include part of the coast to the north of Phoenicia proper as already defined (see Jeffery, *LSAG* p.11); at the same time, Herodotos places Syria Palaestina between Phoenicia and Egypt (III. 5, IV. 39). Conversely Strabo's Phoenicia does not extend north of Orthosia (itself south of Arados), but at the southern end it is said by him to stretch as far as Pelusium on the border of Egypt (XVI. 2. 21).

84. It has been suggested by some scholars that *Phoinike* originally meant *Caria* (see H.D. Müller, *MGS* I (1857) pp. 308-11; I. Levy, *RPh* 29 (1905) pp.309-14; Autran, *Phéniciens* pp.52f., 55; cf. also the German scholars cited above in n. 78). The main reasons put forward are that (a) there was a mountain called Phoinix in Caria; (b) the philosopher Thales of Miletos was said to be Phoenician by descent, and his father (Examues) had a Carian name; (c) a passage in Athenaios suggests that the name *Phoinike* was used for Caria in Korinna and Bakchylides. In addition Levy notes that (d) in a fragment of the poet Choirilos of Samos mention is made of a tribe who speak the

principal home of the people whom they called Φοίνικες, and this name too appears to be used without ambiguity. It is found in Homer as an apparent synonym of Σιδόνες or Σιδόνιοι,[85] and many later Greek authors apply it unequivocally to the Semitic seafaring people whose chief cities were Sidon and Tyre, and who established settlements in various parts of the Mediterranean world.

Phoenician language dwelling in the mountains of the Solymoi (located by various classical authors in Lycia). At first sight the cumulative force of these pieces of evidence may seem strong; but when they are examined they are not nearly so convincing as one would suppose from Latte's brief statement that "der name Phoinikien haftet ursprünglich an Karien" (*RE* X.2 col. 1461). (a) The place-name Phoinix is very widely attested, being found not only in Caria but also in Crete, Epeiros, Achaea, Messenia, Kythera, Sicily and the Lipari islands (cf. *RE* XX. 1 s.vv. Phoinix and derivatives). This wide occurrence is not surprising in view of the many meanings which φοῖνιξ had in Greek and one cannot therefore attach any great significance to its presence in Caria. (b) The tradition of Thales' Phoenician ancestry is most plausibly explained by the fact that there were "Cadmeians" among the original colonists of Ionia; see How and Wells on Hdt. I. 170, with the passages from Diog. Laert. and Hdt. quoted by Kirk and Raven in *PreP* pp.74f., where it is concluded that "Thales' 'Phoenician' ancestors were probably Cadmeians from Boeotia and not full-blooded Semites". There is nothing remarkable in a Carian name for his father, since clearly there was intermarriage between the Ionian colonists and Carian women. (c) The passage in Athenaios (*Deipn.* IV. 174 F) is both isolated and obscure; while the Greek appears to say that the land Caria might once have been called by the name *Phoinike* (so Frisk, *GEW* II p.1032), the sense of the context requires the opposite, i.e. that the land *Phoinike* might once have been called by the name Caria; but even if the former interpretation were accepted, it need be only a poetic extension of the name from the mountain Phoinix to the hinterland (so Meyer, *GAMey* II (ed. 1, 1893) p.147). (d) Choirilos of Samos (*Persika* fr. 4 Kinkel *EGF*) is referring to an ally of Xerxes at the time of the Persian Wars, and if his testimony is accepted as of historical value it would appear to relate not to an extension of the geographical term *Phoinike* to Lycia, but to a Phoenician settlement in historical times on the coast here, something which would not be implausible in view of the Phoenicians' overseas expansion around the 9th to 8th centuries B.C. and their settlement in Cyprus (cf. Rawlinson on Hdt. I. 173, though he places the Phoenician settlement too early).

The most therefore that one can infer is that the name *Phoinike* may have been occasionally applied by poets to Caria, but there is nothing to indicate that this usage was widespread (indeed general Greek usage argues strongly against this), or that it was the original meaning of the term.

85. See for example *Il.* XXIII. 743f.; *Od.* XIII 272 and 285, XV. 415-25. On Homer's failure to mention Tyre see Carpenter, *HVA* p.50; Lorimer, *HM* pp.67, 80; and on the Phoenicians' own names for themselves see below n.87.

But while its use by Greek authors is reasonably clear, the origin of the word itself is exceedingly obscure, and much has been written on the subject.[86] It appears not to have been a name used by the people of Tyre and Sidon or their neighbours,[87] and such oriental etymologies as have been suggested are unconvincing.[88] Most recent scholars have sought an explanation from within Greek, but here too there are difficulties. The word φοῖνιξ, together with many related forms (for which see Liddell and Scott ed. 9, pp.1947-8), occurs from Homer and Hesiod onwards in several senses, chiefly (a) the colour *red,* (b) the *palm tree,* (c) the mythical *bird* "Phoenix", and (d) as a *proper name* for both places and persons. The last two of these meanings provide no obvious explanation for the use of Φοῖνιξ in its ethnic sense, and

86. On the origin of the name see esp. Speiser, *NP* (1936), Bonfante, *NaPh* (1941), Astour, *JNES* 24 (1965) pp. 346-50, Frisk, *GEW* II (1970) pp.1032-4, Muhly, *HAP* (1970) pp. 24-34 and Chantraine, *NPNP* (1972). The subject has also been treated in P. Arnould's short thesis *EONP* (Louvain, 1963), which contains some useful references to the 19th and early 20th century theories, though many more recent discussions have escaped notice. I am very grateful to M. Arnould for supplying me with a copy of his work. On φοῖνιξ in the sense of the mythical bird see further Van den Broek, *MythP* pp. 51-66; on the connexion of the word with writing see Ch. VIII and n. 190; on the-ιξ suffix see Chantraine, *FNG* p.382.

87. The inhabitants of Phoenicia are called in the Bible either Ṣîḏōnîm, Σιδώνιοι, Sidonians, or Kᵉnaʿnîm, Χαναναῖοι, Canaanites, and this seems to accord with their own practice (see Paton, *PhHa* p. 887, Harden, *Phoen.* p. 22; cf. Muhly, *HAP* p. 27).

88. There is no obvious word in Phoenician or the W. Semitic language group from which the term Φοῖνιξ can be derived. The old conjecture connecting it with Egyptian *Punt* (a country on the shore of the Red Sea) has long been given up (cf. Arnould, *EONP*), and the derivation from Egyptian *Fenkhu* is also unconvincing (see Speiser, *NP* pp.122f., Muhly, *HAP* pp.30f.; cf. also Lorimer, *HM* pp.84f.).
A new though highly speculative suggestion has recently been made by Astour (*JNES* 24 (1965) pp.346-50; cf. *HS* pp.146f.), who connects Φοῖνιξ with the Hebrew personal name *Puwwā* (cf. the Gentilic *Pûnî*), Ugaritic *pwt* (probably a substance used in dyeing) and Arabic *fuwwa* (dyer's madder). But apart from having only a very partial phonetic correspondence with Φοῖνιξ, the word *fuwwa* and its cognates seem to refer to a quite different type of red dye, derived from the plant madder (cf. Koehler-Baumgartner, *LVTL* p.754), and it is difficult to see why this should be especially applied to the Phoenicians when the dye for which they were famous was obtained from the shell-fish murex. See further Van den Broek, *MytP* pp.64f. (with support for Astour) and Muhly, *HAP* pp.30f. (with criticisms of the hypothesis).

Movers' old suggestion (*Die Phönizier* II. 2 (1850) pp.1-4) of Phoenicia as "the land of the palms" is now generally discredited. As to the possibility of an extension from the meaning "red", we have already seen above (pp.87f.) that the interpretation of the name Φοῖνιξ as including *Cretan* arose in the early part of this century from Fick's hypothesis which connected the adjective with skin-colouring. There are many reasons why this hypothesis must now be abandoned,[89] but the origin of the name remains unexplained, and we must ask whether there may still be room for the inclusion of Cretan among its oldest meanings.

Of the many alternative suggestions which have been made connecting the ethnic use of Φοῖνιξ with the colour *red*, the one which commands widest support (cf. Lorimer, *HM* (1950) p.85; Kardara in

89. Fick's conjecture undoubtedly owes much to outdated ethnographical theory, which oversimplified the contrast between the supposedly blond, fair-skinned "Aryan" race of mainland Greece and the dark-skinned peoples of the Mediterranean. Thus Fick himself writes: "Φοίνικες sind 'die Rothäute', alle Nachbarn der Griechen, die im Gegensatze zu der helleren eigenen und der Hautfarbe der Indogermanen den brünetten Teint der alpinen, hettischen und semitischen Rasse zeigen" (*VO* (1905) p. 123). The hypothesis must also be seen in the context of Ridgeway's theory of fair-haired Achaean invaders, to which unfortunately neither the Greek usage of the epithet ξανθός (on which see Burn, *MPG* pp.38-47) nor modern interpretation of the linguistic and archaeological evidence for the coming of the Greeks to Greece lends any support.

Evidence for any marked difference in skin-colour between the Mycenaean Greeks and the Minoan Cretans is totally lacking. When it was first put forward, Fick's theory was seemingly supported by the representations of red-coloured Cretans in the frescoes of Knossos, but there are two important objections to this use of the fresco evidence. First, in the matter of skin-colouring we are dealing with an artistic convention, probably borrowed from Egypt (cf. Schachermeyr, *MKAK* p.191): if Cretan men are "redskins" because of their colour in the frescoes, their women appear to be of a different race, since they are panted white! Second, and perhaps more important, the Mycenaeans themselves painted men red in their own frescoes (e.g. in the fresco of warriors and horses from Mycenae, illustrated in *Ath. Mitt.* 36 (1911) col. pl. X; cf. also the Tiryns huntsmen, the Mycenae siege-scene, and the lyre-player and other frescoes from Pylos). There is then no evidence that the Cretans were of redder (or darker) skin than the Mycenaean Greeks. We do not even know that there was any marked difference in skin-colouring between the later Greeks and the Semitic Phoenicians, a supposition upon which the hypothetical transference of the term *Phoinikes* from Cretans to Phoenicians depends. For all these reasons Fick's hypothesis must be abandoned.

95

AAA 3 (1970) p.97) is that which understands the name as having first had the sense "purveyors of red dye", thus connecting the Phoenicians of Canaan with the art of purple-fishing and dye-making, for which they were undoubtedly famous in antiquity.[90] It is of interest to note that certain Akkadian texts from the Hurrian town of Nuzi in Mesopotamia refer to Canaan as a source of purple, and the name "Canaan" and the word for "purple" in these are so similar as to presuppose a definite connexion between them.[91] While nothing has yet been found in Phoenicia proper to prove that this activity began as

90. The derivation of Φοῖνιξ from the art of purple-dyeing is mentioned as early as 1837 by Gesenius, *SLPM* I p.338 n. In recent times it has been supported by Arnould, *EONP,* Speiser, *NP* pp.124-6, Maisler, *BASO* 102 (1946) p.7, Albright, *RCHC* (ed. 2, 1961) p.337, and Gray in *Peake* (1962) p.110. These last four authorities all suppose the term to be a translation of "Canaan" (see n. 91); cf. also Muhly, *HAP* esp. p. 34.

Other explanations are, as Speiser puts it, colourful indeed, and they range from hypothetical red paint or tattooing of the Phoenicians to red precipitations in the sea; the name *Phoinike* has even been derived from the rising (i.e. red) sun. The only alternative suggestion from the meaning red which needs to be taken seriously is the derivation from skin-colour, advanced in the 19th century by Pietschman and recently supported by such writers as Harden, *Phoen.* pp.21f., Carnoy, *DEMG* s.v. Phoinix, and Chantraine, *NPNP* p.9. The chief objection to it is the lack of any evidence that the ancient Phoenicians had a skin of a colour which might be termed φοῖνιξ (cf. n. 89 on Fick's theory, and Astour's criticisms in *HS* p.152).

It is to be emphasised that the connexion between the ethnic use of Φοῖνιξ and the colour red or purple is clearly established by Greek usage and does not depend on the once generally accepted affinity with θείνω, φόνος etc., which lacks the support of the Mycenaean evidence, with initial p-, not q-, being found there. Astour is wrong to rule out a Greek derivation on these grounds. See further Muhly, *HAP* esp. pp.25-34.

91. The documents in question, which date from the 15th and 14th centuries B.C., refer both to *(māt) kinaḫḫi,* "the land of Canaan", and to a substance *kinaḫḫu,* "red-purple wool" (see von Soden, *Akkadisches Handwörterbuch* I p.479b, and Koehler-Baumgartner, *LVTL* p.444). There has been much discussion about the origin of the term *Canaan,* which presents closely analogous problems to *Phoinike,* and it is debatable whether the name *Canaan* is to be derived from the term *kinaḫḫu,* itself possibly Hurrian, or whether, as now seems more likely, the product "purple dye" was named after the land of Canaan, for which another etymology must then be sought (see Albright, *RCHC* (ed. 1, 1942) p.25 and n. 50, and Maisler, *BASO* 102 (1946) pp.7-12).

early as the Bronze Age,[92] there has come to light at Ras Shamra in Syria both epigraphic and material evidence for a purple dye industry there in the late Bronze Age (Thureau-Dangin in *Syria* 15 (1934) pp.137-46; Schaeffer, *CTRS* pp. 22f. and "Une industrie d' Ugarit — la pourpre" in *AAS* 1 (1951) pp.188-92, with details of further texts). If therefore the Phoenicians were so called by the Greeks because of their manufacture of purple dye, it is possible that they received this appellation as early as the Bronze Age. It might also be possible that the name was applied to other makers of the dye in the same period.

Literary and other evidence for the purple dye industry exists for a number of sites in the Aegean, though often the date of the oldest working at these is not known.[93] In the Bronze Age purple-working is attested at Troy, where Blegen reported layers of crushed murex in Troy VI (*AJA* 41 (1937) p.582), at Aghios Kosmas in Attica, where Mylonas found murex shells clearly broken for dye extraction in LH II and LH III levels (Mylonas, *AK* (1959) p.156), and in Minoan Crete, where the industry is attested archaeologically at Knossos, Palaikastro and the little island of Kouphonisi off S.E.. Crete (cf. also the

92. Vast heaps of murex-shells have been seen by travellers at both Tyre and Sidon, but the working of these is not readily datable archaeologically (for the deposits see Jackson, *GDSP* p.6, D'Arcy Thompson, *GGF* p.209; cf. Jensen, *JNES* 22 (1963) p.106. Evidence for the murex dye-industry has also come to light during the recent excavation of an early Iron Age Phoenician temple at Sarepta (between Tyre and Sidon), a site whose very name has been derived from a Semitic word for dyeing (Muhly, *HAP* p.35; cf. *Times* for August 22nd 1972). It is interesting to note that Egypt knew the art of purple-dyeing from the 13th century B.C. (see Schneider, *RE* XXIII.2 col. 2009, where it is suggested that the Egyptians might have learnt the art from Phoenicia).

93. On the literary evidence see esp. Besnier, in Daremberg and Saglio, *DA* IV. 1 cols. 769-778; and on the industry in general see Jackson, *GDSP*, D'Arcy Thompson, *GGF* pp.209-18 (with copious references). For more recent work see Schneider, *RE* XXIII.2 cols. 2000-2020; Jensen, *JNES* 22 (1963) pp.104-18; Jidejian, *Tyre* pp.143-59. A murex dyeing-works of Hellenistic date has been excavated on Delos: see Bruneau in *BCH* 93 (1969) pp.759-91, where there are also listed other possible dyeing-works from classical Greece and Crete.

occurrence of murex in Minoan deposits at Kythera).[94] While this evidence must not be pressed, it would seem that Minoan Crete was one of the earliest producers of purple dye — the first clear evidence for its working goes back as early as MM II times — and it has been suggested by Miss Lorimer (*HM* p.63) that the Phoenicians may even have learnt the art from Crete. Similarly F. Schachermeyr writes: "In Kreta scheint das Färben mit Purpur zu allererst aufgekommen zu sein" (*MKAK* p. 225) and " ... dürfte die Purpurgewinnung überhaupt von unserer Insel ihren Ausgang genommen haben. Jedenfalls kann man hier nicht mehr, wie das noch so häufig geschieht, von einer 'Erfindung' der Phoiniker sprechen" (*MKAK* p. 228).[95]

We must conclude that the obscurity of the origin of the name Φοῖνιξ at least allows us to suppose that it could once have included Cretan among its meanings, though not for the reasons put forward by Fick. But such an understanding of the name differs so radically from its regular sense in classical and later Greek, that one would be reluctant to accept it as a likely meaning unless there were some compelling reason to do so. The scholars who have upheld the Cretan view of the Kadmos legend believe that such a reason is to be found in the archaeological evidence, to which we must now turn. The interpretation of the legend which Hall, Burn and Myres put forward needs to be understood in the context of their belief that shortly before

94. For murex at Knossos see Evans, *PM* IV p.111 n. 5; for Palaikastro see Dawkins and others, *BSA* 11 (1904-5) p.276 (crushed murex in LM deposits), Bosanquet, *JHS* 24 (1904) p. 321 (MM deposits); for Kouphonisi see Bosanquet, *BSA* 9 (1902-3) pp. 276f., *BSA* 40 (1939-40) pp.71f. (crushed murex in MM contexts); for murex in Minoan contexts at Kythera see Coldstream and Huxley, *Kythera* (1972) pp.36f., cf. p.282. A possible Minoan dyeing-works has been excavated at Myrtos in Crete, but there is no material evidence that this was used for murex (see Warren, *Myrtos* esp. pp. 262f.). For possible references to purple-dyeing in the Knossos tablets see Chantraine, *NPNP* pp. 11f. on *po-pu-re-ja* etc.

95. Any comments on the origin and spread of the Bronze Age murex industry are, in our present state of knowledge, bound to be highly speculative. Thus Speiser, who adopts a Greek derivation for Φοῖνιξ, suggests that the word was brought to Syria by Mycenaeans attracted by the excellent supplies of purple there (*NP* p.125), while Astour, who proposes Semitic derivation for both φοῖνιξ and πορφύρα, believes that the words may have been brought to Greece by Bronze Age Phoenicians attracted to the Aegean by its wealth of murex (*JNES* 24 (1965) p.350)!

the beginning of the late Bronze Age, Crete colonised or conquered the mainland of Greece. Present-day scholarship is united in the opinion that no such colonisation or conquest took place. But earlier in this century it was the generally accepted view, and it is worth considering why it was then so widely received, why it is now rejected, and whether any of the evidence once used in its support might be relevant to the Cretan interpretation of the Kadmos legend.

When Evans first excavated at Knossos between 1900 and 1914, very little was know about the antecedents of Mycenaean civilisation on the mainland, and there had been much debate about the relation of Mycenaean culture to other known ones of about the same date, especially those of the orient. The Minoan civilisation revealed by Evans and others in Crete was much more similar to that of the mainland than anything discovered before, and for a brief period the civilisations of the two areas were thought of as identical (Evans actually described his first finds at Knossos as Mycenaean: see *BSA* 6 (1899-1900) pp. 3-70 passim). Before long however it was realised that Minoan civilisation was older than Mycenaean, and so it came about that the Mycenaean civilisation of the mainland began to be regarded as an offshoot or provincial variant of Minoan, or indeed as but a late and decadent phase of it (see for example Evans in *JHS* 32 (1912) p.282; Dussaud, *CivP* (1910) pp.121f.; Baikie, *SKC* (1910) p.53). Naturally scholars soon attempted to explain why Minoan culture was adopted in this wholesale manner on the mainland, and an early suggestion was that of an extensive Cretan colony established after an attack or invasion (Forsdyke in *JHS* 31 (1911) p.117 and ib. 34 (1914) p.155). The view met wide acceptance and, in spite of opposition, was maintained by Evans all his life.[96]

It was not until the 1920's that this view was seriously challenged. Two factors led to its gradual abandonment: first, a growing awareness of the differences between Mycenaean and Minoan culture; and second, the increased knowledge of pre-Mycenaean Greece, to which

---

96. For Evans' views see esp. *JHS* 32 (1912) pp.282f., *Times Literary Supplement* July 15th 1920 p.454 (referring to "wholesale invasion from oversea"), and *PM* II (1928) p. 168. As late as 1935 he still wrote of "a very real wave of Conquest" (*PM* IV p. 283). Pendlebury continued to support the idea of colonisation in *AC* (1939) p.225.

Wace and Blegen contributed so much, showing that there was a continuity between the Middle Helladic and Late Helladic (or Mycenaean) periods in such matters as pottery-making and burial customs; we can now see that to speak, as did Evans, of "the abrupt and wholesale displacement of a lower by an incomparably higher form of culture" (*JHS* 45 (1925) p.45 n. 4) was an exaggeration of the position. We need not here trace in detail the stages by which the hypothesis of Cretan domination came to be abandoned, but some brief recapitulation of the arguments against it may be useful. First, as has just been mentioned, Mycenaean civilisation shows many features which distinguish it from Minoan: for instance, in pottery decoration there is a tendency to stylise, and in fresco painting and certain other arts an un-Minoan liking for violent and warlike subjects; mainland Greece also differs from Crete in its fortified citadels, in the use of the *megaron* in its palaces, and in the widespread occurrence of tholos tombs; other differences have been noted in dress, burial customs etc. Second, there is no evidence for any destructions, such as one would expect from an armed invasion, at the beginning of the Late Helladic period. And third, northern Crete suffered from a severe earthquake in Middle Minoan III, and would, it is argued, hardly be in a position to colonise the mainland. It is also maintained by some that in the Shaft Graves at Mycenae, where the earliest and clearest signs of colonisation were alleged, there are other new features in the finds not easily explicable in terms of Cretan origin or influence.[97]

In view of such arguments, the hypothesis of a general Cretan conquest or colonisation to explain the rise of Mycenaean civilisation is rejected by present-day scholars. It would appear at first sight that its rejection must entail the abandonment also of the interpretation of the Kadmos legend put forward by Hall, Burn and Myres. But it must be remembered that, while a general Cretan domination of mainland Greece is now considered very improbable, the Minoans certainly

97. For these points and other arguments against the theory of Cretan conquest see Harland, *PelBA* esp. sect. VI; Nilsson, *MMR* (ed. 1, 1927) pp. 11-24; Karo, *SchM* pp. 342f.; Kantor, *AegO* esp. pp.49-55; Schachermeyr, *Archiv Orientalní* 17.2 (1949) pp. 331-50; Lorimer, *HM* pp.18f.; Furumark, *SIAH* esp. pp. 186-91; Stubbings, *CAH* ed 2, fasc. 18 (1963) p.9.

seem to have established settlements on some of the Aegean islands, most notably Rhodes, and probably also Melos and Thera, at all of which it is intriguing to note that there were later traditions of settlement by Φοίνικες.[98] Furthermore there has recently come to light evidence for Minoan activity on the island of Keos, and for a Cretan colony at Kythera, believed by its excavators to have been established at the beginning of the Middle Minoan period and to have lasted till ca. 1450 B.C.;[99] both these islands are only a short distance

98. For a Cretan colony on Rhodes (in LM IA) see Furumark, *SIAH* esp. pp. 179f.; for Melos, ib. pp.199f. Recent excavations on Thera (see under Marinatos in Bibliography) have amply demonstrated the extent of Minoan influence there in frescoes, imported vases, architecture, etc., and Luce has concluded that the settlement of Akrotiri is "likely to have been a Minoan colony or dependency, possibly the seat of the Minoan ruler of the island" (*EA* t p. 105). Strong Cretan influence on Thera (and Melos) was argued, even before the present excavations, by Scholes, *BSA* 51 (1956) pp.37f., Huxley, *CL* p.2; cf. also Matz, *CAH* ed. 2, fasc. 12 (1964) p.44. For the literary traditions of Kadmos and other Phoenicians on Rhodes see above Ch. II esp. p.30 and Ch. IV pp.78 and 81; for Phoenicians on Melos see Festus s.v. Melos (pp.124f.) and Steph. Byz. s.v. Melos, and cf. also Crusius in *Roscher* II, col. 867; for Kadmos and his Phoenicians on Thera see above pp.19, 32. Though it is tempting to link these and other tales of *Phoinikes* in the islands (cf. Thuc. I. 8 and also n. 99 on Phoenicians at Kythera) with Minoan settlements, one must be very cautious, as (a) there is no universal correspondence between traditions of *Phoinikes* and the distribution of Minoan remains in the islands; and (b) it has recently become clear that Semitic Phoenicians in the historical period visited Rhodes, and certain of the stories of Phoenicians in this island might therefore be more plausibly associated with this period (on Iron Age Phoenicians in the Aegean see further Ch. VIII). Nevertheless, neither of these arguments is conclusive against the theory, especially since it is quite possible that the stories of Phoenicians in different parts of the Aegean might preserve the memory of events or circumstances which belong to more than one period of history.

99. For Minoan influence on Keos (imported pottery, Linear A graffito, statues of women in Cretan dress) see Caskey, *Hesperia* 31 (1962) esp. pp.272, 281, and *CAH* ed. 2, fasc. 45 (1966) pp.16f., 24. E. Vermeule doubts whether Keos was a Minoan colony in the proper sense (*GBA* p.120), but the archaeological evidence combined with the literary tradition found in Bakchylides of Keos (Ode I. 112ff. Snell) that Minos conquered the island does make some sort of Minoan settlement or even conquest seem very likely (cf. Stubbings, *CAH* ed. 2, fasc. 18 (1963) p.4). For a Cretan colony on Kythera see Huxley and Coldstream, "Kythera, first Minoan colony", *ILN* for Aug. 27th 1966 pp.28f., and their full publication *Kythera* (1972) esp. p.309. Kythera, as well

from the Greek mainland. All this suggests that the possibility of some Minoan settlement on the mainland itself cannot be excluded, as indeed has recently been postulated for Messenia.[100] The question which interests us here is whether there might be any justification for the view that Thebes was such a settlement. In other words, are there observable among the archaeological remains at Thebes any special Minoan features which might support the view of a Minoan presence there?

The ancient city of Thebes lies directly under the modern town, and so far only rather limited and sporadic excavations have been possible. In the first decades of this century the Greek archaeologist A. D. Keramopoullos excavated in the centre of the town part of a substantial Mycenaean building, known since his reports as "the House of Kadmos", and a large number of tombs mainly outside the Kadmeia proper on the hills Ismenion and Kolonaki. Other brief, unpublished excavations followed, but it is only recently, since 1963, that work has been resumed by Greek scholars at various sites made accessible by building operations within the town. More extensive and systematic excavation of Thebes is much to be hoped for, and any conclusions based on the present evidence are bound to be tentative; nevertheless sufficient material is available from both the old and new

as Rhodes, Thera and Melos, has associations with Phoenicians: Steph. Byz. (s.v. Kythera) derives its name "ἀπὸ Κυθήρου τοῦ Φοίνικος", and Hdt. reports a cult which he believed was founded by Phoenicians (cf. Ch. II with n.39). It is also interesting to note that Kythera was famous in antiquity for its murex deposits, from which its name Πορφύρουσα was said to be derived (Steph. Byz. loc. cit., referring to Aristotle), and that murex has been found in recent excavations there (see n. 94). For very early oriental finds on Kythera and a possible reference to the island in an Egyptian text see Huxley in *Kythera* p.33.

100. See Hood, *HH* (1967) p.76, where it is suggested that "actual colonies of Cretan settlers may have been established in Messenia at the beginning of the Late Bronze Age as they were in some of the islands", and cf. also id., *The Minoans* p.52. Marinatos too believes that Messenia had Minoan settlers: see his paper summarised by Luce, *EAt* p.175, and cf. *Excavations at Thera* I p.1, though the extent of Minoan settlement in the Mediterranean expressed there is altogether too widespread.

excavations to make some historical survey both possible and useful.[101]
It is clear that Thebes was inhabited in both the Early and Middle Helladic periods: EH and MH sherds, including matt-painted and Minyan wares, were found by the earlier excavators, and recent work has revealed further Early and Middle Helladic remains including a cemetery with cist-graves and an EH building which contained a cache of bronze tools. Evidence for occupation throughout the Late Helladic period has been found in the tombs excavated by Keramopoullos, and a small number of Sub-Mycenaean and Protogeometric graves indicate that the site continued in use after the end of the Bronze Age.[102]
In the central area itself the principal remains appear to be mainly of LH III (or LH II-III) date. Only a small number of rooms of the so-called House of Kadmos (or "Old Kadmeion") have been excavated (see the plan given by Schober, *RE(T)* (1934) cols. 1435f.), but the character of these — store-rooms, corridors, workshop — fits in well with the interpretation of the building as part of a Mycenaean

101. Reports on Keramopoullos' excavations appeared in *PAAH* for the years 1910, 1911, 1912, 1921, 1922-4, 1927, 1928, 1929, in *AE* for 1909, 1910, 1930 and in *AD* 3 (1917), the whole of which was devoted to the archaeology and topography of Thebes. Useful general accounts of the work are Schober, *RE(T)* (1934); Catling and Millett, *SIST* (1965) pp.3-15 and Raison, *VIPA* (1968) pp.5-15 (the last two with discussions of chronology and summaries of the excavations up to 1964). Cloché's study *TBOC* (1952) is brief and sketchy on the prehistoric period; cf. Burn's remarks in *JHS* 73 (1953) p.173. Unpublished excavations are mentioned by Furumark, *CMP* p.52, and others.
    The new excavations since 1963, which are mostly of a rescue nature, are being carried out at a great number of small sites (sometimes as many as 20-40 different ones in a single year) in both the centre of the town and the suburbs: for the topography of these see Pharaklas in *AD* 22 (1967) B.1 (*Chron.*) pp. 247-57 with his Plan 8 and, for the remains in the centre of the town, cf. also Spyropoulos' plan in *AAA* 4 (1971) p.33. Preliminary reports on the new excavations have appeared annually in *AD* since 1964, and summary accounts are available in *ILN* for Nov. 28th and Dec. 5th, 1964, and in *AR* and *BCH* from 1963-4 on. Several useful short articles have also appeared in *AAA*: see esp. under Spyropoulos in Bibliography. Full bibliography of new work on Thebes is given twice yearly in *Teiresias* (from 1970 on).
    102. Desborough, *PgP* pp.195f.; *LMS* pp.121f. Thebes seems to have been occupied more or less continuously from ancient to modern times; for the first evidence for Neolithic occupation, in the suburb of Pyri, see Fraser, *AR* for 1970-1, p.15.

palace. The architectural remains included a suite identified as the women's quarters, containing fresco fragments similar in style to those from the palaces of Tiryns and Knossos. Other finds were a large amount of Mycenaean pottery, some gold jewellery and the famous group of 28 stirrup-jars inscribed in the Linear B script. The recent excavations have produced further remains of the palace ("New Kadmeion") at a site immediately adjoining the part excavated by Keramopoullos (the Tzortzis property at the junction of Pindar Street and Antigone Street), including a "treasure-room" where the remarkable discovery of a substantial number of engraved oriental seals was made (these seals will be discussed in detail in Chapter VI). There have also come to light new fresco fragments and notable finds in precious materials, especially ivory, and the first Linear B tablets from Thebes, found at two quite separate sites in the town. Some of these tablets date apparently to an LH IIIA.2 (or early IIIB) context, which would make them the earliest Linear B tablets yet to be found on the mainland.[103] Other recent finds at various sites include a large chamber tomb with frescoed decoration, an incised plaque apparently depicting a boat, a bathroom with bath-tub, and remains of what appears to be an oil-store.[104]

Traces of burning were found both by Keramopoullos and the recent excavators at several points within the town. Although there has been controversy over the date of the destruction level found by

103. The earliest group of tablets are those from the site in Pelopidas Street named the "arsenal" by its excavators (see Platon and Stassinopoulou-Touloupa in *ILN* for Dec. 5th 1964 pp.896f.; cf. also Daux in *BCH* 92 (1968) pp.856-62, and, for full publication of the texts, see Chadwick, *Minos* 10 (1969) pp.115-37. The tablets of the second group, found at a site between Epameinondas and Gorgias (Metaxas) Streets, are thought by their discoverer to date to around the end of LH IIIB: full publication is awaited; for preliminary reports see Spyropoulos, *AAA* 3 (1970) pp.322-6 and *Kadmos* 9 (1970) pp.170-2.

104. For these finds see Fraser in *AR* for 1970-1 p.14 and Spyropoulos, *AAA* 4 (1971) pp.161-4 (chamber tomb with frescoes); Spyropoulos, *AD* 24 (1969) A (*Mel.*) pp.47-50 with pl. 42 (incised plaque); id., *Kadmos* 9 (1970) p.170 (bath-tub); Pharaklas, *AAA* 1 (1968) pp.241-4 (oil-store).

Keramopoullos,[105] the new excavations make it clear that Thebes continued to flourish well into LH IIIB, and that the final destruction of the palace is certainly not to be placed earlier than this period. Thus the general picture which one gains is that Thebes followed the normal mainland development (cf. Keramopoullos, *AD* 3 (1917) pp.5, 62), with marked prosperity and importance during the Late Bronze Age. But although the prevalent character of the finds is typically Mycenaean, a sufficient number of unusual features have been brought to light to make it worth enquiring whether indeed Thebes shows particularly close links with Crete.

Earlier in this century Burn drew attention to the "characteristically Cretan" architecture of the palace, to the Minoan character of the frescoes, and to the occurrence of Minoan writing in Boeotia, and other scholars, including Evans and Persson, used the discovery of apparently Cretan pottery at Thebes as evidence for the presence of Cretans there. As we shall see below, the arguments which they put forward do not now provide sufficient grounds for belief in a Minoan conquest or settlement in Boeotia. At the same time other possible indications of links with Crete have emerged from recent work, which suggest that the whole question needs reconsidering.

---

105. Keramopoullos originally placed his destruction level just after the end of the Late Aegean II period (*AE* for 1909 cols. 105f.), and an early date (LH IIIA.1 or around 1400 B.C.) has been accepted by many scholars, including Furumark, who re-examined the pottery (*CMP* p.52; *SIAH* p.264, n.4), Persson, *RTD* p.132, J. Bérard, *RCEM* pp.23, 54f., and Stubbings, *CAH* ed. 2, fasc. 26 (1964) p.6. But Mylonas has repeatedly suggested that the destruction was not until LH IIIB in the 13th cent. (*AE* for 1936, esp. p.70; *Hesperia* 31 (1962) p.302, and elsewhere), and a IIIB date, ca. 1300 B.C., was favoured by Catling and Millett in their study of the stirrup-jars, though they hesitated on account of Furumark's conclusion (*SIST* p.14). The question has been complicated by the discovery in recent excavations of two destruction levels, both dated by their discoverers to LH IIIB (see *AR* for 1964-5 p.15; *ILN* for Nov. 28th 1964, p.860; ib. Dec. 5th 1964, p.896), so that it is not clear whether Keramopoullos' destruction is distinct from these, and therefore possibly still LH IIIA, or if it is to be identified with the earlier of the IIIB destructions. Raison's recent detailed study of the stirrup-jars and other pottery from Keramopoullos' excavation makes the latter assumption more likely (see *VIPA* (1968) esp. pp.5-7, 46-53), but there is still difficulty over the dating of the frescoes (see n. 107), and no firm conclusions can be drawn without further excavation and fuller study of the pottery excavated in recent years. The dating of the initial foundation of the palace also needs clarification.

First there is the matter of the architecture and decoration of the Theban palace. It is too early yet to draw any definite conclusions about this, since the palace remains are only very partially excavated, but it may be noted that it was large, possibly the largest on the mainland (cf. Marinatos, *AAA* 1 (1968) pp.9f.). It had what appears to be an oil-store with drainage channels, circular pits (? reservoirs) and stirrup-jars containing a black substance believed to be burnt oil. Attention has been drawn here to the close parallel with the oil-store at the palace of Mallia (see Pharaklas, *AAA* 1 (1968) pp.241-4, who takes this as evidence for a probable similarity of the Theban palace with those of Crete). Furthermore certain close-fitting terracotta water-pipes or drains found by Keramopoullos have their nearest parallel at Knossos (see *AD* 3 (1917) pp.327-9, referring for a parallel to Evans, *BSA* 8 (1901-2) pp.13f.).[106] In addition it may be noted that the principal Theban fresco so far discovered, the Procession of Women, shows a remarkably close connexion with Cretan painting and has been taken as the work of Knossian artists.[107] On the other

106. On the Knossian water-pipes, which come from more than one part of the palace, see further Evans, *PM* I pp.141-3, III pp.252f., IV. p.147. These are of circular cross-section while Keramopoullos' are semi-circular, but otherwise the similarities are striking.

107. See Reusch, *ZRF* esp. pp.46f.; Rodenwaldt, *JDAI* 34 (1919) p.99 with his n. 2; cf. also Evans, *PM* IV pp.740f. A small fragment of a Shield Fresco has also been found, apparently of the type known earlier at Knossos and also at Tiryns: see Rodenwaldt, loc. cit.; Reusch, *AA* for 1953 cols. 16-25; for a similar fresco from Mycenae see now *AR* for 1970-71 p.10 and fig. 16. The Cretan character of the frescoes was one of the arguments originally used by Burn in support of his idea of Minoans at Thebes and elsewhere (*MPG* p.77).

The dating of the Theban frescoes is not clear: Evans, Rodenwaldt and other older scholars dated them early on stylistic grounds, and a date around 1500 B.C. was supported by Miss Reusch in her study of them (*ZRF* pp.41-6). Marinatos argued for a lower date, around 1450 B.C. or later (*Gnomon* 29 (1957) p.536), and several more recent scholars have expressed the view that they belong to the LH III period (e.g. Matz, *CEG* p.204; Vermeule, *GBA* p.190). Much depends on how long one supposes the frescoes were on the walls before their destruction and the date of the destruction of the palace (see n. 105). Raison has recently argued that the very early dating on stylistic grounds is unreliable, and tentatively places the Theban frescoes after 1425/1400 B.C., which would accord with his IIIB dating of Keramopoullos' destruction level (*VIPA* esp. pp.56-8 with n. 236 there).

hand, the absence of a *megaron* from the palace remains, which has sometimes been used as evidence of Cretan influence (Burn, *MPG* p. 77; Schober, *RE(T)* cols. 1453f.; Vian, *Or. Theb.* p.232) is a dangerous argument which could be disproved by further excavation.[108]

Secondly there is the appearance of the Linear B script at Thebes. The original discovery by Keramopoullos of the inscribed stirrup-jars not unnaturally led scholars to suppose that there may have been Cretans at Thebes, especially when the close affinity of the writing on the jars with examples of Linear B from Knossos had been recognised by Evans. Soon after their discovery the philologist C.D. Buck, while opposing Evans' idea of a general Cretan domination of the Greek mainland in the LH III period, wrote that "the simplest explanation (sc. of the presence of the jars) is that there were families of Cretan potters, as no doubt other Cretan artists, in Thebes and elsewhere" (*CPh* 21 (1926) p.23). The possibility of a link between this ancient form of writing and the tradition of Kadmos as a bringer of letters had already been noted by Keramopoullos (*PAAH* for 1921 p.34), and was especially taken up by Rhys Carpenter, who wrote: "It is not unreasonable to hold some Minoan settler in mainland Greece responsible for the (apparently not very wide) diffusion of the Cretan linear script; and if Professor Myres states the case correctly, the Cadmeans arrived from the sea about 1400 B.C., were 'red-skins' and sea-bred mariners connected with the new dynasty established about the same time in Crete" (p.7 of "Letters of Cadmus" in *AJPh* 56 (1935) pp.5-13). It must of course be remembered that these statements were made at a time when the Theban stirrup-jars were the chief evidence for Linear B writing on the mainland. The whole picture has since been transformed by the discovery of tablets at Pylos and Mycenae, as well as by the decipherment of their language as Greek.

108. The dangers of drawing too many conclusions from the plan of the Theban palace (and in particular from the apparent absence of a *megaron*) are well illustrated by the fact that Pharaklas has recently stated that there is no compelling reason to make us suppose that the Theban palace was like the other mainland ones from the Peloponnese (*AAA* 1 (1968) p.244), while Spyropoulos writing in the same journal, has expressed his confidence that the *megaron* will soon be found and has even indicated the precise quarter of the town where he expects it to be (*AAA* 4 (1971) p.37).

But although the presence of the script in itself can no longer justify belief in any special Cretan influence, it is perhaps worth mentioning that some of the new Theban tablets (those from the site in Pelopidas Street) would appear to be the earliest example of Linear B tablets on the mainland (cf. above p.104 with n.103), and it is universally recognised that the script (though not the language) of the Linear B documents is derived from Crete. It may also be noted that the second set of tablets (see n.103) appear to deal with wool (Spyropoulos, *Kadmos* 9 (1970) p.171; on the importance of the wool-industry at Knossos see Killen in *BSA* 59 (1964) pp.1-15).

Thirdly we may consider the pottery from Thebes. It is evident that certain references by the earlier scholars to the presence of Minoan pottery arose from the fact that, at the time they were writing, truly Minoan pottery could not be readily distinguished from Mycenaean wares made under Cretan influence,[109] and it is much to be hoped that the pottery from Thebes may be further studied to see if any truly Cretan examples can be identified.[110] Certainly a Cretan origin seems very likely for one major group of pots — the 28 stirrup-jars already mentioned in connexion with their inscriptions. H.W. Catling and A.

---

109. Minoan pottery from Thebes is mentioned by Evans, who refers to sherds and other pottery found by Keramopoullos as LM IB, and uses this evidence to support the idea of the foundation of a Minoan palace at Thebes around 1500 B.C., which, as he put it, "sealed the Cretan conquest of Boeotia" (*PM* III (1930) p.416; cf. *PM* IV (1935) p.283); by Persson, who refers to "a great quantity of Cretan pottery (Palace style)" at Thebes to justify the view of a Cretan settlement there, which he thought was founded by the Minoans to gain a foothold in the interior after they had already mastered Argolis and Attica (*RTD* (1931) p.132); and by Myres, who mentions the discovery of apparently LM II pots in tombs on Aghia Anna (i.e. the Ismenion) in support of his theory of a Cretan Kadmos (*YWCS* for 1911, p.27). Certainly some of the pottery referred to by Myres appears to be of mainland origin, as can be seen by a comparison of the published pieces (*AE* for 1910, cols. 212ff.) with the relevant motifs in Furumark's *MP*. See further next note.

110. Raison has recently re-examined some of the pottery from Keramopoullos' destruction level, and he clearly treats this as Mycenaean (*VIPA* pp.46-53); but although he refers to the LM material mentioned by Evans (*VIPA* p.58 n. 235), he does not discuss its origin. Hope Simpson also apparently treats the older Theban material as Mycenaean, and does not mention any Minoan pottery (*GMS* p.121, citing Furumark, *CMP*).

Millett have argued, from a spectrographic analysis of their clays, that the majority of these (23 in all) are composed of types corresponding most closely with those of certain East Cretan sites.[111] This idea of a Cretan provenance for the jars, though it has been questioned,[112] fits in well with the fact that several of them have a light-on-dark decoration ("a wholly Minoan form of decoration", Boardman, *OKT* (1963) p.76), and the occurrence in their inscriptions of place-names found also on the Knossos tablets.[113] All these facts taken together make it extremely likely that this substantial group of jars was imported from Crete.

Finally we turn to the matter of burial customs. It has been noted that the tholos tomb is so far absent from Thebes, and that the recently discovered chamber tomb with frescoes is unique (see Spyropoulos, *AAA* 4 (1971) pp.161-4). Specific links with Crete are suggested by the occurrence of larnax-burials which are extremely rare on the mainland but characteristic of Crete. As long ago as 1940 C.F.C. Hawkes referred to "clay bath-tub coffin-burials in the Cretan manner" to support his idea of a Minoan colony at Thebes (*PFE* p.351; it may be noted that Hawkes rejected the idea of Minoan colonists elsewhere on the mainland), but at the time he wrote only

111. See Catling and Millett, *SIST*. It should be noted that according to this analysis the jars are not a homogeneous group, but that several different factories appear to be represented including one at Thebes. For earlier work by Catling and others see *BSA* 58 (1963) pp.94-115, esp. p.109 on material from Thebes.

112. In particular Raison has questioned the validity of Catling and Millett's analyses, and has doubted the Cretan origin of the jars (see *VIPA* pp.193-209, esp. pp.207f., and pp.237-40). But his objections have met with a detailed reply from Catling and Millett in *Archaeometry* 11 (1969) pp.3-20, and it seems likely that their conclusions should be accepted (cf. Chadwick, *Minos* 10 (1969) p.119; McDonald and Olivier cited by Palmer, *Kadmos* 11 (1972) p.46). See further Pelon, *REG* 81 (1968) pp.562-7, esp. p.565 for criticism of the limited nature of Raison's own clay analyses. Recent excavation has brought to light new evidence for inscribed jars from Crete itself (see Tzedakis, *Kadmos* 6 (1967) pp.106-9 on sherds from Chania; Fraser, *AR* for 1968-69 p.32 on a jar from Knossos; further discussion by Palmer, *Kadmos* 10 (1971) pp.70ff.).

113. See Palmer, *M&M* pp.167f. and, more fully, *Kadmos* 11 (1972) pp.27-46; cf. also Chadwick, *Minos* 10 (1969) esp. pp.117-9. It may be noted that Cretan place-names have also been identified on certain other jars from the mainland (see Palmer and Chadwick, locc. citt.).

one fragment of a larnax had been discovered at Thebes (see Keramopoullos, *AD* 3 (1917) p.92). Recently several new fragments of larnakes have come to light from Theban tombs, as well as a further possible fragment with fine painted decoration from a site in Pindar Street.[114] Moreover a very large number of complete burial larnakes with quite remarkable painted decoration (including scenes with mourning women and bull-leaping have been discovered at the Boeotian site of Tanagra.[115] As Mrs. Vermeule has stressed, larnakes of this type represent "a dramatic departure from normal Mycenaean burial custom" (*JHS* 85 (1965) p.124), and it is difficult to account for their presence unless one is to suppose that a group of people accustomed to larnax-burial had settled in eastern Boeotia during the LH III period.[116] Tanagra is nearly twenty miles from Thebes and might therefore seem an unlikely site to be invoked in connexion with

114. For new clay larnax fragments at Thebes see *AD* 22 (1967) B.l (*Chron.*) p.227, site no. 4 (Church of the Archangels in the Kolonaki area), and ib. p.228, no. 6 (Mycenaean tomb on the Megalo Kastelli or Gerokomeion Hill). For the small painted fragment, which is decorated in the "palace style" with part of a large fishing-net and fishes, see *AD* 24 (1969) B.l (*Chron.*) p.183 pl. 193a; also *AR* for 1970-71 fig. 27. This could be from either a larnax or a large vase, and is a surface find.

115. The first examples, some twelve known from irregular excavation, were published by E. Vermeule, *JHS* 85 (1965) pp.123-48. Exploration by the Greek Archaeological Service has resulted in the discovery of well over 30 more, many of them painted, in tombs from near Tanagra; for these see esp. Spyropoulos, *AAA* 3 (1970) pp.184-97; id., *Archaeology* 25 (1972) pp.206-9; and Orlandos in *Ergon* for 1971 pp.11-21. The large number of burial larnakes from Tanagra contrasts with the very small number, less than a dozen, from the whole of the rest of Greece apart from Thebes and Crete (see Vermeule, op. cit. p.124 with her n. 3); on the popularity of the larnax in Crete see Rutkowski, *BSA* 63 (1968) pp.219-27, esp.223, where he notes the occurrence of over 500 funerary examples of LM III date.

116. Cf. Vermeule, *JHS* 85 (1965) p.137, though she is very cautious on the question of origin. The larnakes published by Mrs. Vermeule appear, from their decoration, to date from the later LH IIIB period, and first indications are that the newly discovered ones from Tanagra itself are from about the same date. A full stylistic analysis of these would be most valuable, and in particular a comparison with painted Cretan examples, especially those with representational decoration (for some recently discovered examples from Armenoi Rethymni, including scenes of bulls, a hunt (?), and a woman or goddess with raised arms, see Tzedakis, *AAA* 4 (1971) pp.216-22; for other Cretan examples with human figures see Vermeule, op. cit. pp.135f.; for a selection with animals, birds and plants see Marinatos, *CM* pls. 126-7).

the Kadmos legend; yet it is precisely this place which is said by Herodotos to have once been the home of the Gephyraeans, who were among the Φοίνιχες who came over with Kadmos.[117]

All this evidence needs to be assessed very carefully. The features showing Cretan influence are of varying and often questionable dates, and alternative explanations, besides Cretan settlement, are certainly possible. Nevertheless the amount of evidence for special Cretan influence at Thebes is sufficient to raise once again the possibility of some Minoan settlement there, and in this connexion it is worth pointing out that there are other links in mythology and cult between Boeotia and Crete besides the hypothetical identification of Φοίνιχες with Minoans.[118]

---

117. See Hdt. V. 57f.; Strabo IX. 2. 10. For Gephyra as a name for Tanagra cf. Steph. Byz. and Et. Magn. s.v. Gephyra; on the tenuous connexion between Phoinix, the tutor of Achilles, and Tanagra see above n. 64.

118. Attention was drawn to these in my communication to *Teiresias* 2 (1972) pp.2-5, but as this review is of limited circulation, it seems worth summarising the main points here. According to Apollodoros Rhadamanthys, the son of Europê, fled from Crete to Boeotia and lived as an exile at Okaleai, where he married Alkmene, the mother of Herakles (Apollod. II. 4. 11; cf. III. 1. 2). His tomb was shown near a spring called Kissousa outside the neighbouring town of Haliartos (Plut. *Lys.* 28), and Cretan rites were celebrated there. Kallimachos asks: "Why does Haliartos, the city of Kadmos, celebrate the *Theodaisia*, a Cretan festival, by the water of Kissousa?" (*Aitia* fr. 43. 86f. Pfeiffer); the rest of the passage is fragmentary, but the poet also refers to Cretan ships bringing incense, to the spring of Rhadamanthys, and to traces of his legislation. A further link between this area and Crete is provided by Plutarch (loc. cit. above): he remarks that the Cretan storax-plant grows near the spring and Rhadamanthys' tomb, and that the people of Haliartos take this as proof that Rhadamanthys once lived there. It is curious to note that the storax, which was used for the production of incense, balm and medicines, is well known in other sources as an oriental plant (e.g. Mnesimach. fr.4. 62 Kock) and Herodotos attests that its products were imported to Greece from Phoenicia (Hdt. III. 107; for its occurrence in Crete as well as in the orient see also Plin. *N.H.* XII. 124f.).

Other links between Crete and Boeotia are Kadmos' own genealogical relationship with Europê, Minos etc., and the tradition that Europê herself was hidden by Zeus near Teumessos in Boeotia (Antimachos fr.3 Wyss; Paus. IX. 19. 1; Demeter was invoked under the title of *Europê* at Lebadeia: see Paus. IX. 39. 5). A hero or god named Phoinix is attested epigraphically in Crete, his name standing in a list between Britomartis and Amphiona (!), but it is not known whether he was connected with Europê or the Kadmos cycle (see Wüst in *RE* XX.1 col. 413; Astour, *HS* p.142). Two linguistic links may also be

What then may we conclude about the theory that the legend of Kadmos might reflect a memory of the coming of Minoan Cretans to Thebes? From the standpoint of the literary evidence, the chief difficulty in the way of this hypothesis is that it appears to contradict the legend itself. *Prima facie* Φοῖνιξ does not mean Cretan, and Fick's reason for supposing that it might once have done so, i.e. the "redskin" theory, is unsound. Yet this difficulty is not insuperable: we have seen how the obscurity of the name's origin and in particular its suggested association with the once widespread purple dye industry at least allow the possibility that the legend of a "Phoenician" Kadmos might have arisen from such historical events as were reconstructed by Hall, Burn and Myres. As to the archaeological evidence, the view held by these scholars, that there was a general Cretan domination of the mainland, is no longer acceptable. Yet the possibility of a Minoan settlement at Thebes, perhaps only on a small scale, cannot be entirely ruled out, even though at present there is no decisive evidence to support it. If future excavation were to disclose clearer indications of unusually close links with Crete, the notion of a Minoan Kadmos, and even of Gephyraeans (from Crete) at Tanagra, might not seem wholly beyond the bounds of reason.

At the same time it must be recognised that any plausibility which the Cretan hypothesis may have is necessarily dependent on its comparison with available alternatives: if for example it could be shown that the presence of oriental people at Thebes in the Mycenaean period was very unlikely, the Cretan theory would gain

noted: (a) according to Hesychios (see above n. 72) κάδμος was a common noun in Cretan; and (b) the name Φοινικήια for letters, whose first use is ascribed by Herodotos to Ionians living around Boeotia (Hdt. V. 58f.; cf. his use of Καδμήια γράμματα in the same passage), is paralleled by the terms ποινικαστάς, ποινικάζεν on a recently discovered inscription from Crete of ca. 500 B.C. (see Jeffery and Morpurgo-Davies, *Kadmos* 9 (1970) esp. pp.152f.; cf. also Ch. II, n. 32, Ch. VIII, n. 190).

Links such as these would easily be explicable if we knew that there had been a Cretan settlement in Boeotia (cf. Persson, *RTD* p.132), but it must be stressed that one cannot simply assume that they go back to the Mycenaean Age (as Vian, *Or. Theb.* pp.232f.). Evidence of this sort is open to many different interpretations (cf. below Ch. VII on similar oriental material, and Ch. IX, n. 209), and it would be unwise to attach too much importance to it as an indication of immigration.

some measure of attractiveness as a result.[119] For this reason we must now consider historical interpretations of the legend of Kadmos which allow Φοῖνιξ to be understood in a more conventional sense.

119. Apart from the oriental hypothesis to be considered in detail in subsequent chapters, the two main alternatives to the Cretan interpretation are (a) the idea that *Phoinike* and *Phoinikes* originally had a very loose meaning; and (b) the hypothesis that the legend of Kadmos represents a migration from Illyria to Thebes (for these see Ch. III, pp.57f.).

(a) *The idea of a very loose meaning for "Phoinike" and "Phoinikes"*

This hypothesis lacks any good support either in the classical usage of the terms (see above p.92 with n. 83), or in the conjecture favoured by Autran and others that *Phoinike* originally meant Caria and only later became extended to have a wide meaning (cf. n. 84). It might nevertheless be sustained by reference to the idea, discussed earlier in this Chapter, that the name *Phoinikes* was originally applied to purple-dyers, and might thus have once included not only Cretans, but other peoples of the Bronze Age known to have engaged in purple-fishing and dyeing. But though this hypothesis certainly cannot be excluded, the possible meanings for the term are so wide (e.g. Trojans, Mycenaeans, Egyptians, Syrians (from Ras Shamra) and conceivably even Carians - see Hom. *Il.* IV. 142 with Didymos' commentary) that it cannot be tested archaeologically by reference to the remains at Thebes. For this reason it has here seemed preferable to concentrate on the Cretan hypothesis, for which relevant archaeological evidence is available, and which has the further advantage that the Cretans seem to be the *first* known makers of the murex-dye.

(b) *The Illyrian hypothesis*

This hypothesis never won wide support, and is open to the major objection that Kadmos in the literary sources is never said to have come from Illyria, but only to have withdrawn there after his reign at Thebes (cf. above Ch. II). It rests upon a few place-names (e.g. the occurrence of the name Φοινίκη for a town in Epeiros), and is not supported by archaeological or historical evidence (for further brief criticisms see Vian, *Or. Theb.* pp.132f.). More detailed consideration does not therefore seem worth-while. It may in addition be noted that Sakellariou's modified form of the Illyrian theory, by which it is suggested that Kadmos may be a "Pelasgian" hero from Illyria (see above Ch. III), is likewise very speculative: we know very little about who the Pelasgians were, and Kadmos' supposed connexion with them depends upon isolated details found only in late sources (e.g. the fact that the name supplied for the man from whom Kadmos bought his cow was Pelagon).

113

CHAPTER VI

BRONZE AGE PHOENICIANS AT THEBES?

The most natural meaning of Φοινίϰη in the story of Kadmos is that which the Greeks themselves normally gave to the word, that is, Phoenicia proper or possibly Phoenicia and the parts of the Levantine coast immediately north and south of it (cf. above p.92). But many scholars have found insuperable difficulties in the way of understanding Φοινίϰη in this sense, and either have conjectured, as we saw in the last Chapter, a different meaning for the term, or have proposed explanations of how the tradition might have arisen from circumstances other than historical fact (cf. above pp.52-6). The purpose of the present Chapter is to reconsider some of the main difficulties that stand in the way of accepting the presence of oriental people at Thebes as the historical basis for the tradition of Kadmos' Phoenician origin.

The first major difficulty that has been felt concerns the date of Phoenician expansion overseas. It was once believed that as early as the middle of the second millennium B.C. the Phoenician cities of Tyre and Sidon had sent out large numbers of colonies and settlements all over the Mediterranean world and even beyond,[120] but sceptical scholars challenged this view, and at the end of the nineteenth century K.J. Beloch vehemently attacked the idea; he argued that far from maintaining a very early thalassocracy over the Aegean, as had once been believed, the Phoenician cities did not expand overseas until well into the first millennium, that even then they only traded in the

---

120. For the view of very early widespread Phoenician settlement abroad see Movers, *Die Phönizier* (1841-56); Kenrick, *Phoenicia* (1855), esp. pp.69-156; Lenormant, *LPC* II (1874) pp.313-437; Duncker, *GADun* V (1881) pp.42-55; Rawlinson, *HPhoen* (1889) pp.89-129. On Phoenician influence outside the Straits of Gibraltar see esp. Thackeray, *REPS* I (1843) pp.4-17, and on older theories of Phoenicians in Britain see Glyn Daniel, *IP* p.21.

Aegean without founding settlements, and that they were preceded in their marine enterprise by the Greeks. His date for the Phoenician expansion was the eighth century B.C., and he continued to maintain these views in the new edition of his *Griechische Geschichte,* which included (in Vol. I.2 (1926) pp.65-76) a revised version of the article of 1894 cited above on p.53. As a result he rejected the possibility of Phoenicians at Thebes; for him Kadmos, like Phoinix, was originally a god, "der als Lichtgott seine Heimat im Lichtland Φοινίκη hat" (op. cit. p.62). Similar objections over the date of the Phoenicians' expansion and the nature of their relations with the Greeks were made by J.U. Powell, who, however, followed Hall in concluding that the Cadmeians of legend were not Semites but Minoans (*PhE* (1911) pp.44f., 53). More recently the question has been taken up by Rhys Carpenter, who concluded that the old idea of Phoenicians trading and settling in the Mediterranean in the second millennium B.C. is a "hopeless illusion": Kadmos' palace at Thebes has turned out to be Mycenaean; the letters found there Aegean; Phoenician seafaring is not to be denied altogether, but this activity has been projected back in time by a trick of fancy: "The Phoenicians whom we see coming to the Mediterranean in the second millennium are real Phoenicians, but they are in actuality sailing through the years just previous to 700 B.C." *HVA* (1933) pp.41-65, esp. pp.42 and 49). Even in the eighth century B.C. the Phoenicians were, in his view, traders and not settlers in Aegean waters.

The second major reason for rejecting the possibility of Phoenician settlers at Thebes has arisen from the geographical situation of the city. Thebes, it is argued, lies inland in an agricultural area; it is most unlikely that the Phoenicians should have chosen to occupy such a site (so, for example, Meyer, *GAMey* (ed. 1, 1893) II p.152; for others who uphold this view see below p.129). It is true that Victor Bérard, the pre-eminent supporter of the Phoenician cause, attempted to show that Thebes occupied a position on a cross-roads of trade routes, and that Boeotia was in effect an isthmus between three seas (*Ph. Od.* I (1902) pp.225-33), but the evidence for Thebes' position as a trading city was examined in detail by A.W. Gomme, who concluded that many of the routes between Thebes and the sea were not easy, that there were difficulties for navigators in approaching the

Boeotian harbours, and that Thebes lay off the main route for Phoenician traders sailing west and was not at all likely to have depended on trade in the Mycenaean period ("The topography of Boeotia and the theories of M. Bérard" in *BSA* 18 (1911-12) pp.189-210). This argument appeared to be borne out by the fact that successive excavations at Thebes failed to bring to light any Phoenician remains there. Thus as early as 1909, in arguing for the interpretation of Kadmos and the Φοίνικες as Aegeans (see above p.87), Sir Arthur Evans wrote: "The prehistoric past of Boeotia now proves not to be Phoenician but Minoan, and no single trace has come to light of Semitic colonization nor even of a single object of Phoenician import" (*SM* I (1909) p.56). Similarly the lack of any Phoenician remains at Thebes was stressed by Dussaud and Keramopoullos (see above p.54), Autran (*Phéniciens* (1920) p.8), and Carpenter (*HVA* (1933) p.42). It has been repeated right up to the recent discoveries at Thebes, as we can see from Vian's passing allusion to "cette Cadmée sur laquelle on n'a pas réussi encore à déceler des traces d'influence phénicienne" (*Or. Theb.* p.54).

At first sight these arguments are indeed formidable; but much new evidence from both Greece and the Near East has come to light in recent years which makes a re-examination of them necessary and worth-while.

We begin by considering the date of Greek relations with the Phoenicians. It has now become generally accepted that there was no Phoenician thalassocracy or widespread colonisation in the Aegean in the early Iron Age. It is rather believed that there was very little contact between Greeks and the historical Phoenicians before the ninth to eighth centuries B.C., and that even at that date the main Phoenician settlements were outside the Aegean — in Cyprus and in the Western Mediterranean at sites such as Carthage, Lepcis Magna and Sabratha in North Africa or Gades in Spain.[121]

---

121. For a 9th or 8th century date for Phoenician activity in the West see Carpenter, *AJA* 62 (1958) pp. 35-53; Harden, *Phoen.* esp. p. 63; Warmington, *Carthage* (Pelican ed., 1964) pp.25-36; Carter, *AJA* 69 (1965) pp.123-32; and Muhly, *HAP* esp. pp.44-6. It should be noted however that certain oriental specialists prefer a higher date for the beginning of the colonisation, most notably Albright, *RCHC* (ed. 2, 1961) p.348; id.,

But if we look back earlier than the beginning of the Iron Age, we find that there is again a period of contact between Greece and the East, and it has indeed become abundantly clear that in the latter part of the second millennium (ca. 1600-1100 B.C.) there was considerable trading contact between the peoples of the Aegean and those of the eastern end of the Mediterranean from Cilicia to Egypt. The extent of this trade is indicated by the "internationalism" of Late Bronze Age art, which can be seen in mainland Greece as early as the Shaft Graves of Mycenae, not only in such well known objects as the inlaid daggers discovered by Schliemann, but also in the "duck vase" of rock crystal from Grave Circle B, which uses a motif found in both Egypt and a number of sites in Syria and Palestine.[122] The borrowing of artistic motifs continues throughout the Late Bronze Age, and is particularly striking in ivory objects, precious metalwork and gem-cutting. The artistic influence would appear to be reciprocal; Aegean artists take over such motifs as the griffin, sphinx and pairs of antithetically placed animals, while their oriental counterparts make use of the running spiral, the "flying gallop" and other Aegean designs.[123]

CAH ed. 2, fasc. 51 (1966) pp.40-3 (10th cent.); Eissfeldt, *RE* XX.1 (1941) col. 363 (from 1200 B.C. on); and Moscati, *WPh* (1968) p.97 (before the 10th cent. B.C.). For one who still believes in a Phoenician thalassocracy see Baramki, *PhPh* (1961) p.10, where we find reference to "a new and virile nation of seamen which quickly stepped into the gap left by the displaced Achaeans, and established a thalassocracy over the Eastern basin of the Mediterranean and the Aegean. For a period of 400 to 450 years the Phoenicians held complete sway over the high seas" (cf. ib. p.59). The role of the Phoenicians in the Aegean will be discussed further in Ch. VIII.

122. For the "duck vase" see esp. Mylonas, *AMyc* pp.144-6, and *MMA* pp.190f. The Egyptian examples of the motif are collected by Hermann, *ZASA* 68 (1932) pp.86-105, and the whole subject is treated at length by Sakellarakis in *AE* for 1971 pp.188-233, with reference to more recently discovered examples from both Greece and the East. Cf. also Iakovidis, Περατή II (1970) pp.344f.

123. For internationalism in art see esp. Kantor, *AegO;* Webster, *MycH* esp. pp.27-31; and W.S. Smith, *IANE*. Over recent years a number of detailed studies of individual motifs have appeared: see esp. Dessenne, *Le Sphinx* (1957) and, for the griffin, Leibovitch, 'A*tiqot* 1 (1955) pp.75-85; Dessenne, *BCH* 81 (1957) pp.203-15; and Bisi, *Il Grifone* (1965). For the duck's head motif see previous note, and on ivory-carving see further Kantor, *JNES* 15 (1956) pp.153-74.

There is also the evidence of imported artefacts. Mycenaean pottery appears in Egypt in LH I, in other parts of the Levant in LH II, and in the LH III period (especially IIIB) is extremely widely distributed not only at coastal sites but also inland.[124] Nor are oriental artefacts in Greece lacking: scarabs, cylinder seals and Canaanite jars are among the more easily identifiable; other imports included raw materials such as ivory, gold, lapis lazuli and probably bronze, as well as ostrich eggs and faience from Egypt.[125] Further new evidence for Late Bronze Age trade has become available from the underwater exploration of shipwrecks, and in one such recent "excavation" off Cape Gelidonya the remains of a ship were recovered with its cargo of copper ingots. Its contents included oriental artefacts such as scarabs, weights and a cylinder seal, tools for bronze-working, and Mycenaean pottery (see G.F. Bass, "Cape Gelidonya: a Bronze Age shipwreck" in *Trans. Amer. Philos. Soc.* n.s. 57 (1967) pt. 8).

The linguistic evidence must also be mentioned. Several Semitic loan words have been noted by Ventris and Chadwick in the Linear B documents, including the garment χιτών, the condiments κύμινον,

124. On the Mycenaean pottery from the Levant see Stubbings, *MPL* (1951) together with Hankey, *MPME* (1967) on more recent finds from additional sites including Tell Sukas on the Syrian coast, Hazor, an important Canaanite town in Galilee, and Amman, a long distance inland on the far side of the Jordan. There is also a brief discussion in Amiran, *APHL* pp.179-86. The large amount of excavation currently being undertaken in Israel has resulted in the continual discovery of further Mycenaean finds there: for some recent examples see Dothan, *Ashdod* I p.83, II-III pp.25f., 82; and under Biran (Tel Dan) and Kochavi (Tel Aphek) in the Bibliography.

125. For oriental imports to Greece and Aegean trade with the Near East in general see Pendlebury, *Aegyptiaca* (1930); Dussaud, *Iraq* 6 (1939) pp.52-65; Wace, *Mycenae* pp.107f.; Lorimer, *HM* pp.52-102; Nilsson, *MMR* (ed. 2, 1950) pp.385f. n. 60; Grace in *AegNE* (ed. Weinberg) pp.80-109 and Amiran, *APHL* pp.138-42 (on the "Canaanite jar"); and Vermeule, *GBA* esp. pp.254-7; cf. also Hutchinson, *PC* pp.311f. on "Reshef" figurines in Greece.

σήσαμα, and κύπαιρος, and the metal χρυσός.[126] These words alone are sufficient to disprove Carpenter's claim made in 1933 that none of the few Phoenician words is "demonstrably older in Greece than the seventh century B.C." (HVA p.45). There is then abundant evidence for extensive trade between Greece and the orient in the Late Bronze Age. It remains to consider in more detail Greek relations with the Phoenicians themselves, or, to be more accurate, their West Semitic ancestors and predecessors in Phoenicia and adjacent areas.

The evidence at present available from Phoenicia proper is disappointingly slight: Bronze Age Tyre and Sidon are virtually unexplored; what is known about them from documentary sources (most notably the Amarna letters) suggests that they did not attain their greatest importance until after the end of the Bronze Age.[127]

126. On Semitic loan-words in Greek see Ventris and Chadwick, *DMG* pp.135f; E. Masson, *RESG* (1967), esp. pp.27-9, 37f., 51f., and 57f., where Mycenaean borrowings are postulated; and Muhly, *HAP* p.22. Astour (*HS* pp.340-44) further proposes to identify a large number of Semitic proper names in the Linear B documents, but his suggestions must remain very hypothetical, since perforce they are based on etymological conjectures rather than contextual analysis. C.H. Gordon's proposed decipherment of Linear A as a Semitic language (see Bibliography) must likewise be regarded as very speculative: compare the discussions of Pope in *Antiquity* 32 (1958) pp.97-9 and Chadwick, ib. 33 (1959) pp.269-78; for one who accepts the identification see Astour, *HS* pp.344-7 with detailed references to Gordon's publications (other scholars favouring his decipherment are listed by Gordon, *Forgotten Scripts* (Pelican ed., 1971) p.168 n. 32).

Further evidence of contact between Greece and the East is provided by references to Aegean people in Egyptian documents (and by representations of them in Egyptian paintings): see esp. Vercoutter, *EMEP* on the identification of *Keftiu* and the "Isles in the midst of the Sea"; on some specific Aegean place-names recently identified in a text from the reign of Amenophis III, see Kitchen, *Orientalia* 34 (1965) pp.1-9, id., *BASO 181 (1966) pp.23f.*, Astour, *AJA* 70 (1966) pp.313-7, and Muhly, *HAP* p.61 with his n. 316 for bibliography.

127. For a summary of our knowledge of Tyre and Sidon in the Late Bronze Age see the relevant sections in Jidejian, *Tyre* (1969), *Sidon* (1972) with the bibliographies there, and Eissfeldt's articles in *RE* XX.1 (1941) s.v. Phoiniker, esp. cols. 355-65, and ib. 2nd ser. VII.2 (1948) s.v. Tyros, esp. cols. 1882-6. The remarkable fact is how little can be said of these cities: such recent works as Gray, *Can.* (1964) and Culican, *FMV* (1966) make no more than brief mention of them, and Hankey actually describes two recently discovered Egyptian inscriptions at Tyre as "giving the first solid evidence of Late Bronze Age Tyre" (*MPME* p.122).

Nevertheless we know that Mycenaean Greece was in contact with these cities from an interesting piece of linguistic evidence which concerns their Greek names. After the Bronze Age the initial sibilants found in these names (z and ṣ) fell together and were both rendered by ṣādê (ṣ), but the Greek names for these towns preserve an opposition current in the second millennium B.C.[128] It would therefore seem likely that the apparent absence of Mycenaean imports at Tyre and Sidon is caused by the limited amount of excavation of the early levels of these sites rather than by lack of Mycenaean contact with them: indeed, excavation of a Bronze Age grave in Sidon has very recently produced the first ever definite Mycenaean import there (Hankey, *MPME* (1967) p.120). It may also be mentioned that Mycenaean wares have been found in some quantity at other sites on the Phoenician coast, including Tell Abu Hawam in the extreme south of Phoenicia proper, and at Sarepta and Gharifeh in the neighbourhood of Sidon (Stubbings, *MPL* (1951) pp.77-82; Hankey, *MPME* pp.121f., referring to a major group of 34 Mycenaean pots all from one tomb at Sarepta); imitation Mycenaean pottery has been found at Qrayeh (el-Bordj) only eight kilometres S.E. of Sidon (Hankey, loc. cit.; cf. Schaeffer, *SCCA* p.76).

Of the other chief Phoenician cities, only Byblos has been extensively excavated, and even here there has been less exploration of the Late Bronze Age phase than of certain other levels.[129] It is shown to have been in contact with Mycenaean Greece by the

---

128. See Friedrich, *ZS* 2 (1924) p.4; id., *Phönizisch-punische Grammatik* (1951)p.9; Albright, *JPOS* 6 (1926) p. 83; id., *AJA* 54 (1950) p.165. In this context it is worth noting that Latin, in addition to *Tyrus* and *Tyrius*, uses also *Sarra* and *Sarranus*, rendered in accordance with the Phoenician form of the name (ṣr) in the first millennium, where the initial consonant is indistinguishable from the s in Sidon (ṣdn).

129. For the excavations at Byblos see Montet, *Byblos et l'Égypte* and Dunand, *FB*, together with Schaeffer's discussion of the chronology in *SCCA* pp.50-72, where the Cretan contacts are also discussed; detailed bibliography is given in Jidejian, *Byblos* (ed. 2, 1971) pp.214-7; see also Hankey, *MPME* p.117 n. 14 on evidence for Byblos' external contacts in the Late Bronze Age. It may be noted that remains of Late Bronze Age Beirut are only just now beginning to come to light, but the finds already include Mycenaean pottery (Hankey, *MPME* pp.119f.).

occurrence of Mycenaean pottery there (see Stubbings, *MPL* pp.53f. and 75-7; Hankey, *MPME* pp.119f.), but although it had attained some importance in the Middle Bronze Age, maintaining close relations with Egypt and having trade contacts with Crete, by the Late Bronze Age its importance as a trading centre seems to have been eclipsed by another port, Ugarit, in North Syria. The discoveries at this site, which a very recent writer has called "probably the first great international port in history" (Culican, *FMV* (1966) p.46) have attracted much attention, and have several times been mentioned by scholars who believe in a historical basis for the tradition of Phoenicians at Thebes (see above pp.60f.). Since the material from Ugarit is not generally well known to classical specialists, and some scholars who have used it in connexion with the Kadmos legend seem to have relied on brief accounts of the site which are now outdated,[130] it seems appropriate to consider the evidence in some detail.

Ras Shamra or "Fennel Head", which is the site of ancient Ugarit, lies on the North Syrian coast some eight miles north of Latakia. Excavations there and at the neighbouring harbour town of Minet-el-Beida or "White Haven" were begun in 1929, and work has continued ever since, interrupted only by the war. Altogether a substantial palace, several habitation quarters and numerous tombs

---

130. Until recently the two most widely available general accounts of the site were those of Gaster in *Antiquity* 13 (1939) pp.304-319, and Schaeffer in *CTRS* (1939). Possibly reliance on these produced the statement found in both Thomson, *SAGS* I (1949) p.376 and Willetts, *CCF* (1962) p.157, that the oldest of the Mycenaean and Minoan objects at the site date from the 17th cent. B.C., and this is used to support their theory that the legend of Kadmos refers to events before 1580 B.C. (cf. above pp.65f.). But in fact it is now clear that the Minoan and Mycenaean phases at Ugarit are distinct: the oldest Cretan imports are MM II and belong to Schaeffer's Level II.2, ca. 1900-1750 B.C. (see Schaeffer, *SCCA* (1948) p.16 and pl. XIII, and the "Corpus céramique" in *Ugaritica* II, esp. p.256), while the Mycenaean pottery is mainly LH III, though one LH II pot has been identified (see Wace and Blegen, *PET* (1939) p.137 and pl. III.5; Stubbings, *MPL* p.53). Several useful general accounts of Ras Shamra are now available, including Drower, *Ugarit*(1968), and, at a more popular level, Courtois, "Les cités états de Phénicie au IIème millénaire" in *Archeologia* 20 (1968) pp.15-25 (almost exclusively on Ras Shamra). I am grateful to the Revd. W. Johnstone, who has taken part in several campaigns at Ras Shamra, for discussing the subject with me.

have been uncovered, and the results of these extensive excavations, including the discovery of a large number of documents in a variety of languages, have proved to be of the greatest importance not only for Near Eastern and Biblical scholarship but also for Mycenaean studies.[131]

The earliest settlement goes back to a pre-pottery Neolithic phase, and habitation continues right through the Bronze Age. C.F.A. Schaeffer, the excavator of Ras Shamra, has divided its history into five main periods, the earliest being Level V and the latest Level I (for the dating of the Bronze Age levels see Schaeffer, *SCCA* (1948) pp.8-39). It is known that Semites were established at the site at least by Level II, which corresponds roughly to the Middle Bronze Age, and is dated by Schaeffer to ca. 2100-1600 B.C. By this time Ugarit already had trading contacts with a wide area, including Egypt, Mesopotamia and Crete, and diplomatic relations with Egyptian pharaohs of the Twelfth Dynasty are attested. The best known period of Ugaritic history and the one most relevant to our study is Level I, corresponding roughly to the Late Bronze Age, ca. 1600-1200 B.C., and subdivided by Schaeffer into three phases. This is the time of the great struggle for power in North Syria between Egypt, the kingdom of the Mitannians, and the Hittites. Ugarit itself seems first to have come under Egyptian influence, and after Tuthmosis III's conquest of North Syria in the fifteenth century even had an Egyptian garrison. But Hittite and Mitannian influence is also attested, and there seem to have been Mitannian and Hurrian elements in the population as well as Semitic people of various groups.

The second phase of Level I is brought to an end by a violent destruction, dated by Schaeffer to 1365 B.C., and apparently identical with that mentioned in one of the Amarna letters (no. 151 in Knudtzon's edition), in which Abimilki of Tyre writes that Ugarit is

---

131. Preliminary reports have regularly appeared in the journal *Syria*, and more detailed studies in Schaeffer's series *Ugaritica* I-VI (1939-1969). The texts are published by Virolleaud and Nougayrol in *Ugaritica* V and *PRU* (see Bibliography). Further study of the texts has been carried out by numerous scholars, including most notably C.H. Gordon (see his *UG, UH, UL, UM,* and *UT* cited in the Bibliography).

destroyed by fire. Schaeffer attributed the destruction to an earthquake, and this view has been widely accepted, though it has recently been suggested that it might be connected with the campaigns of the Hittite king Suppiluliumas in North Syria in the early fourteenth century (see A.F. Rainey in *The Biblical Archaeologist* 28 (1965) p.110). Whatever the cause of the destruction Ugarit made a rapid recovery, and the following phase (Level I.3) is even more prosperous than the preceding. Mycenaean pottery appears in large quantities, both at Ras Shamra itself and its new harbour town of Minet-el-Beida. To this period belongs the palace with its nine interior courts, 12 staircases and 90 rooms including library and sanctuaries, described by Schaeffer as "une des plus vastes et des plus luxueuses demeures royales jusqu'ici connues des pays de la Méditerranée orientale et du Proche Orient en général" (*Syria* 31 (1954) pp.16f.). The wealth of the town is attested both by its physical remains and by the documents.

These are of particular interest, comprising as they do diplomatic correspondence, administrative texts, private letters, religious and literary texts, and business records. They are chiefly in Akkadian, the *lingua franca* of the Near East at this date, and Ugaritic, a Semitic dialect not previously known to scholars; but a number of other languages are attested at the site, including Sumerian, Hurrian, Egyptian, Hittite and a type of Cypro-Minoan. These documents mean that the history of Ugarit in its last phase is better known than that of other Canaanite sites in this period, and its complicated relations with Egypt and the Hittites can be traced: see especially Liverani, *SUEA* (1962); Drower, *Ugarit* (1968). Ugarit continued to be occupied till the late thirteenth century, when it was violently destroyed, perhaps by the Sea Peoples; after this it never regained its importance.

We must now ask what light these discoveries at Ras Shamra cast on Mycenaean relations with the East, and on the problem of Greek references to Phoenicians in the Aegean. The most important fact to be established is undoubtedly the presence at Ugarit during the Late Bronze Age of a Semitic people whose language belongs to the same group as later Phoenician and Hebrew, and whose religion, mythology and culture were exceedingly close to those of the historical Phoenicians — so close that some scholars have not hesitated to call them Proto-Phoenician or even Phoenician.[132] The archaeological evidence shows that this major centre of Canaanite culture was in contact with the Mycenaean world, as can be seen not only by the precious metalwork of Level I.2 at Ras Shamra (gold patera and bowl) and the famous ivory relief of a goddess from Minet-el-Beida, but also in the occurrence of corbelled tombs with dromoi, which present close analogies in certain features with Grave Rho from Circle B at Mycenae and the Royal Tomb of Isopata in Crete.[133] The clearest evidence however for contact with some part of the Mycenaean world is the Mycenaean pottery, which appears in such large quantities in Ugarit's last period (Level I.3, ca. 1365-1200 B.C.) that Schaeffer writes of the

132. For the use of the terms "Proto-Phoenician" and "Phoenician" as applied to the Semitic people of Ugarit see Schaeffer, *CTRS* pp.7, 26, 57 etc., and the works of Dussaud, Gaster, Virolleaud and others, cited in the bibliography of Ras Shamra in *Ugaritica* I pp.147-207.

The appropriateness of the term "Canaanite" for the people of Ras Shamra has been criticised (see esp. Rainey in *IEJ* 13 (1963) pp.43-5); and it should be noted that it has been adopted in this Chapter in accordance with the usage of such scholars as Gray in *Can.* passim and K.M. Kenyon in *Amorites and Canaanites* (1966) esp. pp.58f., and it is to be understood in a general cultural sense.

The classification of the Ugaritic dialect has likewise been the subject of some debate: earlier scholars took it as a direct ancestor of Hebrew and Phoenician (see the authorities quoted by Schaeffer, *CTRS* n. 144 on pp. 90f.), but it is now generally understood as an independent Semitic language or dialect, belonging to the same broad group ("West Semitic") as Hebrew and Phoenician (see the discussions of Gordon, *UM* pp.120-3; Albright, *CAH* ed. 2, fasc. 54 (1966) pp.16f. (where it is classed with the "North Canaanite" group); for further discussion see the authorities cited by Rainey, op. cit. p.45 n. 15).

133. For the gold patera and bowl see esp. Schaeffer, *Ugaritica* II pp.1-48, and for the ivory of a goddess see *Ugaritica* I p.32 and pls. I and XI. The exact relation of the vaulted tombs of Ras Shamra and Minet-el-Beida to those of the Aegean is obscure: Schaeffer himself understood the tombs as being of Aegean origin and as evidence for Cretan or Mycenaean settlers (see esp. *Ugaritica* I pp.68, 73; cf. also Evans, *PM* IV pp.770-84); but other scholars have rather supposed that the influence is in the reverse direction, and that the Aegean tombs with the greatest similarity to those of Ugarit, namely the Royal Tomb of Isopata and the more recently discovered Grave Rho at Mycenae, were built under the direct or indirect influence of Canaanite prototypes (see Vermeule, *GBA* p.125). The dating of the various tombs requires some clarification (compare the discussions of Westholm, *AIRRS* 5 (1941) pp.57f., Mylonas, *AMyc* p. 164, Hutchinson, *PC* p.292 and Vermeule, loc. cit.).

city as "inondée de produits mycéniens" (*Ugaritica* I (1939) p.99). In addition to the Mycenaean vases, which include ritual vessels, a substantial number of Mycenaean figurines have been found.[134] It has been suggested on the basis of these Aegean contacts that there were Mycenaean colonists resident in Ugarit.[135] Is it possible also that the people of Ugarit themselves visited the Aegean for the purpose of trade or settlement?

They are certainly known to have engaged in seafaring. Evidence for the extent of this activity comes from documents excavated at Ras Shamra and belonging to the last phases of its history (Level I.3). Since many of these are only recently published, it is worth mentioning the principal texts and giving some outline of their contents.[136] They include the well known "naval gazette" where warships are listed with the names of their captains, their place of origin and the number of

---

134. For the Mycenaean pottery and figurines from Ras Shamra see Schaeffer's "Corpus céramique" in *Ugaritica* II pp.131-301, together with Stubbings, *MPL* pp.53, 61f., 71-5. For more recent finds see Hankey, *MPME* pp.112f. and Schaeffer, *Ugaritica* V pp.765f. with pls. III-VII.

135. For Schaeffer's view of Mycenaean (and Minoan) settlement at Ugarit see *JDAI* 52 (1937) esp. p.140; *CTRS* pp.12, 26; *Ugaritica* I Ch. II passim. His interpretation has been disputed by Liverani and Astour (see *HS* pp.352-5), on the grounds that no Mycenaean Greek proper names have been identified in the documents of Ugarit, and there are no certain references in the texts to the presence of Aegean peoples in the city (Dhorme's old identification of *yman* as Ionia is now generally abandoned: see Astour, loc. cit. and Cassola, *IMM* pp.20, 41f.). But though it is perhaps rash to speak of "une véritable colonisation mycénienne" (Schaeffer, *Ugaritica* I p.99), some sort of Mycenaean settlement seems likely in view of the occurrence of figurines and ritual vessels at the site (cf. Stubbings, *MPL* p.71; Webster, *MycH* pp.9, 66; and Cassola, loc. cit.). The exact source of any settlers within the Mycenaean world remains to be determined; Stubbings noted a striking prevalence of Cypriot features in the pottery included in *MPL* (see there, esp. p.74).

136. References are to the excavation numbers of the texts. This list is not comprehensive: further texts mentioning ships and seafaring may be found by consulting the glossaries of Gordon, *UT* and of the relevant volumes of *Ugaritica* and *PRU*, though their interpretation is sometimes obscure. For Canaanite seafaring see Astour, *HS* pp.106f., 348f. with notes, Bass, *AHS* pp.22f., and, in more detail, Sasson, *JAOS* 86 (1966) pp.126-38, though he surely goes too far in speaking of "definite proofs of a Canaanite 'thalassocracy' " in the Late Bronze Age (op. cit. p.128; cf. Muhly's criticisms, *HAP* p.43).

126

men who went on each ship (RS 8.279; cf. T.H. Gaster in *PalEQ* for 1938 pp.105-12), a list of types of ship (no. 5 in *Syria* 12 (1931) pp.228f.), a list of workers including shipbuilders (RS 14.01 in *Syria* 28 (1951) p.167) and a letter to the king of Ugarit requesting him to equip a ship (RS 18.147, *PRU* V (1965) pp.87f.). A notable text (RS 16.238; cf. *Syria* 31 (1954) pp.38f. and *PRU* III (1955) p.107) refers to a merchant ship's passage to *Kptr*, most plausibly to be identified with Crete;[137] another refers to a ship on its way to Egypt being overtaken by storm (RS 18.31, *PRU* V pp.81-3). Other recently published texts mention the lading of cargo (RS 18.119, *PRU* V p.74) and the payment to the king of Byblos for a ship (RS 18.25, *PRU* V pp.129f.), and allude to "the ship (or ships) of the king" (see the brief fragment RS 18.291, *PRU* V p.75; cf. Gordon, *UT* (1965) p.283 no. 2057, who refers to this as a fragment of a catalogue of ships; for another apparent catalogue of ships see RS 18.74, *PRU* V pp.109f. = *UT* p.286 no. 2085). Finally, in three important texts the Hittite king requests a ship for the transport of grain to Cilicia (RS 20.212; cf. *CRAI* for 1960 p.165 and *Ugaritica* V p.731), the king of Ugarit writes to the king of Alasia at the time of the Sea Peoples' invasions and complains that all his ships are in Lycia (RS 20.238; cf. *CRAI* for 1960 pp.165f. and *Ugaritica* V p.87), and the last king of Ugarit is asked by one of his officers to equip 150 ships (RS 18.148, *PRU* V pp.88f.).

The significance of these documents needs to be carefully weighed: in many of them only a small number of ships are involved; for instance the fragment of the "naval gazette" actually lists only three ships, and the total of enemy ships to which reference is made in RS 20.238 is only seven. At the same time it should be observed that some of the ships are of considerable size: 90 men are mentioned as

---

137. For *Kptr* as Crete see Schaeffer, *Syria* 31 (1954) pp.38f. (on RS 16.238), Dussaud, *CRAI* for 1938 pp.537f., Gordon, *UT* p.422 no. 1291 and elsewhere, and Gray, *Can.* p.46. The identification rests upon the similarity of the name to the Egyptian term *Keftiu* (cf. also Biblical *Caphtor* and *Kaptara* of the Mari texts), which is most plausibly interpreted as referring to Crete or at least some part of the Aegean world: see the detailed discussion in Vercoutter, *EMEP* (1956); for a new reference to *Kptr* in a mythological text see *Ugaritica* V p.570.

going on board one of the ships in the "naval gazette", while it has been estimated that the grainship of RS 20.212 would have held 500 tons. Such ships, as Astour has stressed (*HS* p. 348) would be capable of long voyages, and a likely example is provided by the text referring to *Kptr*. Furthermore, by the end of our period at least, the existence of a substantial fleet is implied by the mention of 150 ships in RS 18.148.

In the light of this evidence from Ras Shamra it needs to be reconsidered by whom the international trade of the Late Bronze Age was conducted. One can hardly doubt that much was in the hands of the Aegean people themselves, but it is at least possible that a proportion of the oriental imports to Greece was brought by Near Eastern seafarers including Canaanites.[138] It would seem then not at all implausible to suggest that some of the Greek traditions of Phoenicians in the Aegean could refer to Bronze Age people from North Syria,[139] and this proposal receives additional support from the fact that one of the industries of Ugarit was the manufacture of purple dye from the murex, an activity for which the later Phoenicians of Tyre and Sidon were famous and from which the very name "Phoenician"

138. There is a fair amount of evidence for other oriental seafaring: see Février, "Les origines de la marine phénicienne" in *RHPh* n.s. 10 (1935) pp.97-124; id., *La Nouvelle Clio* 1 (1949) pp.128-43; Säve-Söderbergh, *The Navy of the Eighteenth Egyptian Dynasty* (1946); Landström, *Ships of the Pharaohs* (1970) esp. p.89; and the more general discussions of Barnett, *Antiquity* 32 (1958) pp.220-30; Casson, *SSAW* (1971) Chs. II-III; and Bass, *AHS* (1972) Ch. I; Bass himself interpreted the Gelidonya wreck as Syrian (*CGBS* (1967) p.164 and *AHS* pp.23f.; so too Astour, *HS* p.349 n. 2), but the possibility cannot be excluded that it might be Cypriot (cf. McCann, *AJA* 74 (1970) p.105) or even Mycenaean (cf. Cadogan, *JHS* 89 (1969) pp.187f.).

For Mycenaean and Minoan seafaring see Marinatos, "La marine créto-mycénienne" in *BCH* 57 (1933) pp.170-235, together with Hutchinson, *PC* pp.91-100; Casson, *SSAW* pp.30-5, 40-2; see also Laviosa, "La marina micenea" in *ASAA* 47-48 (1969-70) pp.7-40 with a comparison of Mycenaean and contemporary oriental ships. For the view that the extent of Mycenaean shipping has been overestimated and that the Phoenicians (i.e. Syrians or Canaanites) must have played a major part in the maritime trade of the Late Bronze Age see esp. Bass, *CGBS* pp.74-7, 165-7.

139. We may compare the suggestion that the Phoenicians who appear in the *Odyssey* are Bronze Age sailors from Syria, including Ugarit (see Stella, *ArchClass* 4 (1952) pp.72-6; id., *Il poema di Ulisse* (1955) pp.38f.; cf. also Stubbings in *CH* pp.542f.). For a different view see Muhly, *HAP* pp.29-31; Coldstream, *GGP* p.390.

has been derived by many scholars (see above p.96 and n.90).

We now turn to the second major difficulty that lies in the way of accepting "Phoenicians" at Thebes as a historical basis for the Kadmos legend, namely the situation of Thebes itself and the apparent absence of Phoenician remains there. As to the geographical situation the most curiously contradictory views have been held. On the one hand it has been used as an argument against the reliability of the tradition: one early writer went so far as to say that "Thebes, situated at a distance from the sea, in a rich fertile valley only adapted for agriculture, and which never had any trade, was the very last place that a commercial people like the Phoenicians would have selected to colonise" (Keightley, *MAGI* (1831) p.293), and similar views have often been put forward (cf. K.O. Müller, *OM* (1820) pp.117f.; Rawlinson, *Phoenicia* (1889) p.62; Meyer, *GAMey* (ed. 1, 1893) II p.152; ib. (ed. 2, 1928) II.1 p.255 n.; and Schober, *RE(T)* (1934) col. 1454). On the other hand V. Bérard maintained the direct opposite, writing that "la seule topologie nous fournirait une preuve d' origine pour cette fondation phénicienne" (*Ph. Od.* I (1902) p.225). For him Boeotia was mainland Greece's "grand bazar" and "centre des routes commerciales", and possession of Thebes was, in his argument, essential for the "thalassocratie phénicienne" in which he believed. Hardly less extravagant claims were made by T.G. Tucker in *The Seven Against Thebes of Aeschylus* (1908), where he writes: "That it (sc. Thebes) in some way received a Phoenician settlement is now scarcely to be doubted. Its position is one upon which the trading and exploiting Phoenicians would be eager to seize if they could." In his view "nothing could be more likely" than a Phoenician settlement at Thebes (op. cit. pp.xiif.).

What are the facts about the position of Thebes? It is certainly not the evident centre of trade routes that V. Bérard claimed, nor the most obvious place to expect close contacts with the orient, and Gomme rightly pointed out the dangers of looking at a map and calculating the distances without allowing for such factors as the difficulties of the terrain and the barrenness of the hills in southern Boeotia (*TBTB* pp.193-206). This is why statements such as that of Astour that Thebes is "merely 12 miles from the Gulf of Corinth and 15 miles from the Euripos" (*HS* p.150; cf. Jidejian, *Tyre* p.37) are misleading. But

129

on the other hand its communications are, as Gomme himself admits, not so difficult as to deter very eager traders, and Heurtley, who examined the south Boeotian coast personally, revealed at least one route which Gomme had overlooked (see *BSA* 26 (1923-5) pp.41f.).

Gomme also criticised Bérard for talking of trade routes without considering at what date such trade existed, and he noted how unimportant such places as Chalkis, Attica and Megara were in the period for which Bérard was postulating Phoenician trade from these places (*TBTB* p.208). This principle is sound, but the conclusions which Gomme based upon it need some modification in the light of more recent archaeological work in Boeotia and adjacent areas: not only has abundant Mycenaean pottery been found in Euboea and Attica (for which see, for example, Stubbings in *BSA* 42 (1947) pp.1-75 for Attica, Hankey in *BSA* 47 (1952) pp.49-95 for Chalkis, and Popham and Sackett, *ELE* (1968) for Lefkandi on Euboea), but also in a recent study of Boeotia Mycenaean remains have been noted at numerous points along the Boeotian side of the Euboean Gulf and also at the various havens on the south Boeotian coast (see Hope Simpson, *GMS* (1965) pp.120-9).[140] All of this must weaken Gomme's argument from the lack of reference in classical sources to these coastal sites. We may conclude then that certainly local trade from these places would have gone through Thebes, and that some

140. While no one could claim that Boeotia was ever a major seafaring state, it is worth noting that its interest in seafaring in ancient times was not entirely negligible: in the Homeric Catalogue of Ships Boeotia contributes 50 vessels, and their complement of 120 men, if such a figure could be trusted, would make the Boeotian galleys "the largest warships recorded until the invention of the trireme" (Casson, *SSAW* p.59). But such evidence must be used with great caution, as the figures from the Catalogue may be far from reliable (so Page, *HHI* pp.151-4), and it is not possible to date the Boeotian section of the Catalogue with certainty (Hope Simpson and Lazenby suggest that its description fits Mycenaean rather than historical Boeotia (*CSHI* p.33; cf. pp.168f.), though we cannot press this point). Other possible evidence for Boeotian interest in seafaring in Mycenaean times are the incised drawings of boats or ships from Hyria (see Casson, *SSAW* figs. 25, 32) and Thebes (see Ch. V with n. 104 above), and the recent discovery of clay model boats from a tomb at Thebes (see *AD* 22 (1967) B.l (*Chron.*) p.228). We must also add the very fact that Agamemnon's fleet traditionally assembled at Aulis rather than at an Argive port (Aulis had no importance in classical times, but has produced Mycenaean remains: see Simpson and Lazenby, *CSHI* p.19).

long-distance trade both by land from Attica to the north and by land and sea from the north coast of the Peloponnese across Boeotia to Euboea might well have passed through it.[141] This view of the geographical situation of Thebes is well in accord with the conclusions of several recent writers, all of whom have tended to emphasise her favourable position for trade.[142]

It remains to consider the archaeological evidence from Thebes itself, much of which was not available to Gomme and his predecessors. The old excavations of Keramopoullos produced, as we have seen in Chapter V, evidence for at least commercial relations with Crete, as well as certain small artefacts made from ivory and other precious materials which may be presumed to have originated outside Thebes; but the most striking evidence for overseas contacts has come from the recent excavations. More ivories have been found at different sites in the city, including some whose workmanship shows oriental affinities,[143] and a Canaanite jar was among the contents of a tomb recently excavated on the Megalo Kastelli (or Gerokomeion) Hill.[144] Most remarkable of all is the collection of oriental sealstones

---

141. For details of this last trade route see Heurtley in *BSA* 26 (1923-5) esp. pp.43-5. It is interesting to see that Eutresis, which lies on one branch of it, has proved to be an important Bronze Age site.

142. See Cary, *GBGH* (1949) pp.70-3 with map; Philippson, *DGL* I (1951) pp.519f. (where it is suggested that Gomme had exaggerated the difficulties in the route from the Euboean Gulf to the Gulf of Corinth); Stubbings, *CAH* ed. 2, fasc. 26 (1964) p.4; Hope Simpson, *GMS* (1965) p.122; Vermeule, *KD* (1972) p.185, cited below in n. 147. In this connexion it is worth mentioning that in early Hellenistic times Thebes was apparently a trading-centre for the *Carthaginians* and had a Carthaginian official in the city to protect her interests (see Grimal, *HRR* p.76; Picard, *DCH* p.180). On the presence of Jews in Byzantine times see below n. 148.

143. Two substantial furniture legs have no known correspondence in Mycenaean or Minoan furniture, but resemble certain oriental designs (see Richter, *FGR* (1966) pp.6f.). For correspondence between another Theban ivory and an Assyrian text see Nougayrol in *Syria* 42 (1965) p.234 n. 1.

144. This tomb is of particular interest, since it contained fragments of two larnakes (cf. n. 114 above), as well as 11 complete vases, a three-handled jar of glass-paste, an iron ring, a steatite lamp, fragments of 5 alabaster vases, seals, bronze spear-heads, bone and gold objects and fragments of lead: see *AD* 22 (1967) B.l (*Chron.*) p.228 with pl. 160; cf. *AR* for 1968-9 p.18.

mentioned in Chapter V: in all about a hundred cylinders of agate and lapis lazuli were found in the context of LH IIIB pottery at the "New Kadmeion" or Tzortzis property site. The first reports indicate that some 30 of the engraved seals are unquestionably of oriental origin, 13 of them bearing cuneiform inscriptions. The publication of these seals, which is in the hands of J. Nougayrol and E. Porada, is eagerly awaited, but some information has been made available about their origin and date.[145] They appear to be of mixed type: some are Babylonian, some pre-Babylonian, a fair number Kassite, others Mitannian, and one Hittite seal has also been identified. Others are of as yet undetermined Aegean character, possibly with Cypriot affinities. The dates of the seals vary, the earliest being one assigned to the third millennium, the latest being the Kassite seals, probably all before about 1300 B.C. Details of three of the inscribed seals have been published, and one of these can be precisely dated from its inscription which reads:. "Kidin-Marduk, son of Ša-ilimma-damqa, the chief of Burraburiyăs, king of totality" (M.T. Larsen's translation). Burraburiyaš is the name of two or possibly three kings of the Kassite dynasty of Babylon, but the one mentioned on this seal can be identified by his title as the last king of this name, the author of some of the Amarna letters, who reigned in the first half of the 14th century B.C. (1375-47 according to the chronology favoured by Roux, *AI* (1964) p.232). Thus the evidence of the seals themselves fits reasonably well with the date of their archaeological context of LH IIIB (1300-1230 B.C., Furumark). From the reports of the excavators it appears that the seals belong to a later phase of the palace than that excavated by Keramopoullos, but one also destroyed by fire. They seem to have been kept in a box and to have fallen from an upper storey when the palace was destroyed. They were found above a burnt stratum, below which were fresco fragments and architectural remains on a different alignment from those

145. For the Theban seals see Larsen in *Nestor* July lst 1964 pp. 335f.; Falkenstein in *Kadmos* 3 (1964) pp. 108f.; Lambert, ib. pp.182f.; Daux, *BCH* 88 (1964) pp. 775-9; ib. 90 (1966) pp. 848-50; Platon and Stassinopoulou-Touloupa in *ILN* for Nov. 28th 1964 pp. 859-61, together with Porada, *AJA* 69 (1965) p. 173; Megaw in *AR* for 1965-66 p.12 and Touloupa and Symeonoglou in *AD* 20 (1965) B.2 *(Chron)*. pp.230-2, summarising E. Porada's preliminary classification.

excavated by Keramopoullos.

Some scholars have concluded from these seals that the legend of a settlement from the orient has been proved true. Thus the directors of the new excavations suggested that Thebes was settled by Mycenaeans returning from the East.[146] Other scholars have not hesitated to postulate Semites at the city: J. Fontenrose writes "So the Kadmos legend appears to reflect a Phoenician (Canaanite) settlement at Thebes after all, just as the Greeks themselves always said" (*CPh* 61 (1966) p.189), and J.M. Sasson remarks that the discovery of the seals at Thebes, where a Phoenician foundation was recognised in the legends, "strongly suggests that this city was a commercial depot for the Canaanites" *(Journal of the American Oriental Society* 86 (1966) p.135 n.53). Others have brought the figure of Kadmos personally into connexion with the seals: thus N.G.L. Hammond writes of their discovery as confirming the legend of Kadmos at several points, and adds that "this uniquely fine collection of cylinder seals was clearly a royal heirloom, brought by Cadmus and lost in the sack by the Epigoni" (*HGHam* (ed. 2, 1967) p.654). B. Hemmerdinger even proposes a derivation of the name Kadmos from that of Kidin-Marduk occurring on the seal mentioned above, and exclaims "*Kadmos devient donc un personnage historique!*" *(REG* 79 (1966) p.698, his italics!).

But one must be very careful about leaping to conclusions such as these. The hypothesis that the seals were brought to Thebes by those who used them is one explanation among several that are possible. For example some of the seals might have been presented to the rulers of Thebes as diplomatic gifts, and E. Porada has suggested that the Kassite seals, including the unengraved lapis lazuli cylinders, could

---

146. It is perhaps worth quoting the exact words of Platon and Stassinopoulou-Touloupa here: "The originally incomprehensible phenomenon of a settlement which was established by the East (Phoenicia) and which had a strong Mycenaean character can now be explained in a logical, predictable way: Old Minoan-Mycenaean settlements along the Phoenician littoral by the 'edge of the sea' (in the words of the Bible), established a colony (Thebes) in a most suitable point for the creation of an industrial and trading centre which supplied the centres of the East" (*ILN* for Dec. 5th 1964 p. 897).

have been sent to Thebes as a gift by one of the Kassite kings of Babylon (see the summary of her paper in *AJA* 70 (1966) p.194); this would however explain the origin of only part of this heterogeneous group of seals. Another suggestion is that the seals might have reached Thebes simply in the course of trade, as has been argued by G.E. Mylonas, who writes that "their presence indicates the antiquarian tendencies of a *wanax* who could have accumulated them in the course of normal commercial enterprises".[147]

However this collection of seals came together — and the exact circumstances will never be recovered — it is worth noting that the number of oriental seals here far exceeds the total of imported cylinder seals found up till now in the whole Aegean area (see L.R. Palmer and O.R. Gurney in *The Times* for July 17th 1964). They do at least provide indisputable proof of contact between Thebes and the Semitic orient, and it can no longer be argued that there has been found at Thebes nothing which might have been brought by "Phoenicians".

Let us now attempt to summarise our conclusions about the possibility of a Phoenician or oriental settlement at Thebes in the Late Bronze Age. In the past this idea seemed most implausible, if not impossible, for two reasons: first, the date of the Phoenician overseas expansion could not be placed earlier than the ninth or eighth centuries B.C.; and second, Thebes' geographical situation was held to be unsuitable for a trading people like the Phoenicians, and no specifically Phoenician objects were found during Keramopoullos' excavations there. But in the light of our present knowledge of Greece and the Near East in the second millennium, neither of these reasons appears to be so strong as was once believed. Such a general claim as that there was "no contact between Greeks and Phoenicians earlier than 750 B.C." (Carpenter, *HVA* p.60) could not now be made

---

147. See Mylonas, *MMA* (1966) p.204 n. 68; cf. McDonald, *PITP* (1967) p.353, where it is suggested that a wealthy Theban king might have had his agents collect the seals, perhaps as models for gem-cutters. Mrs Vermeule finds nothing surprising about the occurrence of oriental objects at Thebes, writing that "in such a large and famous city as Thebes, dominating the cross-roads to the south and east and with a strong command of coastal opportunities, Anatolian and Levantine treasures and ideas are precisely what one would expect" (*KD* p.185)!

without explicitly restricting its scope to the Greeks and Phoenicians *of the Iron Age*. We have seen how there is abundant evidence to prove that the Greeks of the Late Bronze Age were in contact with West Semitic or Canaanite people who may reasonably be regarded as the forerunners of the historical Phoenicians; and since these and other oriental people were active seafarers, it cannot be supposed that they would have been incapable of transporting themselves to Greece and settling there. With regard to the situation of Thebes, it has to be admitted that it is not in the least like the typical sites occupied by the Phoenicians of the Iron Age, who chose islands, promontories or easily defensible coastal sites both in their homeland and when colonising overseas (see Harden, *Phoen.* (1962) pp.25-43); nor is it the most obvious site to be chosen by a trading people from abroad seeking a centre for marketing their goods (as used to be the picture, largely based on Herodotos and Homer, of the Phoenicians). But today no one could say that "it never had any trade" (see above p.129), and certainly it had good agricultural land which would be attractive to colonists.[148] It must be remembered that the Kadmos legend says nothing about a trading settlement: it would be equally possible to

148. See Cary, *GBGH* p.71 on Boeotia's agricultural productivity. It may also be noted that murex-fishing is attested in classical sources on both sides of Boeotia, i.e. at sites on the Euboean Gulf, including Anthedon, and on the Corinthian Gulf at Bulis, where in the time of Pausanias more than half the inhabitants were said to be engaged in murex-fishing (Paus. X. 37. 3; cf. the discussions of Besnier, *DA* IV. 1 p.775 with other ancient references, and Philippson, *DGL* I p.456). Murex is found in many parts of the classical world and it would be dangerous to press its occurrence as an argument for either Phoenicians or Minoans in these areas. It may nevertheless be relevant to observe that under the Byzantine empire (around the 12th cent. A.D.) Thebes became one of the most important industrial centres in western Europe for a time and was famous for its silk and purple-dyeing (Pounds, *HGE* (1973) esp. pp.214, 296f.). It was also said (by Benjamin of Tudela) to have a resident community of some 2,000 Jews, and while this number could well be an exaggeration (so Pounds, *HGE* pp.252, 273), it may be compared with those then recorded for other "large" cities such as Salonica (500), Corinth (300) and Chalkis (200); see Heurtley and others, *SHG* pp.49f. and Schober, *RE(T)* cols. 1491f. with further references. It is curious that silk production first came to Constantinople, Thebes, and other centres in Greece through the agency of Syrian merchants from such places as Tyre, Beirut and Sidon, which were themselves famous for their silk at this period (see Runciman, *ByzC* p.171 and T. Talbot Rice, *ELB* p.128).

interpret its historical nucleus as the coming of a small group of refugees to Thebes, or even as a larger immigration or conquest.[149] The history of Ugarit and other Syrian and Canaanite sites of the second millennium provides plentiful occasions when upheavals occurred which could have given rise to population movements abroad or to the flight of refugees.[150]

At the same time it must be stressed that there is no archaeological or documentary proof that any such movement did take place. If Canaanite settlement of any size occurred at Thebes, one might reasonably look for confirmation in some signs of Canaanite material culture (such as cult figurines or temple architecture), and even if only a small group of refugees settled at Thebes, one might expect to find their personal effects. Unequivocal evidence has not been forthcoming; but Mycenaean Thebes is still only very partially excavated, and we have seen in recent years how new finds can alter the picture. The seals from Thebes are to be dated to a period when Mycenaean trade with the orient was at its greatest. The true explanation for their presence *could* be that they had belonged to Semites or other orientals resident in the city, but alternative interpretations are also possible, and until the full publication of the seals too much speculation is inadvisable. For the present our

149. It is of interest to note that there are ancient references which suggest that Kadmos was thought of as a refugee (see Isokr. X. 68) or as a military conqueror: see the versions of Palaiphatos and Konon discussed above pp.39-41, and cf. Pausanias' allusion (IX. 19. 4) to "Κάδμον καὶ τὸν σὺν αὐτῷ στρατόν". Tacitus clearly imagined Kadmos as coming with a fleet: compare his reference to "Cadmum classe Phoenicum vectum" and his mention of Phoenician sea-power at that date (*Ann.* XI. 14).

150. For instance, the military campaigns of Tuthmosis III (early 15th cent.) must have caused some displacement of persons in Syria, and equally the later conflict between Suppiluliumas and Ramses II. Other possible causes of migration are natural disaster, such as the great earthquake postulated by Schaeffer ca. 1365 B.C., or political upheavals. In addition migration might have been caused by the large-scale population movements of Hurrians, Amorites and others which we know took place early in the second millennium (cf. Roux, *AI* Ch. 14, esp. pp.212-4), or the immigration of the Philistines and other Sea Peoples about the end of the 13th century, not to mention the entry of the Hebrews into Canaan. The latter two events may however be rather late for the postulated arrival of the Cadmeians at Thebes, if their coming is to be placed before the Trojan War (cf. below n.185).

136

conclusion must be that, while the results of archaeological, documentary and linguistic research do not prove the existence of a Bronze Age settlement at Thebes from the East, which would provide the most obvious historical basis for the legend of Kadmos, they do not exclude it, and there is no doubt that today it is much more plausible than it was two or three decades ago.

CHAPTER VII

SUGGESTED ORIENTAL PARALLELS TO THE MOTIFS
OF THE KADMOS LEGEND

In the last two Chapters we have been concerned with the basic questions of whether the Kadmos legend might reflect a Cretan or oriental settlement at Thebes, and our primary evidence has been archaeological, though we have also been able to use that of language and historical documents. But there is a radically different type of evidence which must also be considered, namely that of mythological motifs, cults and proper names. Such material has frequently been mentioned by scholars as lending support to the literary tradition of a Phoenician settlement at Thebes; [151] but very recently an attempt has been made to use it as an independent source for Greek prehistory. M. C. Astour in his book *Hellenosemitica* (1965) has made a detailed study of the motifs and onomastics of several Greek legends, comparing them throughout with Semitic parallels, and he seeks to draw from this study inferences about events in the Mycenaean Age.

---

151. Many 19th century scholars made use of the evidence of proper names for which a Semitic origin had been adduced (e.g. Kadmos, Europê, the epithet Ismenios of Apollo, and the Kabeiroi), of the cults of Thebes and Boeotia believed to be foreign (e.g. Athene Onka, Aphrodite Ourania and the Kabeiroi), and of motifs such as the seven gates of Thebes, Kadmos' guiding cow, Zeus' role as bull, and Kadmos' association with "Phoenician" letters: for details see Brandis, *Hermes* 2 (1867) pp.259-84; Rawlinson, *HHer* II (ed. 4, 1880) p. 92, on Hdt. II. 49; Duncker, *HGDun* I (1883) esp. pp.72f.; cf. also the discussions of Busolt, *GG* I (ed. 1, 1885) p. 52 with his n. 2, and How and Wells on Hdt. IV. 147. For some recent examples see Fontenrose (cited above n.72) on the name of Kadmos, and Thomson (cited below n.172) on a parallel in motif.

The use of this type of material is very old, and is particularly striking in the works of the 17th century scholar Samuel Bochart, "always ingenious and fruitful in conjectures" (so Banier, *MFA* III (1740) p. 408), who proposes many Semitic etymologies both for personal names, place-names and epithets connected with Kadmos and Thebes, and for common nouns in the Boeotian dialect (see *Chan.* (1646) esp. Chs. 16-19).

Astour himself describes the principles of his method (*HS* pp. 69-71): he believes that it is wrong simply to rationalise myths to find history, and instead argues that the important elements in the stories are their basic themes or motifs. Where these are identical or similar in the Greek and Semitic worlds, he believes that they must have been transferred from the orient to Greece in the Mycenaean period. He pays special attention to elements in the stories which do not play a properly intelligible role, on the assumption that they are likely to be relics or survivals of the myth in its original milieu, retained in their new context even when not strictly necessary. This method is first used in an analysis of the Danaos story, and then in other legends including most notably that of Kadmos (on which see *HS* pp.113-224). Astour particularly maintains that it is not the Phoenician label in a myth which is decisive but its contents (*HS* p.112).

The results of his analysis are remarkable: so many Semitic motifs and names are identified, that it is concluded that there must have been one major West Semitic settlement in Argolis, the centre of the Danaos myth cycle, and another in Boeotia, the centre of the Kadmos legend and its related myths. On these Astour sums up his conclusions thus: "This agglomeration of Semitisms cannot be historically explained except by assuming that *an important West Semitic settlement had taken place in Boeotia in the early Mycenaean age.* These settlers became Hellenized and merged with the inhabitants of the country, but their Semitic influence remained visible in two domains that are particularly conservative: in toponyms and in mythology" *(JNES* 23 (1964) p.200, our italics. This article, published shortly before *Hellenosemitica,* embodies the same conclusions and material about Kadmos as the book; cf. especially *HS* pp.220-4).

Astour's work is important to our study for two reasons: first, with regard to the Kadmos legend itself, we should (if Astour were right) at last have proof of a historical basis for the story in a Semitic settlement in Boeotia, the very place where a Phoenician foundation was traditional; and secondly, from the point of view of methodology Astour would appear to have brought to the fore a potential source of information hitherto neglected by prehistorians. We shall here attempt to make an assessment of both these aspects of his work, and for this purpose it will be necessary to examine in detail some of the

140

specific parallels to the Kadmos legend which he has adduced from oriental sources and then to make some more general comments on the method of his book.

What then does Astour believe about Kadmos? In analysing what he calls the "mythological essence" of the hero he writes as follows: "His name and almost all his adventures and attributes are Oriental and originated in W-S [West Semitic] myths of the god of sunrise, strongly influenced by the image of the Sumerian Ningišzida" (*HS*pp. 158f.). This striking conclusion is elaborated later in his section entitled "A Glance at the Tribe of the Cadmeians", where we are told that "the eponymous hero and ideal founder of the city (sc. the Kadmeia) was the homonymous god Qadm, the W-S personification of sunrise, dawn and morning-star, the head of the group of the 'good gods', protectors of seamen and givers of fertility, who had absorbed the essential characteristics of the Sumerian serpent-god and dragon-fighter Ningišzida" (*HS* pp.222f.). Nor, in Astour's view, is Kadmos an isolated figure: "all characters linked with him by the myth have the same origin" (*HS*p.159). Thus Europê, Kadmos' sister in the later tradition, is identified as a West Semitic goddess of night, sunset and the evening-star (*HS* pp.131-9); Harmonia, Kadmos' wife, is compared to the Akkadian goddesses Bêlit-ṣêri and Bêlit-êkallim (Ugaritic *B'lt-bt*), as well as to the female of the entwined snakes in the symbol of Ningišzida (*HS* pp.159-61); Semele, Kadmos' daughter, is identified as *Ṣml*, the Mother of the Eagles, in the Ugaritic poem of *Aqht* (*HS* pp.169-72); Aktaion, Kadmos' grandson by Autonoe, is said to be *Aqht* himself in the same poem (*HS*pp.164-8); Ino, another daughter of Kadmos, is identified with the Semitic goddess Derceto-Atargatis, herself a modified form of Asherah of the Sea, known at Ugarit (*HS* pp.204-9); and finally numerous Semitic elements are found in the myths, cult and epithets of Dionysos (*HS*pp. 173-204), in the place-names of Boeotia and in the personal names of other heroes associated with that area (*HS* pp.212-7).

At first sight the sheer number of Semitic motifs and etymologies adduced appears overwhelming, and one is inclined to think, in spite of certain reservations, that some cumulative force must be acknowledged. But when the evidence for the identifications is examined closely, it is found that Astour has laid himself open to a number of grave criticisms. This becomes apparent as soon as detailed consideration is given to the oriental parallels which he proposes for the two key figures of Kadmos and Europê. Our discussion of these may be divided conveniently under three heads.

(1) Kadmos (Qadm) and Europê as solar and astral divinities

We saw above (p.141) that Astour identifies Kadmos as a god Qadm, who is described as the West Semitic personification of sunrise, dawn and morning-star and the head of the group of "good gods", while Europê is similarly said to be the goddess of night, sunset and evening-star. But when the oriental evidence is examined, it is found that there are no single West Semitic divinities with all these characteristics. Astour's statements rest upon a series of hypothetical identifications, which must be considered in turn. A Babylonian god ^dQa-ad-mu is attested, but his function and identity are almost totally unknown.[152] The statement that Qadm is the West Semitic god of sunrise etc. depends upon the identification of this Babylonian god ^dQa-ad-mu with an Ugaritic god *Šḥr* (conventionally spelt Shachar). It is worth noting that the only evidence for this identification consists of one fragmentary Ugaritic text (*UM* 75),[153] quoted by Astour, *HS* p. 154), in which *šḥr* appears as parallel to *qdm,* and since in Ugaritic poetry parallelism is normally strictly observed, and *Šḥr* appears in other Ugaritic texts as a god of dawn, Astour concludes that *qdm* (whom he identifies with ^dQa-ad-mu on the basis of linguistic similarity) must also be the god of dawn and have all the characteristics and attributes of the god Shachar. But this involves many unjustified assumptions. *Šḥr* in West Semitic is not only a proper name but also a common noun (cf. Hebrew *šaḥar,* "dawn"), and there is no evidence that in the Ugaritic text in question it is anything but a common noun. The same applies to *qdm,* which is a common noun with various meanings in both Hebrew and other Semitic languages, including

152. The only information known about him seems to be that one text refers to him as "vizir of Sataran", a serpent deity (Astour, *HS* (ed. 2, 1967) p.392), but this does not help his identification with *Šḥr* as the god of dawn.

153. To facilitate comparison with Astour's discussion reference is here made to Ugaritic texts by their numbers in Gordon. *UM* (1955).

Ugaritic. It will be found that in the same text as is cited by Astour *qdm* is taken to mean "east wind", and *šḥr* taken as a common noun by both Gordon (*UT* (1965) p. 476, no. 2208, p. 489, no. 2399; the same interpretation also in his earlier works) and Driver (*CML* p. 71, and Glossary s. vv. *qdm* and *šḥr*). Furthermore the text is so fragmentary that one wonders whether it is wise to base any important deductions on it. Driver renders the first eleven lines as follows:

```
"    .      .      .      .      .      .      .
     .      .      .      .      .      .      .
            .      .      .   of the earth
            .      .      .      .      .   to us (?)
5)   .      .      .      .      .   them
     .      .      .      .      .      .
            .      .   like (heat at) dawn,
            .      .   like the east-wind.
     [They] destroy us, El our father;
10)  they devour (our) liver(s) like insects(?)
     they gnaw our breasts like worms (?)."
```

(*CML* p.71).

Gordon's translation is even less illuminating.[154] This then is the evidence for the existence of a West Semitic god Qadm, the personification of sunrise, dawn and morning-star. It rests upon the identification of the Babylonian god ᵈQa-ad-mu, about whom virtually nothing is known but his name, with the Ugaritic god Shachar, and the

---

154. Gordon's rendering is as follows:

```
     [        (2 lines broken)        ]
3)   [                    ] of the earth
     [        (2 lines broken)        ]
     [                ] you
     [                ] like the dawn
     [                ] like the east-wind
     [                ] 'Il, our father,
10)  The liver, like - - they devour
     [        ] like - - - they bite
```
(*UL* p. 53)!

evidence for this is lines 7 and 8 of the text just quoted.

We may next consider upon what grounds *Kadmos* is identified with *qdm* or Shachar. Astour's starting point seems to be the etymological evidence of the names of Kadmos and Europê. It was long ago suggested that Kadmos might be derived from the Semitic root *qdm* meaning "in front", and hence "of old" and "the east", and Europê from Semitic *'rb,* meaning "to enter", "to set" (of the sun) (see above p. 58 with notes 60, 72 and 73). Astour argues in favour of these derivations (see *HS* pp. 128-131, 152f.), and further proposes a complicated series of identifications (*HS* pp.132-6, 153-5), in which he first shows that the people of Ugarit had a divinity of the sunset named *'rb špš* (*UM* 9. 9), whose sex was unknown, but whom he identifies with a goddess of the night, *ll,* who appears in another fragmentary text from Ugarit (*UM* 104), where she is said to "enter the sunset". Next he suggests the further identification of the divinity *'rb špš* or *ll* with the Babylonian goddess Ishtar, whose planet was Venus. Venus, as once pointed out by V. Bérard, in its aspect of evening-star was thought by the Babylonians to be female, while as morning-star was imagined as a separate male deity. This divinity *'rb špš,* alias *ll* alias Ishtar, is then identified, in spite of the difference in sex, with a god appearing in a well known Ugaritic text (*UM* 52), namely *šlm* (Shalim). The root *šlm,* meaning in Hebrew "intact", "complete" or "at peace" (cf. *šālēm* etc.), in Akkadian means "dusk", and this seems also to be its meaning in Ugaritic. Shalim in the text just mentioned is the brother of Shachar (*Šḥr*), dawn, the divinity identified by Astour with *qdm.* By these stages we reach the conclusion that Europê must be Shalim and that Kadmos must be Shachar, alias *qdm,* the god of dawn, sunrise and morning-star.

It is noticeable that in the series of identifications just described no obvious similarity of motif is visible: Kadmos searches for Europê (in the version of the story current in the fifth century and later), but in nome of the oriental myths cited by Astour does the motif of a search of the dawn for the dusk or of the evening-star for the morning-star appear. Conversely, while Astour has shown that there were several oriental divinities of sunset, dusk, evening-star etc. (or one divinity if we accept all his multiple identifications), it is remarkable that there is nothing in the story of Kadmos and Europê as such to indicate that either figure was associated in any way with sunset, sunrise etc. The only possible hint of this is an etymological gloss of Hesychios (flor. fifth century A.D.): Εὐρώπη· χώρα τῆς δύσεως. ἢ σκοτεινή. The source of the gloss is unknown, and while it could represent ancient tradition, it could equally be the result of learned speculation.[155]

Only one real similarity of motif is adduced by Astour in this section: it is the fact that Europê in the monuments is frequently represented with a veil, and both the Babylonian goddess Ishtar and the Ugaritic goddess of the night in *UM* 104 are said to be veiled. But, as Astour himself admits, the detail of Europê's veil is *Hellenistic* (see Babelon in *RA* 20 (1942-3) pp.125-40; cf. Bühler, *Europa* p.59). It is not shown on early representations of the heroine such as the famous metope from Selinus, the fine late Archaic gem recently illustrated by Boardman (*Greek Gems* (1970) pl.345), nor yet on the early vases (see, for example, the Caeretan hydria illustrated in Devambez, *Greek Painting* pl.52). A veil is in any case a common motif in representations of divine and semi-divine personages, and can surely have little claim to provide us with any clue to Europê's original role.[156]

To conclude, no convincing evidence for Kadmos and Europê as solar or astral divinities is present either in the motifs of their story or the oriental sources adduced by Astour. The most striking part of his argument is his discussion of their names, particularly that of Kadmos. Here we must admit that none of the proposed alternative derivations

155. The reference in Hesychios does not necessarily presuppose a knowledge of Semitic '*rb*, as for instance assumed by Allen, Halliday and Sikes in *The Homeric Hymns* (ed. 2, 1936) p.240; Hesychios or his source may rather have reached the meaning "dark" for Εὐρώπη by connecting it with εὐρώς "mould", "dank decay". Compare the neighbouring entries in his lexicon, εὐρώεντος· σκοτεινοῦ, ἀπὸ τοῦ εὐρῶτος and εὐρωπόν· σκοτεινόν, πλατύ, and cf. also Platnauer on Eur. *Iph. Taur.* 626. This fact must weaken Astour's arguments for the derivation of Europê from '*rb*, since he regards Hesychios' testimony as "incontestable" (*HS* p.129).
156. Astour states that the wind-blown veil was first introduced by the Sidonians (*HS* pp.134f.), but in fact it appears slightly earlier on the coins of Knossos than those of Sidon, and may well be an artistic development from older representations of Europê holding her billowing mantle (see Bühler, *Europa* pp.57-60 with her fig. 3). Even if Astour were right that the motif of Europê's veil originated in Sidon, this need be only the result of late syncretism, since it was here that Europê was identified in Hellenistic times with Sidonian Astarte, the same goddess as Ishtar (cf. above p.38).

145

from Indo-European is fully convincing (for the various suggestions see nn.72 and 73), and while the vocalisation of the name Europê presents serious difficulties to the suggested connexion with Semitic 'rb (see *HS* pp.129f.), the association of Kadmos with *qdm* (qadm) is phonetically good. But it must be emphasised that although a Semitic etymology for the name Kadmos is plausible, this does not mean that the identification of the hero with a solar or astral divinity necessarily follows: the name could simply mean "the man from the East", or Kadmos could be merely the eponymous hero of the tribe Kadmeioi or Kadmeiones, "the Easterners".[157]

(2) Kadmos, the Kabeiroi and the "good gods"

The second main identification made by Astour (see above p. 141) is that of the "good gods", of whom Shachar and Shalim are said to be the heads, and the Kabeiroi of Samothrace, with whom Kadmos, though not Europê, was associated (for details of the comparison see *HS* pp.155f.). There is indeed a superficial similarity between these "good gods" and the mysterious gods known variously to the Greeks as Kabeiroi, Μεγάλοι Θεοί, or Samothracian gods (on the name Kabeiroi see n.75), but when the evidence is examined in detail it is not so convincing as one would suppose from Astour's writing. Very little is known about the "good gods", who appear in only one text (*UM* 52), of uncertain interpretation. Let us consider each of Astour's three points of comparison between these gods and the Kabeiroi, namely (a) their number, (b) their function as protectors of seamen, and (c) their role as givers of fertility.

157. Astour has a good discussion of Kadmeioi as a possible tribal name (*HS* pp. 221-3). He shows that the meaning "Easterners" for an ethnic would be well in accord with the Semitic usage: the Old Testament actually mentions a tribe Qadmonites, i.e. Easterners (*qadmōnî;* Gen. 15. 19), and several times refers more loosely to the eastern peoples as *bᵉnê gedem* ("sons of the East"). He also well counters the objection of Beloch that a people coming from the East would more appropriately call themselves "Westerners" by comparing the usage of "Norsemen" and "Normans" for Northerners in England, S. Italy and Sicily (see *HS* p.223 n. 4; cf. Mitford, *HGMit* I (ed. 2, 1789) p. 89 n. 39!). Where however we must disagree with Astour is in supposing that the name Kadmos must have belonged to a god of sunrise etc. as well as being the eponym of the tribe.

(a) First Astour says that the Kabeiroi seem to have been originally seven in number, and that the full number of the "good gods" was seven (*HS* p.155). But it is in fact quite uncertain what the original number of the Kabeiroi was. One author, Philo of Byblos (64-161 A.D.), refers to seven, but the scholiast to Apollonios of Rhodes says that they were originally two, while Pherekydes alludes to nine, and other sources state numbers between four and fifty. B. Hemberg, who has carried out a detailed study of the Kabeiroi and related gods, concludes that the number and names of the gods were quite uncertain: "... wir eine verwirrende Mannigfaltigkeit der Namen, eine unbestimmte Anzahl der Götter und verschiedene Kombinationen gefunden haben" (*Kab.* (1950) p.100).

In addition, when the crucial Ugaritic text is examined, it will be found that even the number of the "good gods" is not certain. Indeed it is a matter of great controversy. The text (*UM* 52) is basically a frank and sensuous description of how El, the father of the gods, seduces two women, and how they give birth to two children, Shachar and Shalim. Because of its sensuous nature, it is generally interpreted as referring to a "ἱερὸς γάμος", and there are indications that it was used in ritual. So much is generally agreed, but there is no consensus of opinion about details. The birth of the children is twice described in the text; in one passage (R. ii 17-19 Driver) they are called Shachar and Shalim; in the other, which follows closely upon it (R. ii 24-7), they are called the *n'mm*, "gracious" or "good" gods. Most scholars assume that the gracious gods and Shachar and Shalim are one and the same, and that the passage is describing the same event twice. This view is supported by the general run of the text, which begins by invoking the "gracious gods", and ends by describing their monstrous appetites (on this interpretation see Driver, *CML* pp. 22f. and 121-5; Gaster, *Thesp.* pp. 225-37, though cf. note 158). But Cyrus Gordon understands the text as describing the birth of two separate pairs of gods, i. e. four gods in all (see *UL* pp.57-62). Astour accepts that Shachar and Shalim are "good gods", and that these two passages refer to the same event, but

---

158. In the revised edition of this work (*Thesp.* (ed. 2, 1961) p.406) Gaster treats the "gracious gods" and Shachar and Shalim as separate sets of divinities.

interprets another passage, which actually occurs between the two descriptions of giving birth, as referring to a *fivefold* repetition of the union. The passage, which consists of one line and one word, is both fragmentary and obscure. Gordon renders it:

"They again [   ]
count(s) to five [   ]"

(*UL* p.61 = *UM* 52. 56-7).

Driver and Gaster both attempt a fuller rendering, and interpret the passage as a rubric addressed to the reciters of the text. We quote Driver's translation, giving it its context:

"By kissing and conceiving, [by] embraces and
yearning - *it shall again*

23)   *be recited (up) to five (times) by the troupe [and
by] the leaders (?) of the assembly* - both
of them travail and bear (children); they bear
gracious gods, twin figures
born in one day, sucking the teats of the breasts
of the [two]."

(*CML* p.123, R. ii 22-5; the sentence within parenthesis, here in italics, corresponds to the passage quoted above from Gordon's translation). This line (57 of Gordon and 23 of Driver) is the only evidence adduced by Astour in support of his assertion about these gods (*HS* p.155) that "their full number was seven"! It depends not only on the assumption that this phrase

"*yṯbn* [   ]
yspr lḫmš lṣb [   ] *šr pḫr*" (Gordon's text)

refers to a fivefold repetition of the union, but also on the quite unwarranted supposition that the five repeated unions each resulted in the birth of *one* child, in contrast to the earlier one union (or is it two?) which produced a pair of gods (being the result of the simultaneous seduction of two women). But the text, which continues at some length after the passage discussed, nowhere mentions any more offspring; it never gives their names, their sexes, or even their number.

This study of the text which is Astour's source for his statements about the "good gods" has, it is hoped, made one thing abundantly clear: the assertion that the "good gods" are seven in number rests upon very dubious evidence. When we add to this the fact that the

148

number of the Kabeiroi is equally uncertain, then the only conclusion which can be drawn is that the comparison between the numbers of the gods as made by Astour is wholly worthless.

(b) Secondly, Astour compares the role of the "good gods" and Kabeiroi as protectors of seamen (*HS* pp. 155f. and 223). Here again the comparison is dependent on the interpretation of a few difficult words in this text (*UM* 52), and if the rendering of these words adopted by Astour is rejected, then the similarity no more exists. The words in question are "*agzrym bn ym*" (*UM* 52, lines 58-9; Driver R. ii 24-5), understood by Astour as "islanders, sons of the sea". It will be useful to see what other renderings have been put forward for these words. The first word "*agzrym*" is recognised by Ugaritic scholars as being from the root *gzr* (cf. Hebrew *gazar*, "to cut up"), but there is no general agreement as to its meaning in this text. Gordon in an early work suggested "islanders", but he italicised it as uncertain, and in his later works does not adopt it (compare *UL* p.61 and *UT* p.379, no. 570). Aistleitner renders it "images" (*WUS* p.65 s.v. *gzr*), while Driver suggests "twin figures" (*CML* pp.123 and 134). Much depends on the rendering of the following phrase "*bn ym*", which is also difficult. Since vowels are not indicated here, it is not possible to tell whether *ym* should be interpreted as *yām*, "sea" (cf. Hebrew *yām*) or *yôm*, "day" (cf. Hebrew *yôm*). Both meanings are found elsewhere in Ugaritic. Gordon and Aistleitner adopt the rendering *yām* (Aistleitner emending the text to make sense), while Driver and Gaster adopt *yôm*, translating "born on one day" (Driver), or "one day old" (Gaster). When the text is so uncertain, no comparison based upon it can be regarded as very safe; but here as in the case of the number of the gods Astour gives little indication of the uncertainties involved.

(c) Thirdly, Astour draws attention to the connexion of the "good gods" with fertility and the similar function of the Kabeiroi. Little can be said on this. The association of the "good gods" with fertility is very vague and tenuous, deriving purely from the fact that they are said to be the sons of El, whose sexual unions are described in this text and who is generally connected with fertility. But the concept of a god or gods who give fertility is so commonplace that borrowing of the idea must be very doubtful. There is nothing unusual about this function of the Kabeiroi as fertility gods: they are very similar to other groups of gods, such as Korybantes, worshipped by the Greeks (cf. Hemberg, *Kab.* p.300). The role of the "good gods" is perhaps somewhat closer to that of the Dioskouroi, who share their astral connexions, and with whom they have more than once been compared (Gaster, *Thesp.* pp. 228f.; cf. Driver, *CML* p.23).

Each of Astour's points of comparison between the Kabeiroi and the "good gods" is therefore open to question, and the first so doubtful that it cannot be admitted as evidence. One must conclude that the *rapprochement* between the Kabeiroi and the "good gods" does little to support the identification (based largely on etymology) of Kadmos and Europê as gods of dawn and dusk.

(3) Kadmos and Ningišzida

The third and last of the main comparisons in Astour's discusssion of Kadmos is that between him and the Sumerian god Ningišzida (cf. above p.141). Here he notes no less than four motifs which they have in common, namely (a) sunrise, (b) dragon-fighting, (c) city-foundation and (d) serpent, and he concludes: "these four common motifs show that, though Cadmos' immediate prototype was the W-S god *Šḥr/Qdm,* the deeper roots of his image and essence go back ... to the remote Sumerian past" (*HS* p.157).

At first sight with a number of motifs in common it looks as if the thesis of a Greek borrowing from the orient is plausible; but once again there are difficulties in Astour's view. (a) Kadmos' only connexion with sunrise is through his proposed identification with Shachar / *qdm,* and this as we have seen above (pp. 141-6) must be considered very doubtful. (b) Although Kadmos' role as a dragon-fighter is well attested, that of Ningišzida is uncertain, since he is not apparently mentioned in any text nor depicted in art as such.[159] It is curious therefore that Astour should single out this Sumerian god as Kadmos'

---

159. The only evidence for Ningišzida as a dragon-fighter seems to be the fact that his attribute is sometimes the dragon, a strange hybrid creature, part lion, part bird, sometimes winged and with a scorpion's tail; on this cf. Frankfort in *Iraq* 1 (1934) pp. 10f. and Langdon, *MARS* pp.284f.

oriental prototype, when there are many other much better attested examples of the theme of dragon-fighting both at Babylon and in the West Semitic cultures. If borrowing of the motif is to be postulated, one of these would seem a more likely source,[160] but in view of the widespread attestation of the motif in folk-literature independent occurrence may seem more plausible. (c, d) The motifs of city-foundation and serpent, in contrast to the last two discussed, are attested for both Kadmos and Ningišzida, but here again we must bear bear in mind the possibility of independent occurrence, since both are very commonplace ideas, appearing in many cultures, and frequently found in Greek thought.[161] Once again, to postulate borrowing from

160. For the fight of a god and dragon at Babylon cf. the combats of Marduk and Tiamat, and Ninurta and Labbu. In the W. Semitic sphere it occurs at Ugarit (Baal and Yam) and in Hebrew mythology (Yahweh and Leviathan). The theme is treated in detail by Fontenrose in *Python*, with discussion of both oriental and Greek examples (e.g. Apollo and Python, Zeus and Typhon, Perseus and the sea-monster). Fontenrose believes that the story of Kadmos' fight with the dragon shows marked affinities with the Canaanite myth and suggests that it is a variant of it (*Python* pp. 319f., 466f.), but though this view is possible, his arguments are not so convincing as to rule out the possibility of independent invention; on Fontenrose's work see further Vian, *Or. Theb.* pp.95-9, where some pertinent criticisms of his treatment of Kadmos are made; on the motif in folktale see Thompson at the places cited above (p.42), and cf. Fontenrose's own appendixes 3 and 5 on the combat theme in China, Japan, and America, and in Germanic mythology.

161. For the motif of city-foundation (c) in Greek mythology compare Perseus at Mycenae, Sisyphos at Corinth, Kar at Megara, and the rival legend of Amphion and Zethos at Thebes (see also n. 165). Ningišzida's role (see *HS* p.157 n. 4) in assisting Gudea (flor. ca. 2100 B.C.) build a temple is not at all closely analogous to Kadmos' own foundation of Thebes. The motif of serpent (d) is extremely well attested in Greek myths, since the serpent is, as Rose has said, "the regular accompaniment of heroes and of some, especially chthonian, deities" (*OCD* s.v. serpents, sacred). On snakes in Minoan and classical Greek religion see further Nilsson, *MMR* (ed. 2) index s.v. snakes; Picard, *RP* pp. 113f. and passim; Harrison, *PSGR* pp. 17-21, 325-31, 340-9 (for Zeus Meilichios and Asklepios); Rose, *HGM* p.261 (for Kekrops and Erichthonios); and on the story that Kadmos became a snake cf. Rose's suggestion (mentioned above p.43) that the motif expresses the same belief as the alternative version of the hero's end, namely that he was translated to the Isles of the Blest. Since these two ideas are so very well attested in Greek thought, there seems no reason to derive their association with Kadmos from such a remote figure as Sumerian Ningišzida.

Sumer seems unnecessary, and the thesis is all the more unconvincing since there is no evidence that Shachar (let alone the hypothetical god Qdm) was ever regarded as a dragon-fighter or city-founder.

Finally it must be noted that in stressing the similarities between Kadmos and Ningišzida Astour ignores important differences. Thus Ningišzida was not only a serpent-god: he was a vegetation-deity, and especially associated with trees; he was invoked among the gods of agriculture, and has been identified by some with the constellation Hydra; he has also been thought to be a "dying god" like Tammuz, with whom he is associated in the ancient sources, and he is described as the "throne-bearer of the wide nether world".[162] Yet Kadmos is connected with none of these things. Here, as in Astour's comparisons between Shachar and Kadmos and the "good gods" and the Kabeiroi, one is very forcibly reminded of Farnell's basic criticism of the comparative method of mythology, namely its "tendency to be more impressed by resemblances than by differences, even when the resemblances are vague and superficial, the differences essential" (see *PBA* for 1919-20, p.39).

This treatment òf Astour's analysis of Kadmos and Europê has necessarily been long, since only a detailed examination is sufficient to bring out fully the weakness of his arguments concerning these figures. It is possible that some of his other identifications may be more convincing than those which have been scrutinised, but those which the present writer has examined are not encouraging. Obviously it is not possible to discuss all the comparisons at the same length, since this

162. For the characteristics of Ningišzida see Langdon, *MARS* pp.77, 90, 104, 162, 178f., 284, 349; van Buren, *Iraq* 1 (1934) pp. 60-89; Dhorme, *LRBA* pp. 119-121; and Haussig, *GMVO* pp.112f.

would involve writing a book longer than *Hellenosemitica*. It does however seem worth drawing together some general criticisms, which arise directly from the identifications which we have studied and which can be further illustrated by other parts of his book. These fall into five main groups.

(1) *First, many of the proposed parallels of motif are far from exact; indeed, some can only be described as illusory.* In order to produce the figures from whom Kadmos and Europê are said to originate, one continually has to suppose the identification of one oriental deity with another: thus '*rb špš* has to be identified with *Il, Il* with Ishtar, and Ishtar with Shalim to produce the figure from whom Europê is derived. Similarly, Kadmos shares the characteristics of more than one deity: with ^dQa-ad-mu he shares a similarity of name; with Shachar a possible association with fertility; and with Ningišzida a connexion with snakes and city-foundation. Moreover many of the parallels adduced by Astour are themselves doubtful or even non-existent: thus we have seen that Kadmos' role as a god of sun and dawn is extremely questionable, while the supposed parallel in number between the "good gods" and Kabeiroi rests upon such dubious inferences that it cannot be taken as adding any weight to Astour's arguments. This point is further illustrated by the case of Harmonia, who is compared to Akkadian Bêlit-ṣêri, "the lady of the steppe" (*HS* pp.159f.). But what similarity is there between these two figures? Bêlit-ṣêri was scribe to the queen of the nether world, who registered the dead and those doomed to die; Harmonia was given on her wedding a necklace and robe, which were believed by certain Greek writers to be the same objects as those by which several generations later Eriphyle was bribed and which brought trouble to her family (see Apollodoros III. 4. 2 and III. 6. 1-2 with Frazer's notes). This most tenuous association with doom is the sole point of comparison made by Astour, but any resemblance that there is between Harmonia and Bêlit-ṣêri is exceedingly superficial, especially as Harmonia nowhere "caused destruction" to anyone as Astour states. Indeed it seems likely that the necklace and robe in the Harmonia story are simply wedding-gifts of the gods with no fatal qualities (on Harmonia's association with these gifts see further Vian, *Or. Theb.* pp.147-9). Here, as elsewhere, the reader is in danger of being misled by Astour's

153

persuasiveness.[163]

(2) *Second, in many cases the parallels are dependent on the interpretation of single texts, whose meaning is disputed.* This has already been seen in an acute form in the identification of the hypothetical West Semitic god Qadm with Shachar, and in the parallel between the "good gods" and the Kabeiroi as protectors of seafarers; but these are not isolated examples. In seeking an oriental parallel to the image of Teiresias as a blind soothsayer, Astour writes: "In the Ugaritic epic of King *Krt* (Krt: 99-100, 187-188) '*wr mzl ymzl* 'a blind man consults the fate' is stated" (*HS* p.162). But if this text is consulted in its various editions, it will be found that the phrase quoted is exceedingly obcure. It occurs only twice, in practically identical passages (see *Krt* lines 100 and 188 in Gordon, *UL*). Renderings of it vary from "Let ...the blind man give his benediction" (Gray, *KTL* ed. 1), "(even) the blind man will be excited" (Gray, *KTL* ed. 2), "the blind man indeed shall foretell (good) luck" (Driver, *CML*), "the one-eyed man blinks with one eye" (Ginsberg ap. Gray, *KTL* ed. 1), "the blind man *gropes his way* (also Ginsberg in *ANET* p.143), "the blind man falls into the ditch" (Dahood, ap. Emerton [164]), "der Blinde möge auf der Ruhestätte ruhen [?]" (Aistleitner, *WUS* p.180) to what sums it up best of all: "der Blinde ...." (Jirku, *KME* p.88).

---

163. A further example where Astour is misleading is his statement that "wherever Phoenix appears, either as a person or as a toponym, he is clearly connected with Semitic names, myths, and cults" (*HS* p.150). But this is palpably untrue: even if one were to accept every example of "Phoenicianism" adduced by Astour in connexion with the name Phoinix, there are still many places of this name with no obvious Phoenician connexion (for a list of relevant place-names, including many not mentioned by Astour, see *RE* XX. 1 s.vv. Phoinix and derivatives). In other cases, hypotheses are stated as if they were facts: on the name Tektamos, it is stated that later mythographers took an epithet of Europê and "as customary" transformed it into a supplementary character to fill out a genealogy (*HS* p.136); but this is pure surmise, as is the reference to the name Eueres being originally an epithet of Teiresias (*HS* p.162). Throughout, the phrasing is such that superficial similarities are made to seem important, and important differences are glossed over or ignored.

164. See Emerton, "The meaning of the root 'mzl' in Ugaritic", *JSS* 14 (1969) pp. 22-33. Emerton himself comes to no firm conclusion, but favours a meaning of either "lag behind" or "lament", saying that the second is "probably preferable as a working hypothesis"!

(3) *Third, the motifs are often very common themes in folklore or else so true to life that independent occurrence seems the best explanation of any similarity.* We have already noted in our study of Kadmos and Ningišzida that the association of a god or hero with snakes and city-foundation may well have occurred independently in the Greek and Semitic world. The same applies to other motifs cited by Astour as examples of Semitic influence on Greece. Thus the theme of an animal guide in the Kadmos story, which he takes to be a West Semitic borrowing (*HS* pp.157f.) is exceedingly common in folklore (see above p.42f.), as well as being attested by numerous other examples in Greek literature. Even the detail stressed by Astour that the cow must be unyoked is found elsewhere and is easily explicable.[165] Similarly, Euphemos' power of walking on water, which Astour compares to the Spirit of God moving on the face of the waters in Genesis I (*HS* p.121), is a popular motif in folklore, and exactly paralleled by the supernatural gifts of Jason's other companions.[166] These examples could be multiplied many times.[167] What we must not forget is that a mere resemblance of one myth to another is not in itself

---

165. On the reasons why the animal should be unyoked see Brockington in *Peake* pp. 320f., on I Sam. 6. 7-16 (the passage adduced by Astour), and Nineham *GSM* p. 295 on "an ass whereon never man sat" (Mk. 11. 2). The general idea seems to be that an animal intended for sacred or ceremonial use should not have been used before for secular purposes.

The theme of the animal guide is usefully discussed by Vian (*Or. Theb.* pp.77-9), where he cites a large number of examples from Greek literature in which the animal is connected with city-foundation, including not only cow and bull, but also crow, eagle, wolf, hare, rat and other animals.

166. We may compare Stith Thompson's comment: "In Jason's fellow voyagers is to be found a good example of a very popular motif, that of the extraordinary companions" (quoted by Mary Grant, *The Myths of Hyginus* p. 38, on *Fab.* 14). Similarly Halliday notes the parallel between Jason's companions and those of King Arthur, remarking that "one need not suppose any link except coincidence" (*IEFT* p. 17). For walking on the water in particular see further Thompson, *MIFL* D 1841.4.3.

167. Some further examples are: (1) the motif of magic darkness (*HS* pp.117f.), for which compare Thompson, *MIFL* D 908; (2) the blind prophet (*HS* p. 162), a motif true to life, and in folklore: compare Rose, *HGM* p. 195 and Thompson, *MIFL* D 1712. 2; (3) women shouldering water (*HS* p.73), the normal work of women in the orient and in Greece.

evidence for borrowing. As S.H. Hooke wrote, "there are two ways in which the presence of myths in any society may be explained; one is by way of diffusion, and the other is through the independent working of imagination when confronted by similar situations" (*MEM*(1963) p. 16). Obviously it is possible for elements which are common in myth and folktale to be borrowed, but if the thesis is to be convincing much more stringent tests need to be applied than those observed by Astour.[168]

(4) *Fourth, all too often the real similarity is not motif at all but name; and the evidence of conjectural etymology, upon which the similarities of name depend, is exceedingly difficult to evaluate.* Where the parallels of motif adduced by Astour are so weak, one may suspect that the real point of departure lies in the conjectural etymologies, which in some instances form the most impressive part of Astour's evidence (cf. above p. 146 on Kadmos). But it must be emphasised that Semitic derivations are notoriously easy to conjecture with the whole range of Semitic languages to draw upon, and there is often no decisive means of judging between these and the possible alternative derivations from Indo-European and other sources.[169] It must moreover be remembered that vocalisation is uncertain in languages such as Ugaritic, and that proper names, on which Astour largely relies, are particularly difficult, since meaning is rarely important and

168. Halliday has a good discussion of the problem of the diffusion of folktales in *IEFT.* What he shows is that individual motifs may occur widely in different cultures by independent invention, and that in order to postulate borrowing one needs not merely a general resemblance of idea or identity of an individual detail in two areas, but an *identity of structure in the story* (see *IEFT* esp. pp.13-20). Astour however simply assumes diffusion from the orient to Greece for his motifs, and neither seeks to find an identity of structure (something which would be extremely difficult with our present sources) nor discusses the occurrence of similar motifs in other societies.

169. On occasion Astour draws on both East and West Semitic for the formation of a single word; e.g. Atalante is derived from Akkadian *eţlu,* "hero", and the W. Semitic name *'Anta (HS*pp.214f.); in other instances the names for which he proposes oriental etymologies are Greek words for which IE derivations are commonly accepted. Thus there seems no reason to doubt that the name *Harmonia* is derived from Greek ἁρμονία, ἁρμόζω (cf. Sittig, *RE* VII col. 2379), and similarly the proper name *Poikiles* is much more plausibly connected with Greek ποικίλος, ποικιλέω (cf. Höfer, *Roscher* III col. 2600) than with the Semitic terms suggested by Astour (see the next note).

one is very much dependent on phonetic resemblances which may be only coincidental.[170] Sometimes the same Greek word is derived from two or three different Semitic words by various authorities. Thus, whereas Astour derives *Hellotis,* a title of Europê in Crete, from the West Semitic root *halal* "to shine" comparing *Hêlēl ben Šahar,* "Morning-star son of Dawn" in Isaiah (*HS*pp.138f.), H. Lewy derives this title *Hellotis* from a completely different Semitic word, Phoenician *'almat,* "young woman" (*SFG* p.140), while Movers proposes yet another Semitic derivation from a form *'ēlōtî,* meaning "my goddess" (*Die Phönizier* II. 2 (1850) p.80 n. 89). In each case the proposed meaning might seem to suit the character of Europê. When it is so "easy to pull a parallel of some sort out of the Near Eastern hat" (Boardman in *CR* 16 (1966) p.87), the evidence of etymology must be regarded with great caution.

(5) *Fifth, the parallels are drawn from widely separate periods of time in both Greece and the orient.* Throughout Astour tends to assume that both names and motifs must have been borrowed in the Bronze Age. But the possibility must not be overlooked that many could have been borrowed later, for instance in the ninth to eighth centuries B.C., when Greeks are believed to have settled at such places

---

170. For some of Astour's proposed etymologies complex linguistic changes have to be postulated. Thus several alternative derivations are proposed for the name *Poikiles,* including one from the name *Kolpias* of a primaeval wind in Philo, and one from a hypothetical Semitic phrase *pî-kôl,* meaning "womb of all" (*HS* pp.123-6). In supporting the first of these derivations Astour refers to a "metathesis"; but to invoke this term for such a complex set of changes in both consonants and vowels can only be described as fantastic. With the second too there are major difficulties in the vowels. Astour attempts to explain the appearance of *i* for *oi* in the first syllable on the grounds that in the 5th cent. B.C. the pronunciation of these sounds in Greek was "practically identical" (*HS* p.125 n.1); but the dispute over λιμός and λοιμός to which he refers (Thuc. II. 54) is concerned with the true or false recollection of an ancient oracle, and did not arise from any confusion of pronunciation. It was not until about the *ninth century A.D.* that *oi* in Greek finally became pronounced as *i* (Lejeune, *TPG* (ed. 2, 1955) pp. 200f. §217 fin.).

Furthermore often very complicated hypotheses are also necessary to make the supposed Semitic meaning suit the bearer of the name in question: this is abundantly illustrated not only by the example of Poikiles cited above, but also by Astour's discussions of Tektamos (*HS* pp.135f.) and Harmonia (*HS* pp.160f.).

as Al Mina and Tell Sukas on the Syrian coast, and when Iron Age Phoenician seafarers were visiting the Aegean.[171] Some of the themes of which Astour makes use are not attested till Hellenistic or Roman times. One example is the motif of Europê's veil (see above p. 145); others are the pall of darkness encountered by the Argonauts and Euphemos' walking on the water, both of which Astour derives from West Semitic myths of creation (*HS* pp. 117f. and 121), but which are not attested until Apollonios of Rhodes in the Hellenistic period. Even if it should be accepted that these two motifs share a common oriental source with the Priestly account of creation in Genesis I (itself probably compiled in the late sixth or fifth century B.C.), there are many occasions other than the early Mycenaean period when they could have been borrowed. Similarly in the important matter of Kadmos' relationship to Europê, Astour simply takes it for granted that the idea of the two as brother and sister is an original Mycenaean element in the legend; but as we saw in our earlier discussion (Ch. II p. 24 with n.33) the oldest classical authorities give Kadmos and Europê different parentage and it seems likely that no exact blood-relationship was established for them in the early tradition.

We are now in a position to make some assessment of the potential value to the prehistorian of the material used by Astour, and to consider its contribution to the interpretation of the Kadmos legend. It would seem that any attempt to use parallels in motifs and onomastics as a source for Mycenaean Greece is subject to serious difficulties. In the first place this kind of study, when applied to the mythology of Bronze Age Greece and the orient, is radically different from, for example, a comparison between motifs found in classical Greek literature and that of Rome, where one is dealing with a substantial body of extant and datable material and where one knows much about the historical and literary background. As far as the Bronze Age is concerned, we do not possess a Mycenaean literature from which to make comparisons with the orient, but merely inferences about a hypothetical Mycenaean mythology, drawn, often very speculatively,

---

171. See Boardman, *GO* esp. pp.62-7; Riis, *Sukas* I esp. pp.158-62; cf. id. in *Ugaritica* VI 435-50. For Phoenician traders in the Aegean see below Ch. VIII esp. n. 198.

from much later Greek sources. Even the oriental mythology with which this is being compared is imperfectly attested and sometimes obscure, and has to be taken from various periods and cultures. This means that any conclusion concerning borrowing of names and motifs must be very tentative.

Secondly, even granting that some borrowing has taken place, it is exceedingly difficult, if not impossible, to use this for the reconstruction of historical conditions and events. This is well illustrated by Astour's specific historical conclusions: thus concerning the presence of Syrian and Phoenician migrants in Greece, he writes that the "data of onomastics and mythology are *quite sufficient for unconditional acceptance of their historic reality"* (*HS* p.334, our italics). But the truth is that the evidence of motifs and proper names of itself can tell us very little about the date and manner of any transmission, i.e. whether they were diffused in the Early Mycenaean period or later, and whether as a result of a substantial movement of peoples, the settlement of a small group, or through forms of contact involving no settlement at all. Even if the Semitic parallels to the Kadmos legend were much more convincing than we have seen them to be, they certainly need not be explained in terms of "the settlement of a large and strong W-S group in Boeotia", with "many men and a lasting domination over the country" (so Astour, *HS* pp.221, 224). For example, supposing that the Cretan interpretation of the Kadmos legend were right, and that there were no Semitic settlement at all in Boeotia, points of similarity in the mythological traditions of Greece and the orient could nevertheless be explained by a variety of means: some might have arisen from the independent working of the imagination in a similar cultural milieu (cf. Hooke's comment cited above p.156); others might have been introduced to Greece in the Mycenaean period through casual contact with oriental merchants and craftsmen; others again might have been brought back by Mycenaean sailors or settlers returning from the East; others could have been diffused *after* the Mycenaean period either by Phoenician traders, or by Greeks who had settled on the Phoenician coast (see above pp.157f.); we cannot even exclude the possibility that some might have been transmitted in the reverse direction, from Greece to the orient. Where so many alternatives are open, it is clear that a major West

Semitic settlement in Mycenaean Boeotia is not the only conceivable explanation of the facts.

A few more positive conclusions do however emerge from this study. Although the data of motifs and onomastics clearly cannot be considered a primary source for prehistory, they may play a subsidiary role in our discussion. The fact that an oriental origin is at least possible for Kadmos' name and a few of the elements in his story does perhaps add some slight weight to the view that he was originally a Phoenician in the tradition and that the legend may have a genuine historical basis, even though it does not provide any proof of this.[172] Astour's real contribution lies not in finding independent testimony from motifs and onomastics that Semites were settled in Greece, but rather in adducing similarities between Greek mythology and that of the orient whose explanation could lie in oriental settlement in Mycenaean Greece, *if that were already known from other sources to have taken place.*[173]

---

172. Astour is not the only scholar to overrate the historical value of parallels in motif: cf. G. Thomson, *SAGS* I p. 377, where the significance of an Ugaritic parallel to the role of Zeus in the Europê story is much exaggerated. In fact the Ugaritic passage to which he and others refer (see above p.60) in very obscure (see esp. Dussaud, *RHR* 105 (1932) p. 252), and the elements of supposed parallelism are either inexact or commonplace. One must insist that there is no Ugaritic evidence, either archaeological or textual, to "confirm" (so Thomson, loc. cit.) the truth of the Kadmos story.

173. Astour seems to recognise that his historical deductions based on mythology and onomastics alone may be open to criticism without some consideration of the archaeological evidence (see *HS* p.323), but his treatment of the question "Does archaeology contradict Semitic penetration into the Aegean?" (*HS* pp. 323-31) is very unsatisfactory. He quotes the opinions of archaeologists such as Gordon Childe, C.F.A. Schaeffer and C.L. Woolley to show (*inter alia*) that Minoan metallurgy was based on Asiatic traditions, that the Torque-Bearers came from Syria to central Europe, that the Knossian frescoes were derived from Alalakh, and that the potter's wheel was introduced to Crete from the East in the MM period, referring to these as "archaeological proofs" (*HS* p. 334). But however eminent the archaeologists who hold these views, they are hypotheses not facts, and they serve only to refute a view held today by nobody that there was no contact by sea between the Aegean and the East in the whole of the Bronze Age. What Astour needs to win conviction for his thesis is archaeological evidence from the *Late* Bronze Age and from his proposed centres of Semitic penetration, i.e. Argolis and Boeotia; but hardly any material from mainland Greece is considered. We may agree that it is not necessary for people to produce their "ceramic passports" (*HS* p.334) for us to believe in their presence in a country, but one must have some discussion of archaeological evidence of the right date and place.

Finally, however weak Astour's proposed parallels may be judged to be, and however inadequate the material for establishing what he claims for it, it must be emphasised that this does not disprove the occurrence of such events as he postulates. We have seen that on archaeological and other grounds an oriental settlement at Thebes is more plausible than it once seemed (above p.137), and even if all Astour's etymologies and parallels of motif were rejected, this would not rule out the possibility of an oriental presence in Mycenaean Boeotia, though this need not necessarily have been in the period (LH I-II) which Astour seems to favour. This brings us face to face with the whole question of chronology and the problems which it poses.

CHAPTER VIII

SOME CHRONOLOGICAL PROBLEMS

If we allow that the legend of Kadmos might contain some kernel of historical fact, to what chronological period is it most plausibly to be related? A good many scholars both in the last century and in more recent years have sought to answer this question by basing their reconstructions on what the traditions themselves have to say about date, and we therefore begin here. Two sources of information may be distinguished: first, the genealogical evidence concerning the position of the hero Kadmos, and second, absolute dates for the "events" of the legend supplied by ancient chronographers, whose work must be regarded as secondary to the genealogies.

In the present century the idea that the Greek genealogies are basically reliable material for dating has been stated most fully by Sir John Myres, who in his book *Who were the Greeks?* (1930) argues that the pedigrees of the noble families in Greece are carefully preserved, coherent with one another and the other available evidence, and historically trustworthy (see *WWG* esp. pp.297-308 with notes). Myres calculates that the historical events typified by the legend of Kadmos occurred around 1400 B.C. (*WWG* esp. pp.321f., 347), and this fits in with his general scheme by which he reconstructs from the traditions three main periods of resettlement in Greece. His date has been accepted by many scholars: thus both Rhys Carpenter and A. Mentz hold that the introduction of writing associated with Kadmos is to be placed around 1400 B.C.[174] Others similarly estimate

---

174. Carpenter identifies the writing with Linear B rather than the classical Greek script, suggesting that " 'Cadmus' may well have brought letters (though not this later alphabet) to Greece around 1400 B.C." (*AJPh* 56 (1935) p.7; cf. above p.107), while Mentz has in mind the Greek alphabet: "Kadmos führt also um 1400 die Schrift in Böotien ein. ...Es ist einfach die phönikische Schrift" (*RhM* 85 (1936) p. 365). Other scholars who adopt a date around 1400 B.C. as traditional for Kadmos are Nixon, *TRD* pp. 134, 136 (1430 B.C. after adjusting to a date of 1250 B.C. for the Trojan War), and Jackson Knight, *MMHom* p.47 (also 1430 B.C.).

from the pedigrees a date in the first half of the fourteenth century for the coming of Kadmos to Boeotia: for instance in *A History of Greece* (1959; ed. 2, 1967) N.G.L. Hammond has argued that "while the eponymous ancestor or the god at the head of a genealogy marks the back-stop of family tradition, the succeeding names in the pedigree of a dynasty may well be historical", and he wrote (in the first edition) of Kadmos as "founding a dynasty at Thebes from Phoenicia six generations before the Trojan War", which on the basis of a thirty-year generation he calculated to be roughly about 1380 B.C. (op. cit. p.60). In the second edition the "six generations" here have been somewhat arbitrarily reduced to five, and the date lowered to c. 1350, presumably to accord better with the evidence of the Theban seals![175] Likewise J. Zafiropulo has calculated that Kadmos' expedition to Greece took place in 1360 B.C., and he refers to the "dynastie que Cadmos établit sans aucun doute possible à Thèbes vers le milieu du XIVᵉ siècle avant J.-C." (*HGAB* (1964) pp.27f.).

Can we assume from the statements of these scholars that here we have clear evidence for the dating of the historical events associated with Kadmos to 1400 B.C. or a little later? The first fact to be noted is that even if one were to accept the general reliability of the pedigrees, one would need to allow for a considerable margin of error in calculation. Very much depends on the date adopted for the Trojan War, which ranges from the early fourteenth century to Eratosthenes' estimate of 1184/3 B.C. Some variation can arise also from the number of years reckoned to a generation: while the ancients often based their calculations on a forty-year generation (cf. Burn, *MPG* pp.52-5), modern scholars generally count three generations to a century or make one generation equal thirty years or even less.[176] The

---

175. See *HGHam* ed. 2, p.60. According to the Theban pedigree Kadmos lived six generations before the Trojan War (see Table 7, p.166). No significance can be attached to the fact that he visited Thera with "his grown-up nephew" Membliaros (Hammond, op. cit. p.654): see n. 26 above.

176. Compare and contrast J. Bérard, *RCEM* passim; Huxley, *CL* p.36; Holland, *HSPh* 39 (1928) pp.77f.; and Myres, *WWG* esp. p.307. For extensive use of the genealogies and chronographers (though not for Kadmos) see Mylonas, *AMyc* Ch. I, esp. p.15 with n. 44 on the date of the Trojan War.

practical consequence of this is that, when a hero was believed to have lived three generations before the Trojan War, he might still be placed as far back as the beginning of the fifteenth century (in archaeological terms LH II) or as late as the early thirteenth (LH IIIB), while one thought of as living nine generations before the War might belong to any time between the late eighteenth and mid-fifteenth centuries (MH, LH I or LH II).

But there are perhaps more basic assumptions behind this use of the genealogical evidence which must be challenged. How reliable can we expect the genealogies to be, especially when, as often, they are inconsistent among themselves? One finds numerous difficulties and chronological *impasses* which cannot be solved by a criticism of sources, and a coherent picture can be obtained only by an arbitrary choice of version followed. Thus, to revert to Kadmos, this hero was, according to Pherekydes and other authorities from the fifth century B.C. onwards, a contemporary of Danaos, who in the Argive royal pedigree lived *nine* generations before the Trojan War. But in the Theban royal pedigree, attested also in the fifth century B.C. by Herodotos and Sophokles, Kadmos lived *six* generations before the War, while if one calculates according to the Cretan genealogy, which has the authority of Homer, Europê, who was Kadmos' niece or sister in the later tradition, lived only *three* generations before the Trojan War (for these pedigrees see Table 7, p.166). This means that the traditional genealogies themselves provide a discrepancy of as much as *six generations* or about 200 years. Nor is Kadmos an isolated example, for similar difficulties will be found over the genealogical position of many heroes.[177] It is small wonder that Pausanias once declared: "οἱ μὲν δὴ Ἑλλήνων λόγοι διάφοροι τὰ πλέονα καὶ οὐχ

---

177. For example, Teiresias is imagined as contemporary with Kadmos in Euripides' *Bacchae* (and indeed as an old man at the time of the dramatic action), and yet according to Euripides' *Phoenissae* he is alive at the time of Kadmos' great-great-great-grandsons, Polyneikes and Eteokles. Similarly Elektryon, son of Perseus at Mycenae, must have lived a long time, since traditions found in Apollodoros (II. 4. 5 and 6) make him contemporary with both his brother Mestor and Mestor's great-great-grandsons! Notorious difficulties also exist over the genealogical position of Herakles, Minos, Pelops and many others (see Burn, *MPG* pp. 22-5; cf. also the older work of Clinton, *FH* I esp. p.80 on Pelops).

TABLE 7: The date of Kadmos according to the Greek genealogies

Argive pedigree	Theban pedigree	Cretan pedigree
(see Apollodoros	(see Apollodoros	(see Apollodoros
II.1.4 to 4.8	III.4.1; 5.5-8;	III.1.1 to 3.1;
and III.1.1)	Sophokles, *O.T.*;	*Iliad* XIII.445-53
	Herodotos at the	and XIV. 321f.)
	references discussed	
	in How and Wells'	
	commentary, Vol. I	
	pp.438f.)	

Argive pedigree:

KADMOS as the
cousin of
Danaos
|
Hypermnestra
|
Abas
|
Akrisios
|
Danae
|
Perseus
|
Elektryon
|
Alkmene
|
Herakles
|
TROJAN WAR PERIOD
(Tlepolemos, son
of Herakles, fought
at Troy: *Iliad* V.
628)

Theban pedigree:

KADMOS
father of
Polydoros
|
Labdakos
|
Laios
|
Oidipous
|
Polyneikes
|
TROJAN WAR PERIOD
(Diomedes, son of
Tydeus contemporary
of Polyneikes,
fought at Troy:
Iliad IV. 370ff.)

Cretan pedigree:

KADMOS as the
brother or uncle of
Europê
|
Minos
|
Deukalion
|
TROJAN WAR PERIOD
(Idomeneus, son of
Deukalion, fought
at Troy: *Iliad*
II.645ff. etc.)

166

ἥκιστα ἐπὶ τοῖς γένεσίν εἰσι" (VIII. 53.5).

This difficulty in establishing a clear genealogical position for Kadmos and the other variable factors already mentioned (the length of a generation and the date of the fall of Troy) no doubt account in large measure for the great variety of dates assigned to him by the ancient chronographers. The Parian Marble, a chronicle compiled in the third century B.C., places Kadmos' coming to Thebes in the equivalent of 1518/17 B.C. (see *FGrH* II B, 239, A7); but Kastor of Rhodes, a chronographer of the first century B.C., assigns his arrival to the reign of Pandion of Athens, which in his chronology began in the equivalent of 1307/6 B.C. (*FGrH* II B, 250 fr.4,8), while Eusebios (ca. fourth century A.D.) gives various dates for Kadmos and Europê, ranging, in modern terms, from the extremes of 1455 to 1285 B.C., clearly varying according to the source which he is following (on the Eusebian chronology cf. J. Bérard in *Syria* 29 (1952) pp.7f.). With such a wide range of dates, it is all too easy to find an ancient source which will support a particular view of the chronology, as is done, for example, by Mrs. Vermeule when she writes: "In the Early Mycenaean Age, Greek tradition says, Kadmos the Phoenician brought writing to Greece",[178] and by B.H. Ullman, who, in arguing for a Bronze Age introduction of of the Phoenician alphabet to Greece by Kadmos, writes that according to Eratosthenes this event took place in 1313 B.C., and that in his view "this may be right" (*AJA* 31 (1927) p.326; cf. Diringer, *The Alphabet* (ed. 3, 1968) I p.358; but the ascription of this date, here and elsewhere, to Eratosthenes is erroneous[179]).

Yet if one attempts to consider the legendary material as a whole and to assess all the possible alternatives, the difficulties are enormous. There is a great time-lag between the period to which the story is

---

178. See *GBA* p.239; cf. also Pfeiffer's statement "mythical chronology puts Cadmus 300 years before the Trojan War" (*HOCS* p.21 n. 8) and Muhly's assertion "tradition dated Cadmus in the sixteenth century B.C." (*HAP* p. 39). All these writers are presumably following the Parian Marble and ignoring other ancient dates for Kadmos.

179. The date of 1313 B.C., which is given by several scholars for Kadmos and ascribed by them to Eratosthenes, goes back not to him but only to Fynes Clinton, *FHI* (1834): see G.P. and R.B. Edwards, "Eratosthenes and the date of Cadmus" in *GR* 24 (1974).

believed to refer and the first attestation of any traditions concerning date. While we may reasonably assume that many of these traditions, whether in genealogical form or as absolute dates, are older than their first attestation, there is no valid means of determining which, if any, are reliable.[180] As far as Kadmos is concerned, the literary refences provide a much wider range of date than is commonly supposed, and all that can safely be concluded is that this hero was believed by the classical and later Greeks to have lived several generations before the Trojan War.

If the internal evidence of the traditions can provide no secure basis for dating, we are forced to turn to the outside sources. Here much depends on the particular interpretation of the legend which is adopted, especially on the proposed source of any migration. Furthermore different parts of the story can be understood as its essential historical core, and these can suggest very different dates for the postulated events. It is therefore necessary to give separate consideration to the three principal elements which have been distinguished (see above p.43), as having a possible basis in fact, namely the "Phoenician" foundation of Thebes, the introduction of letters, and the various settlements traditionally established by Kadmos in the Aegean.

(1) Kadmos and the foundation of Thebes

A good many scholars believe that Kadmos' traditional foundation of Thebes is to be dated to the beginning of the Mycenaean Age: thus G.L. Huxley, after suggesting that the legend of Danaos refers to events around 1550 B.C., writes: "Another immigrant from

---

180. In the case of Kadmos, reckoning by both the Cretan and the Argive pedigrees is suspect, since his relationship to both Europê (see above p.74) and Danaos (cf. p.29 and Tables 1 and 3) may be comparatively late additions to the story. This leaves only the Theban royal pedigree, but even this might be only an attempt to link Kadmos, through his rather shadowy son Polydoros (see above p.21), with the house of Oidipous with which he was not originally connected. Similar difficulties arise with other heroes; it seems not uncommon in heroic legend for figures of different periods to be brought together regardless of the chronological problems which this poses (see esp. Bowra, *HP* pp.522-4, with examples from the *Song of Roland,* the *Elder Edda,* and Russian and Yugoslav oral poetry).

the Levant at this time was Kadmos, the eponymous ancestor of the Kadmeian dynasty in Thebes; as at Mycenae, the rise of Thebes in the first Late Helladic period can be explained by the arrival of an immigrant dynasty" (*CL* (1961) p.37). Similarly, F.H. Stubbings suggests that there was a series of small-smale invasions of Greece at the beginning of the Late Helladic period, arguing that "there is a case for inferring the arrival in Greece at this time of new rulers from abroad, such as are indeed ascribed by legend to the beginnings of the first heroic age. Some of these immigrant founder heroes are of origins too improbable to be fictitious - Danaus, for example, from Egypt; Cadmus from Syria. The only probable juncture for such immigration which can be recognized in the archaeological record is at the transition from M.H. to L.H.; while in terms of external history no time is so likely as the period of the expulsion of the Hyksos overlords from Egypt" (*CAH* ed. 2, fasc. 4 (1962) p.74 = ed. 3, I.i pp.244f.). A sixteenth century or early Mycenaean date for Kadmos' settlement has likewise been proposed by W. Dörpfeld, L.B. Holland, J. Bérard and M.C. Astour (see above Chs. III and VII).

There are several arguments in favour of this early dating for the coming of the Cadmeians to Thebes. The story of Kadmos ostensibly refers to the foundation of the city, and Nilsson has stressed that this in itself is a remarkable fact, since, although stories of foundation are common for Greek colonies, Thebes is almost alone of the cities of the mother-country in having a "true foundation myth", i.e. a story in which the site of the town is chosen by divine intervention and the origin of the people and the noble families is explained (see *MOGM* pp.122-6). One can hardly suppose that this story looks back to the earliest occupation of Thebes, which was inhabited from the Early Bronze Age or even Neolithic times (see above p.103 with n.102), but it would seem not unreasonable to refer it to the transition from Middle to Late Helladic, a time which in general marks the beginning of an era in Greece, when many changes in material culture were introduced, and when there was a noticeable opening-up of overseas contacts after the comparative isolation of the Middle Helladic period. Furthermore, this is a time when few fortifications are attested, when the civilisation of Greece is less homogeneous and apparently less well organised than in the Late Mycenaean period, and when therefore it is easy to imagine how new leaders might have settled at various Greek sites and have contributed to the rise of Mycenaean civilisation. Thus the very fact that the legend refers to the foundation of the town may seem to be in favour of placing it in LH I.

But it must be admitted that the evidence at present available might also support other interpretations. While certain scholars postulate a new element in the population at the beginning of the Mycenaean period, the majority regard it as more plausible to suppose that the Mycenaean civilisation developed out of the Middle Helladic without any influx of new blood, simply under the influence of fresh contact with Crete and the orient.[181] It is important here to bear in mind the date of the evidence for foreign contacts from Thebes itself, of which very little is as early as LH I. Since in any case Kadmos' "foundation" could not refer to the original foundation of Thebes but only to some subsequent re-foundation or re-settlement (for example, the foundation of the palace), is it possible to relate it to a later phase of the Mycenaean Age?

As far as the Cretan hypothesis is concerned, the objects which most clearly reveal Minoan influence at Thebes — the palace frescoes and inscribed stirrup-jars — are LH II or III (cf. above pp.106-9 with nn. 105 and 107) while the larnakes from Tanagra, which might be taken to indicate Cretan connexions (see above pp.109f.) are datable to LH IIIB. This means that although it is possible to postulate Minoan settlement at Thebes in LH I, as did Hall, Burn and Evans, at the *earliest* period of Minoan contact, the material evidence for this is slight, and the period of *greatest* Minoan influence would rather appear to be LH II or even LH III. It is a moot point which of these

181. For a new element in the population at the beginning of the LH period see Stubbings, loc. cit. above p.169 and *CAH* ed. 2, fasc. 18 esp. pp.11-16. For stress on the continuity between MH and LH and the absence of firm evidence for any invaders see Matz, *CEG* p.163; Chadwick, *CAH* ed. 2, fasc. 15 p.13; Caskey, *CAH* ed. 2, fasc. 45 esp. p.26; and Buck in *Phoenix* 20 (1966) esp. p.207. A few scholars admit the possibility that there might have been a new element at this period, but suppose any fresh arrivals to be of the same stock as the IE invaders believed to have arrived at the end of the EH period; see Wace in *CH* Ch. 12, esp. p.348, and compare Mrs. Vermeule's discussion in *GBA* Ch. 4, esp. p.110. Palmer is exceptional in postulating the first arrival of the Greeks at this period (see above n. 8).

periods would be the most plausible for the settlement connected with Kadmos: reconstructions will vary according to the type of event which is believed to lie behind the legend, and we must consider also the evidence from Crete. If one is thinking in terms of a Cretan colony at Thebes, then this might most reasonably be placed in LM IA, a period of Cretan strength and expansion (cf. Furumark, *SIAH* pp.251-4), though dates later than this cannot be ruled out. If on the other hand one thinks in terms of refugees from Crete, as was once suggested by Myres (*YWCS* for 1911, p.27), then the most plausible period is perhaps that immediately after the fall of the palaces and the destruction (possibly volcanic) of the great Cretan sites, that is, early in LM IIIA in the case of Knossos, or at the end of LM IB in the case of the other Cretan sites. There is no sound criterion for deciding between these various alternatives, and it must be remembered that if there ever was at Thebes a dynasty, however short-lived, of Cretan origin, close links with Crete might have been maintained over a considerable period of time both before and after any period of Cretan domination.

Turning now to the oriental hypothesis, we find that the evidence from Thebes for the date of contacts with the Near East is more clear-cut: the only substantial indication of close relations — the seals from the palace — come from an LH IIIB context (see above p.132). At the same time in assessing the probabilities one must bear in mind not only the specific evidence from Thebes itself, which is very limited, but also the type of event which is postulated and the general history of the Near East. A really large-scale migration from the orient to Greece in the Mycenaean period is unlikely,[182] but if a limited refugee movement from Syria or Phoenicia were to be suggested, then there are several possible occasions ranging from the migrations of the early

---

182. If settlement on *a large scale* from the orient had occurred in Mycenaean Greece, one would expect either more specific traces of it in the archaeological record, or some mention in the oriental documents. But evidence of this sort is lacking, and no good support is given by the linguistic material, since (*pace* Astour) the Semitisms which occur in Greek are comparatively few and explicable as loan-words. A detailed discussion of the precise date of any possible major oriental immigration does not therefore seem worth-while.

second millennium to the period of the Sea Peoples' invasions (cf. n. 150). If a refugee movement from *Egypt* were to be regarded as the origin of the tradition, then the Hyksos expulsion ca. 1570 B.C. provides a suitable, well-attested historical juncture.[183] If on the other hand one has in mind a colony or trading station from the East, then

183. See J Bérard, *Syria* 29 (1952) pp.1-43. The tradition of an Egyptian origin for Kadmos remains very intriguing. One suspects that the homonymy of Boeotian and Egyptian Thebes has played a part in shaping it (cf. above pp.37f.), but it cannot be dismissed solely as a Hellenistic invention (so apparently Vian, *Or. Theb.* p. 32), since a connexion between Kadmos and Egypt is attested as early as Bakchylides and Pherekydes (see above pp.71, 73).

The position may be summarised as follows: a true Egyptian settlement at Mycenaean Thebes is most unlikely. There is a total lack of supporting Egyptian documentary evidence, and a complete absence of any Egyptian objects, even small artefacts, from the site during the Bronze Age (Pendlebury, *Aegyptiaca* p.87; the solitary Egyptian scarab found at Thebes is from a Geometric context). A theory connecting Kadmos with Hyksos refugees has slightly greater plausibility, in that it is easier to imagine how some sort of settlement could have occurred at the end of the comparatively obscure Hyksos period without leaving trace in the documents. Nevertheless if there really were Hyksos at Thebes, one would expect to find at least some scarabs or other artefacts (e.g. Tell el-Yahudiyah jugs) which they are known to have used. Bérard's detailed arguments are not convincing, since he is not sufficiently critical of the Greek literary sources. Thus he builds up his case for the Hyksos period as the only possible one at which the legend of Kadmos can be placed on the basis of five generations between Kadmos and Io (see op. cit. pp.11-16); but we have seen how little reliance can be placed on the exact genealogical data. He also makes extensive use of late and rationalising versions (such as Eusebios' reference to Kadmos migrating from Egypt to Phoenicia and Herodotos' version of the rape of Io: see op. cit. pp.15, 3f.), and many of his philological equations are doubtful; cf. also Vian's brief criticisms in *Or. Theb.* pp.52f. Similarly Holland's theory of Greek-speaking invaders from Egypt (see above p.59), though it avoids the necessity of looking for Egyptian objects at Thebes, involves so many doubtful hypotheses that it cannot be sustained.

It is interesting to note that the connexion between the Greek legends of foreigners and the Hyksos, maintained in the 1930's by Dörpfeld (see above Ch. III), can be traced at least back to the early 19th century: see Heeren, *SPAG* (1829) p.65 and Thirlwall, *HGThi* I (1835) p.76, who refer respectively to the Hyksos as "Arabian nomads" and "the shepherds". See further n.186.

the latter part of the Late Bronze Age (i.e. LH III) is most plausible,[184] when, as was seen in Chapter VI, there was extensive trade between Greece and the orient, and when there is evidence for Canaanite seafaring. Certainly any settlement by Mycenaeans returning from the East (cf. the suggestions of Dussaud and the recent excavators of Thebes, above p.60 and p.133 with n.146) would have to be placed in LH III and probably not earlier than LH IIIB.[185] In the opinion of the present writer the available evidence would seem to offer more support to the idea of a small-scale settlement of genuine Semites from Phoenicia or Syria as a historical basis for the legend than to a theory of Mycenaeans returning from the East, or to the suggestion of an Egyptian dynasty or other foundation from Egypt.[186]

184. It cannot be argued that Greece was too well organised and too well defended for any foreign settlements to have occurred there within the LH III period; such settlement could have been by peaceable means, for instance following trade. At Thebes itself settlement by force of arms is also possible, since there are at least two, possibly three, destructions there within LH III (see Ch. V with n.105), and it would not be inconceivable that the "foundation" associated with Kadmos was a re-foundation after one of these.

185. A difficulty with a IIIB (i.e. 13th cent.) dating for the "foundation" by Kadmos might be that it allows little time for the period of history possibly represented by the other Theban legends (e.g. the expedition of the Epigonoi), and that it brings the foundation very close to the generally accepted date for the Trojan War, which (if Homer's Troy has been correctly identified with Troy VIIa) seems to have occurred before the end of IIIB. This point however should not be pressed, since analogies from well-documented periods show that several major events can occur within a short time, and one need not necessarily postulate more than about half a century between the coming of the Cadmeians to Thebes and the sack of Troy.

186. An Egyptian settlement at Thebes has been postulated recently by Spyropoulos on the basis of a hill there supposedly cut in the shape of a pyramid and with a tomb on its top (see *AAA* 5 (1972) pp.16-27); but the resemblance of the hill to a pyramid seems very slight: see Spyropoulos' fig. 2, op. cit. p.18 (a montage from *AD*3), and contrast the very elaborate stone-built structure of the famous stepped pyramid of Saqqara to which Spyropoulos refers. It must be noted that no Egyptian artefacts were found in the tomb on the hill, and its date (EH II) is far too early to be plausibly related to the Kadmos legend. (The Saqqara pyramid is also very early, dating to the early third millennium: see Edwards, *PE* p. 243, and Ch. II with details of its complex architecture.) The possible Egyptian cults from the classical period at Thebes mentioned by Spyropoulos cannot be thought to add any weight to his argument, since Egyptian cults occur quite commonly in classical and later Greece, especially at sites of commercial importance (on the Theban dedication to Isis etc. cf. Ziehen in *RE(T)* col. 1523).

It must be concluded that the dating of the foundation element is no simple matter, since it is dependent on the precise type of event postulated from the story. Yet there is no objective way of determining from the legendary sources to what event the story may relate, and no guidance is to be obtained from them about the exact period at which any "foundation" is to be placed. All that one can do is to attempt to assess the relative plausibility of the various alternatives, and there is bound to be a subjective factor in any judgement that is made. If the Minoan hypothesis is favoured, then a date anywhere between LH I and LH IIIA (or even IIIB) is possible. The evidence which has emerged in recent years however appears to make the oriental hypothesis more plausible, and in this case the most likely date for the events to which the legend might refer is LH IIIA-B — the period of the Ugaritic texts on seafaring, of the greatest contact between Mycenaean Greece and the East (as witnessed especially by the distribution of Mycenaean pottery there), and of the oriental artefacts found at Thebes.

(2) Kadmos and the introduction of letters

We now consider an element in the legend which at first sight seems to be more easily datable from outside sources, namely the introduction of letters. For many scholars this is indeed the one part of the story which has been proved to relate to a historical event. H.J. Rose, for example, writes: "Here the legend touches fact, for the Greek alphabet is for the most part a modification of North Semitic script" (*HGM* p.185), while J. Day concludes that the Phoenician origin of the Greek alphabet is "the only definite historical element in the legend" (*AJA* 42 (1938) p.125; a similar assessment is made by Sir Paul Harvey, *OCCL* (1937) p.84). But this identification of Kadmos' letters with the classical Greek alphabet presents a major chronological problem. Varied though the traditions are about the hero's date, they are at least agreed that Kadmos is to be placed before the Trojan War, whereas no examples of Greek alphabetic script have yet come to light which can be dated earlier than the eighth century B.C. (see Woodhead, *SGI* (1959) pp.13f. with n. 5, and the authorities cited below in note 188).

Two alternative solutions have been proposed to this problem.

The first is to place the introduction of the Phoenician alphabet in the Bronze Age, as has been maintained by both Ullman and Mentz.[187] But there are strong arguments against this view, which necessitates the unlikely assumption of the existence of the script in Greece for five centuries or more when not a single example is attested.[188] The second solution is to refer the tradition not to the classical Greek alphabet but to some other mode of writing belonging to the Bronze Age. The suggestion which has been most widely supported is that the tradition may refer to the introduction to mainland Greece of the Linear B script. An early exponent of this view was Rhys Carpenter, who in the article quoted above (in Chapter V) adopted the Cretan interpretation of the Kadmos legend, and argued that the "letters of Kadmos" are to be sharply distinguished from the later Greek alphabet. He writes: "Only if, like Herodotus, we are perturbed by the legend of Cadmus of Thebes and, like Herodotus but with much less excuse, are unable to distinguish between Helladic and Hellenic script, can we still pursue the impossible Phoenician mirage into pre-history and confuse the Ionic alphabet with the 'letters of Cadmus the Phoenician' " (*AJPh* 56 (1935) p.13). Others also argue for the identification of Kadmos' letters with Linear B, but without assuming a Cretan origin for the hero. They base this conjecture on different hypothetical misunderstandings of the term φοῖνιξ, which as is well known has several other meanings in Greek besides "Phoenician" (see above Ch. V). Thus G.E. Mylonas writes: "Most probably the legend indicates that the mythical Kadmos introduced letters which were painted *in red color* and so were called φοινικήια. The date assigned to Kadmos, the very beginning of the fourteenth and the end of the fifteenth century B.C., may suggest that these painted letters introduced into Greece

187. See above n. 174 and p.167. In a later article Ullman lowers his date slightly for the introduction of the alphabet, but still suggests "the eleventh or twelfth century B.C. or even earlier" (see *AJA* 38 (1934) pp.359-81, esp. p.380).

188. See the discussions of Carpenter in *AJA* 37 (1933) pp.8-29, Albright, *AP* (rev. ed., 1960) pp.195f., Jeffery, *LSAG* pp.12-21, *Guarducci, EpG* I pp.70-3 and Coldstream, *GGP* (1968) pp. 358f., all of whom favour a late 9th or 8th cent. date for the introduction of alphabetic script to Greece. Very recently however J. Naveh has proposed a date as early as the 12th to 11th cent. B.C., arguing on the basis of the Semitic evidence (see *AJA* 77 (1973) pp.1-8).

may have been the Linear B Script developed outside the mainland, in Knossos" (*MMA* (1966) p.204, our italics). F.M. Ahl on the other hand supposes that the original tradition referred to writing *on palm-leaves,* which, he argues, may have existed along with clay tablets as a medium for writing in the Mycenaean Age (see "Cadmus and the palm-leaf tablets" in *AJPh* 88 (1967) pp.188-94). Various other interpretations have been proposed similarly relating the legend to Bronze Age writing,[189] and the recent discovery of cuneiform script on some of the oriental seals from Thebes has not surprisingly prompted the suggestion that this is what was intended by the tradition of Kadmos' letters (see Zafiropulo, *Mead and Wine* (1966) p.16; cf. Hammond, *HGHam* (ed. 2, 1967) p.654; Guarducci, *EpG* I (1967) p.46).

It is true that these suggestions receive some support from the fact that both cuneiform and Linear B are attested archaeologically at Thebes; but when the evidence as a whole is considered it remains doubtful whether Kadmos' traditional association with letters has anything to do with either of these scripts. The appearance of cuneiform at Thebes is so far limited to an isolated group of seals, which in all likelihood are only imports, and it need not be assumed, as it is by Zafiropulo (loc. cit.), that people at Thebes could read and write cuneiform. And although Linear B was in use at Thebes, as is proved by the discovery of clay tablets there, the idea that the Kadmos legend refers to this involves some further hypothesis of an ancient misunderstanding of φοινικήια. Here the suggestions made by

189. J. Bérard interprets the legend as referring to the first introduction of a linear script to the Aegean (*RCEM* p. 57; cf. also his article in *Minos* 2 (1953) pp. 65-83); but the home of the earliest linear script (Linear A) is Crete, and there is nothing in the traditions to associate "Kadmos" with the introduction of any script there. Marinatos on the other hand tentatively suggests that the legend refers to an "improvement" of the Linear B script by the addition of some Semitic signs allegedly occurring on certain "Canaanite" jars from Greece (see *GD* esp. p.231). But these signs are few, isolated, and of doubtful origin, the longest inscription being merely three symbols (cf. Grace in the article cited above n.125). The suggestion therefore seems unnecessarily complicated and extremely hypothetical.

Mylonas and Ahl must appear rather fanciful,[190] but if on the other hand we appeal to the theory that Φοίνικες may once have meant Minoans, we have to accept that a remarkable coincidence has occurred in that the Greeks on separate occasions learnt two distinct forms of writing from two distinct sets of people, both of whom at the relevant time were called Φοίνικες!

The alternative is to suppose that Kadmos' connexion with letters as attested by Herodotos, Ephoros and other authors refers to what it most obviously suggests, namely the introduction of the Phoenician script. In favour of such a view, it may be argued that (a) there can be no possible doubt that the Greek script of the classical period was derived from Phoenicia or some area of Phoenician culture;[191] (b) this explanation involves no hypothetical assumption of a change of meaning in φοινικήια, but interprets the term in its most natural sense of "Phoenician" (cf. Hdt. V. 58); and (c) the crucial passage of Herodotos implies that the historian himself had in mind some early form of the Greek alphabet.

This last passage (Hdt. V. 57-61) is worth considering in more detail, since it is our earliest as well as our most detailed source for the tradition. Herodotos is considering the origin of the Athenian family named the Gephyraeans, whom he identifies as Phoenicians who came over with Kadmos and introduced many accomplishments including

190. It may be noted that the interpretation of *phoinikeia* as "red letters", without however their identification as Linear B, has been supported recently by several writers including Willetts and Chantraine: for criticisms of this view and of Ahl's theory see G.P. and R.B. Edwards, "Red letters and Phoenician writing" in *Kadmos* 13 (1974).

191. The exact source of the alphabet and the route by which it reached Greece are not known. A view which has met with favour is that it was first introduced by Euboean and other merchants who had been resident at Al Mina on the North Syrian coast, where there was a community of Greeks and Phoenicians in intimate contact (see esp. Woodhead, *SGI* p. 14; Jeffery, *LSAG* pp.10-12; Boardman, *BSA* 52 (1957) pp.1-29). Boardman puts forward an interesting hypothesis connecting this theory with the legend of the Gephyraeans, whom Herodotos believed to be Phoenician, but who themselves claimed to come from Eretria on Euboea (op. cit. esp. p.26; cf. above p.67). But other sources for the alphabet are quite possible, and a strong case can be made for its having been first learnt in Crete from Phoenician traders: see Guarducci, "La culla dell' alfabeto greco" in *GAK* pp.342-54; cf. Coldstream, *GGP* p.359; and Jeffery and Morpurgo-Davies, *Kadmos* 9 (1970) pp.118-54, esp. p.153.

writing (ἄλλα τε πολλὰ ... ἐσήγαγον διδασκάλια ἐς τοὺς Ἕλληνας καὶ δὴ καὶ γράμματα). After some discussion of how this Phoenician script was adapted for the use of Greek, Herodotos says that he himself saw Καδμήια γράμματα inscribed on three bronze tripods at Thebes. He quotes as the readings of the inscriptions three groups of hexameter lines saying that the tripods were dedicated by (1) Amphitryon, (2) Skaios (both of whom Herodotos places at the time of Laios father of Oidipous) and (3) Laodamas son of Eteokles. H. Biesantz has argued that what Herodotos saw here were Linear B inscriptions, supporting this identification with the alleged survival of Linear B in Boeotia on a fifth century kylix now in the Larissa museum (*Minoica* ed. Grumach (1958) pp.50-60). But Mrs. A.D. Ure has shown convincingly that the three so-called Linear B signs are only filling ornaments "by no means unfamiliar on the floral kylikes of Boeotia", and while three space-fillers in a row are uncommon, there was an unusually large space here to fill (*BICS* 6 (1959) pp.73-5). The suggestion that Herodotos had seen Linear B at Thebes is moreover rendered highly improbable by the description of the letters as "τὰ πολλὰ ὅμοια ἐόντα τοῖσι Ἰωνικοῖσι".[192] The most likely explanation of the dedications which Herodotos saw is that they were either examples of a pseudo-archaic Greek script, added to older antiquities by the Theban priests, or genuine archaic inscriptions which had become unintelligible and which were wrongly interpreted by the priests.[193]

To sum up, the possibility that Kadmos' association with writing goes back to the Bronze Age cannot be wholly excluded, since we know that writing was in use in Greece at that period and is attested in more than one form at Thebes. At the same time since the classical Greek alphabet is known to be derived from a Phoenician source, it is

192. Biesantz is unconvincing when he alleges (*Minoica* p.59) that the interpretation of Herodotos' "Cadmeian letters" as the Greek alphabet involves postulating the use of an Ionicising script in Boeotia before the local Boeotian script. As he himself stresses (quoting Pohlenz), Herodotos "epigraphische Studien nicht getrieben hat" (*Minoica* p.58).

193. Cf. Forsdyke, *GBH* pp. 40f.; Jeffery in CH pp.546f.; Grassl, *Hermes* 100 (1972) p.171 n. 7; see also Burn's discussion, *LAG* p.53. It should not be denied however that *some* Linear B inscriptions might have survived the Bronze Age: see Jeffery in *CH* p.547; cf. also Marinatos, *GD*.

most natural to suppose that this was the only form of writing which the Greeks meant when they spoke of the φοινιχήϊα with which Kadmos was associated. Admittedly this interpretation involves supposing that the Greek authors had a confused picture about the date of the script's introduction, but it is a natural desire for nations to claim the greatest possible antiquity for their institutions (cf. Josephus, *Ap.* 1.10), and it was common practice among the Greeks to ascribe the invention of the various arts to legendary heroes. It is therefore easy to understand how, in the years between the adoption of the Phoenician alphabet and the fifth century B.C. when Herodotos wrote, the vaguely remembered introduction of alphabetic writing could be attributed to a figure of the Heroic Age.[194]

(3) Kadmos and the "Phoenician" settlements in the Aegean

The settlements traditionally associated with Kadmos in the Aegean fall into two groups: (a) settlements in the southern Aegean, on Rhodes, Thera and possibly also the small island Anaphe; and (b) those in the northern Aegean, on Samothrace, Thasos and in parts of Thrace (on the traditions see above Ch. II with n.42). The dates to which these traditions might refer naturally vary according to the different possible interpretations of the legend and which group of islands one is considering. If the Cretan hypothesis were to be admitted, then the settlements of the first group could be related to the Minoan activity attested archaeologically on both Rhodes and Thera in the LM I period (see above Ch. V with n.98). There is however no evidence to suggest that Minoan interest ever extended so far as the northerly group, which must make the possibility of Minoan settlement in these places as the basis of the legend very remote.[195] A

194. If one were to accept the arguments of Ullman and Naveh (see above nn. 187, 188) and the introduction of the Greek alphabet could be placed as early as the 12th to 11th centuries B.C., then the gap between Kadmos' supposed date in the Bronze Age and that of the introduction of alphabetic script would not be so great as commonly supposed.

195. For the view that the Cretans regularly travelled as far north as Thasos and its hinterland in search of gold see Sutherland, *Gold* p.51. There has been very little exploration of Bronze Age levels in this area: cf. Desborough, *LMS* p.139; Koukouli-Chrysanthaki, *AAA* 3 (1970) pp.215-222.

similar position is found if the legend is taken to refer to Bronze Age oriental settlement: while there is evidence for Eastern contacts at both Rhodes and Thera (including some exotic new finds in Marinatos' recent excavations),[196] archaeological support for the idea that oriental people ever ventured as far north as Thasos and Samothrace in the Mycenaean Age is lacking.[197]

196. At Rhodes a very large number of *Egyptian* objects have been found (see Pendlebury, *Aegyptiaca* p. vii) and it is likely to have been a major source for exports of Mycenaean pottery to Syria, Palestine and Egypt at least in LH IIIA (see Page, *HHI* p. 16 with his n. 55, referring to Stubbings, MPL; for detailed bibliography of the excavations at Rhodes see Konstantinopoulos, *AD* 24 (1969) A (*Mel.*) p. 176 n. 1). It has even been identified with the notorious *Ahhijawa,* appearing in Hittite texts (see Page, *HHI* Ch. I passim).

The evidence from Thera comes from very recent excavations, not yet fully published. We may mention in particular representations of the oryx beissa and of monkeys, neither of which are nowadays indigenous to the Aegean area (for these see Marinatos, *Excavations at Thera* IV (1971) pls. D and 114-5), a fresco of what has been identified as an African (*AAA* 2 (1969) pp. 374f.), and decorated ostrich eggs (*AAA* 5 (1972) col. pl. II). Furthermore a very recently discovered fresco, of which around 21 feet have been uncovered, apparently depicts a narrative scene with walled cities, ships, fishermen, and a river edged by palm-trees. According to preliminary press reports Professor Marinatos suggests that the fresco may represent a siege scene in *Libya* (see Modiano in the *Times* for March 23rd 1973; and cf. the brief description by Marinatos, *AAA* 5 (1972) pp. 448-50). It is obviously too soon to come to any historical conclusions on these new finds, but it may be noted that there is also a limited amount of evidence for contact with the eastern Mediterranean from older finds on Thera, namely fragments of a Cypriot white slip bowl (see Popham, *BSA* 58 (1963) p.93; fragments of the same ware have also been found on Rhodes, Melos and Crete), and three Palestinian juglets, now in the Thera museum, which may have been found in old excavations on Thera by Nomikos (see under Åström in the Bibliography). It is conceivable that both the foreign artefacts and the taste for exotic animals were brought to Thera by Cretans, but the possibility of more direct oriental activity there certainly cannot be ruled out.

197. In view of our limited knowledge of Bronze Age Thrace, Thasos and Samothrace (cf. n. 195), one cannot make too much of the negative evidence. The traditions associating Kadmos with gold-working and other mining in this area and elsewhere (see above p.32) do merit consideration as having a possible basis in historical fact, but the difficulties in dating the working of ancient mines and the paucity of evidence from the relevant periods make it impossible to come to any firm conclusions. The Thasian mines are discussed further below with reference to the possibility of their exploitation by Iron Age Phoenicians.

This suggests that the possibility should seriously be considered whether some or all of the stories of Phoenicians in the Aegean, if historical at all, might relate not to the Mycenaean Age but, as may be the case with Kadmos' association with letters, to the post-Mycenaean period, or more precisely to the Geometric and Orientalising periods. One point in favour of referring the possible Phoenician settlements in the Aegean to the Iron Age is their geographical position. Unlike Thebes, whose situation is very different from those favoured by the Phoenicians of the early first millennium B.C., the Aegean settlements associated with Kadmos are on islands, or in the instance of Chalcidice in Thrace, peninsulas. Moreover Rhodes in the southern group lies on one of the main routes from Phoenicia to the Western Mediterranean (cf. Cary, *GBGH* pp.100f.; Coldstream, *GGP* pp.380-3), and it has been suggested by some scholars that it was through this island that the Phoenician alphabet was disseminated to Greece (cf. Jeffery, *LSAG* pp. 9, 346f.; Carpenter in *AJA* 42 (1938) p.125 favours a Rhodian as the "inventor" of the script, and mentions Crete and Thera as lying on "the familiar route for the diffusion of oriental motives at the end of the geometric period"). On the other hand although the northerly group of places associated with Kadmos lies well off any route from Phoenicia to her colonies in the Western Mediterranean, Phoenicians could have been attracted here by the wealth of metals, including gold. Herodotos says that he visited important mines on Thasos which he believed were first exploited by Phoenicians (VI. 47), and though doubted in the past (see How and Wells on Hdt. loc. cit. and Lorimer, *HM* (1950) p.76) his statement has now been confirmed at least with regard to the location of the mines, even if there is no evidence as to who first worked them (see Pouilloux, *ET* III (1954) p.18; Salviat and Servais in *BCH* 88 (1964) p.283).

In the present century there has perhaps been a tendency to underestimate the extent of Iron Age Phoenician activity in the Aegean, largely as a result of a reaction against the older view which saw Phoenicians everywhere (cf. Dunbabin, *GEN* (1957) pp.35f., and Albright, *RCHC* (ed. 2, 1961) pp.343-9). Syrian and Phoenician artefacts (most notably ivories and bronzes) are known from both the Aegean islands and mainland Greece from the ninth and eighth centuries B.C. onwards, and may equally well have been brought by

Phoenician as by Greek sailors.[198] It is probable that this trade was more extensive than is indicated by the material remains, since many of the goods exported by the Phoenicians seem to have been perishable wares such as textiles, wood and furniture.[199] Furthermore the types of settlement which are generally believed to have been founded by the first Phoenician traders of the Iron Age were intermittently occupied or temporary trading stations which are not likely to have left many traces archaeologically, as is clearly witnessed by the early levels of the colony at Sabratha in North Africa, where, to quote D.E.L. Haynes' description of the oldest remains, "beaten floors of temporary huts alternate with layers of wind-blown sand".[200]

What material evidence can be adduced for Iron Age Phoenicians at the places associated with Kadmos? Thera offers nothing beyond the fragments of a solitary Phoenician glass vessel (see *Thera* II ed. Dragendorff (1903) p.235, together with Pfuhl in *Ath. Mitt.* 28 (1903) p.238). But at Rhodes many small Phoenician artefacts have been found, there was a local school of ivory-carving under strong Eastern influence, and recently Phoenician pottery has been identified which

198. See Dunbabin, *GEN* esp. p.40. The extent of Phoenician seafaring in the Aegean is discussed most judiciously by Coldstream in *GGP* Ch. 14, esp. pp.348f., 357f., 361, 389f., who concludes that Phoenician traders frequently visited the S. Aegean (Crete and the Dodecanese) in the 8th cent., and that we should not underestimate their part in intensifying the orientalising tendencies in Greek art. For the possibility of Phoenician craftsmen, especially ivory- and metal-workers, resident in Athens, Crete and other parts of Greece around this time see Higgins, *GRJ* p.95; Boardman, *BSA* 62 (1967) esp. pp.57-67; Homann-Wedeking, *Archaic Greece* p.60; and Coldstream, locc. citt. Phoenician art of this period and its influence on Greek art is usefully discussed by Akurgal, *BGA* Chs. V and VI.

199. For these see Harden, *Phoen.* Ch. XI, esp. pp.141-6. Many of the known Semitic loan-words in Greek are for textiles and other perishable objects such as plants and spices (see Masson, *RESG* esp. Ch. II A "Tissues et vêtements" and D "Noms de plantes"). It is salutary here to compare Warmington's comments on the celebrated commerce of Carthage and the scanty traces which this has left in the archaeological record (*Carthage* pp.150f.).

200. See Haynes, *AT* p. 107. At Lepcis Magna, however, the earliest remains appear to be somewhat more substantial; cf. Carter in *AJA* 69 (1965) pp.123-32, esp. p.130.

may well indicate settlement.[201] In the North Aegean Thasos has produced the most interesting evidence: several Semitic proper names are attested on the island, and some seventh century ivories have been found which are undoubtedly of oriental origin.[202] M. Launey, one of the excavators of Thasos, postulated a Bronze Age "Phoenician" settlement there, calculating a date for this of around 1500 B.C. from the genealogical evidence of Herodotos,[203] but his suggestion has been strongly criticised (see n. 74 to Ch. IV), and Vian has gone so far as to say that "cette tradition est dénuée de valeur historique: aucun indice archéologique ne permet de supposer une installation phénicienne dans l'île dès le milieu du second millénaire" (*Or. Theb.*p.66). But it is to be noted that behind the statements of both Launey and Vian there lies an assumption which they have made in common with other scholars that this part of the legend must refer to the Bronze Age; if however the testimony of the genealogies is rejected, then it is quite possible that the traditions of Kadmos and his Phoenicians at Thasos refer not to the Mycenaean period but to the centuries immediately

201. For oriental connexions at Rhodes see Barnett, *JHS* 68 (1948) p.17; Jeffery, *LSAG* p.9; James, in *Perachora* II (1962) pp. 262f. (favouring a Phoenician origin for the numerous Egyptianising objects of faience from there); and Coldstream, *GGP* p. 381 with n. 3 there. The Phoenician pottery is discussed in detail by Coldstream in "The Phoenicians of Ialysos", *BICS* 16 (1969) pp.1-8; cf. also Chapman, *Berytus* 21 (1972) p.178. I am grateful to Mr. T.E.V. Pearce for referring me to this last article.

202. The evidence from both Thrace and Samothrace is so far negative. At Thasos the names of two places Αἴνυρα and Κοίνυρα (which are said by Herodotos to be in the vicinity of the Phoenician mines), are generally taken to be Semitic; see Salviat in *BCH* 86 (1962) p.108 with n. 7 and Dossin's comments cited by Salviat and Servais in *BCH* 88 (1964) p.284. Two Semitic personal names are attested inscriptionally from the island (see Seyrig in *BCH* 51 (1927) p.230 n. 2 and Pouilloux, *ET* III p.20). It is interesting to note that the personal name Kadmos occurs some 12 times on Thasian inscriptions dating from the 5th cent. B.C. onwards. For the oriental ivories see Salviat, *BCH* 86 (1962) pp. 95-116; cf. Akurgal, *BGA* pp. 177, 181-3.

203. See *ET* I esp. pp.195 and 221. Launey believes that "Phoenicians" of the Bronze Age brought to Thasos the cult of Thasian Herakles (cf. above n. 74), and he cites analogies from Canaan for rock-cut "cupules" associated with a rock altar in the Herakleion (op. cit. pp.167ff.). But, as Launey himself notes, this type of installation (presumably for religious purposes) is widespread in the Mediterranean, being found in Crete and North Africa as well as in Palestine, Egypt and other parts of the Near East.

preceding their first attestation.[204]

We must admit, then, that with the exception of Rhodes the material evidence which can be adduced for Phoenicians in these islands at any period is very limited, and one certainly cannot conclude that settlements must have existed solely on the basis of a few Semitic names and oriental artefacts. Nevertheless, there may well have been more Phoenician contact than the physical evidence suggests, and if the literary traditions have any basis in historical fact, they are perhaps more reasonably to be related to the period of Iron Age Phoenician seafaring (about the ninth and eighth centuries B.C.) than to the Mycenaean Age.

There can therefore be no easy answer to the question posed at the beginning of this Chapter. We have seen how the whole matter of chronology is much more complicated than it might seem at first sight. The ancient literary sources, the genealogies and dates given by the chronographers, are too confused to provide any accurate dating, and those scholars who use them for establishing chronology do so either by ignoring the ancient variants or by a choice of version which can only be termed arbitrary. It is generally assumed that the traditions must refer to the period before the Trojan War, since this is not only implied by their content but also explicitly stated by those authorities who attempt to bring these events into relationship with one another; but there is an exceedingly long interval between the sixteenth or even the thirteenth century B.C. and the earliest attestation of the traditions in classical Greek authors. We know that the legend received many accretions during and after the classical period; it is perfectly feasible to suppose that it had received others during the centuries before it is

---

204. It is worth noting the conclusion of Salviat and Servais in their recent study of an inscription from Thasos: "On a toutes raisons d'admettre qu'au début du 1ᵉʳ millénaire et au VIIIᵉ siècle au plus tard, c'est-à-dire avant la colonisation parienne, les Phéniciens furent les initiateurs de la recherche de l'or et de l'argent à Thasos et dans la région de Pangée. ... La légende phénicienne de Thasos est une affabulation de l' époque archaïque avancée, on peut en demeurer d'accord avec Fr. Vian, mais elle transpose, selon nous, en généalogies mythiques, un véritable héritage ..." (*BCH* 88 (1964) p. 284 n. 1).

first attested, and these could include elements reflecting the memory of historical events belonging to the post-Mycenaean period. This is not to suggest that the whole legend originated in post-Mycenaean times, since it would be no contradiction to suppose that some elements in it might refer to the Mycenaean Age, while others reflect events of a much later date.

It is obvious that no adequate chronological scheme can be worked out on the basis of the legendary material alone. But when we turn for help to the outside sources, where archaeology can often supply fairly precise information about date, we are at once confronted by the difficulty of determining to which particular event or circumstance known from archaeology any given part of the legend refers. Two main hypotheses for the interpretation of the Kadmos legend have been considered in this book, namely the Cretan and the oriental. If the Cretan theory were to be adopted, then any date between LH I and LH IIIA would be quite possible as the historical period for Kadmos' "foundation" at Thebes, while the traditions of his settlements on the southerly group of islands could most plausibly be referred to some time in the LM/LH I period, and the introduction of writing could be related to the use of Linear B at Thebes in LH III, or conceivably to its introduction or invention there earlier than this. If on the other hand the natural interpretation of the legend is accepted and the traditions are related to Phoenician or oriental settlement, then in the light of the present archaeological evidence the LH III period would seem more plausible than LH I for oriental people at Thebes, while the tradition of letters and possibly those also of settlements in the Aegean would most reasonably be related to post-Mycenaean times.

CHAPTER IX

CONCLUSIONS: THE VALUE OF GREEK LEGEND FOR THE STUDY OF THE MYCENAEAN AGE

We must now draw together the main conclusions which emerge from the preceding chapters, considering first what the legend of Kadmos itself may have to tell us about the Mycenaean Age, and then turning to the wider implications of this study. Obviously the story as it stands cannot be taken as historical in all its details; it is highly complex, and includes elements which seem likely to belong to the category of religious myth, such as the rape of Europê by Zeus, or to that of folktale, like the slaying of the dragon at Thebes. It is inappropriate to look for a memory of historical events in elements such as these.[205] Furthermore, whatever historical nucleus the legend may have had originally, it has clearly been much elaborated by additions over the years: as we saw in Chapter II, the story is not the same in sources of the fifth century B.C. as it is when related or alluded to by Hellenistic or Byzantine writers, and one must indeed presuppose many earlier centuries of transmission and change between the oldest period to which any part of it may reasonably be taken to refer and its first attestation in classical literature. Some of the factors at work in the elaboration of the story have been traced (above pp.35-42), but it must be confessed that not all can be identified with precision.

Are there any elements in the legend which have the clear mark of being Mycenaean in origin? One very likely Mycenaean element is the

---

205. Thus Tucker rationalises Kadmos' casting of stones among the Spartoi as "stirring up feud among the autochthonous tribes and taking advantage of the situation" (*AesS* (1908) p. xiii n. 2). The same interpretation is found earlier in Lenormant, *LPC* II (1874) pp. 399f., and has recently been repeated by Graves in *GM* I (1955) p.197 n. 5. But this element in the story surely belongs to the category of folktale (cf. above p.42 with n. 45).

mythical rape of Europê;[206] another is the existence at Thebes of a people named "Kadmeioi" as attested in the Homeric epic.[207] But when this much has been said, there is little more about which one can speak with confidence. For example, we cannot be sure that the figure of Kadmos arises from the memory of a real Mycenaean prince, since he might well be a mere eponymous hero, invented as a personification of the Kadmeioi (cf. above p.146 with n.157). It is true that, for the purpose of interpreting the legend in terms of historical events, the hero's personal reality is not important, since the story as whole may be understood as typifying the belief that a "founder" of Thebes came from "Phoenicia". Yet even this part of the story which *prima facie* seems to stem from historical fact (cf. the end of Ch. II) cannot be related with certainty to events of the Mycenaean Age. Some scholars have maintained that the "Phoinikertum" of Kadmos was invented as late as about the sixth century B.C.; the arguments for their belief have been shown to be inadequate (in Ch. IV above), but this enables us to conclude only that the oriental elements in the legend *may* have some historical basis in the Mycenaean Age, not that they *must* do so. All that can be said with assurance is that the information derived from archaeology, language and other sources is consonant with the view that the legend reflects real events. One of the things I have tried to

206. An origin in the Mycenaean Age for the motif of Europê's rape by Zeus in bull form is suggested both by the well-known religious associations of the bull in Minoan Crete (on which see, for example, Guthrie in *CAH* ed. 2, fasc. 2 pp.21f.), and by the apparent representations on glass-paste plaques from Dendra of a woman or goddess riding a bull: for the belief that these depict the story of Europê itself see Persson, *RTD* pp.65, 121; Nilsson, *MOGM* pp.33f.; and Webster, *MycH* p.49; but one should compare also Technau's discussion, "Die Göttin auf dem Stier" (in *JDAI* 52 (1937) pp. 76-103) and Bühler, *Europa* p.25.

207. In both the Homeric epic and Hesiodic poetry the inhabitants of Thebes are always called Καδμεῖοι or Καδμείωνες, and the appellation Θηβαῖος occurs in the *Iliad* only with reference to Hypoplacian Thebes and in the *Odyssey* as an epithet of Teiresias. It is difficult to explain this remarkable fact except by presupposing that the term "Cadmeian" is the genuine ancient name of an early people at Thebes before the Trojan War and the Boeotian occupation of the town (cf. Thucydides' reference to "τὴν νῦν μὲν Βοιωτίαν, πρότερον δὲ Καδμηίδα γῆν καλουμένην" (I. 12. 3) and Gomme's commentary ad loc. (*HCT* I p.118); see also Nilsson, *MOGM* pp.121f., 126, and Schober, *RE(T)* col. 1454 with reference to ·further literature).

show in this book is that, granted the possibility of a historical basis, more than one hypothesis will fit the available evidence.[208]

Two main interpretations have been investigated, and we must now consider which of these hypotheses, Cretan or oriental, is the more plausible. It is clear that the Cretan theory cannot be sustained for the reasons originally alleged (cf. Ch. V, esp. p.95 with n.89 and pp.98-100), but there are some sound arguments in its favour. (1) The term Φοίνικες is obscure in origin, but if its connexion with purple-fishing and dye-making, now favoured by many scholars, is

---

208. We may compare here the legend of Danaos, who traditionally came to Greece from Egypt, and who was associated with Kadmos or related to him genealogically by many classical writers. The chief problem in attempting to identify any historical basis in this story is in determining its essential nucleus and in assigning a precise date or period to any postulated events. For Nilsson "the kernel of this myth was always the murder on the bridal night of the fifty sons of Aegyptus by the fifty daughters of Danaüs", which he attempts to relate to the period of the Sea Peoples' invasions, when a people named *Danuna* appear in the Egyptian records (*MOGM* pp. 64-7; similarly Capovilla has more recently associated the story with the period 1220-1191 B.C.: see *Aegyptus* 39 (1959) esp. pp.293f.). For other scholars the essential element is the coming of a foreigner to Argos from Egypt, and they suggest that the story refers to the beginning of the Mycenaean Age ca. 1570 B.C., when the Hyksos were expelled from Egypt, and when oriental influence is attested in the Shaft Graves at Mycenae which they believe may reflect the presence of new leaders from abroad (see Huxley, *CL* pp.36f.; Stubbings, *CAH* ed. 2, fasc. 18 pp.9-14).

It lies outside our present scope to assess in detail the merits of these interpretations, but it may be noted that the historical problems posed by the Danaos legend are closely analogous to those associated with Kadmos in that (1) Danaos himself may not be a real person, but the eponymous hero of the Danaoi appearing in Homer (cf. n. 67); (2) more than one hypothesis could fit the facts, and there is no firm proof, either in the Egyptian records or in the archaeological sources, for any one particular reconstruction (on problems concerning the identification of the *Danuna* see Page, *HHI* pp.22f. n. 1 (b), and on the view that there is no need to postulate new people at the beginning of the Mycenaean Age cf. n. 181); (3) whereas older scholars once supposed that the whole oriental connexion of Danaos was a late invention (see n. 67), one can now see that the idea of some historical fact behind it is at least consonant with other sources for the Bronze Age (cf. Nilsson, loc. cit.). Another curious point of similarity between the two legends is the way in which both have been taken as relating to Cretan settlement in mainland Greece (see above pp.88f.,91), although as far as the Danaos legend is concerned there is no obscurity in the origin of the term Αἴγυπτος analogous to that of Φοινίκη.

accepted (see Ch. V esp. n.90), it may easily have once included Cretan among its meanings. (2) There is archaeological evidence for extensive Minoan influence on mainland Greece from LM I onwards, and though a general Minoan colonisation cannot now be accepted, some Minoan settlement at certain sites is quite possible (cf. p.102 and n. 100). At Thebes itself Minoan connexions are especially obvious in the palace frescoes, and a Cretan origin for some of the pottery seems extremely probable (cf. pp.108f.). The archaeological record is therefore at least consistent with the idea of a Cretan settlement at Thebes, and some particularly strong Cretan influence there might be argued independently of the legendary sources. (3) If the Cretan theory were to be adopted for the foundation element at Thebes, other parts of the Kadmos legend could be interpreted on similar lines: thus the tradition of writing could be related to Linear B, and the settlements on islands in the southern Aegean to Minoan activity on Rhodes and Thera (see above esp. pp.175f. and 179).

These arguments in favour of the Cretan theory make it attractive, and if an oriental interpretation were impossible or very difficult, then they might well be convincing. But on balance it seems that there is rather more to be said in favour of an oriental Kadmos. (1) Though Thebes might seem a highly improbable place for trading Phoenicians, in fact its geographical situation is not entirely unsuitable for a Bronze Age "Phoenician" settlement, and oriental objects have now been found at the site which could indicate the presence of oriental people there, though this is not the only possible explanation (see Ch. VI esp. pp.131-4). (2) There is extensive archaeological evidence for contact between Greece and the Near East in the Mycenaean period, quite apart from the contribution of language and literary motifs (see Chs. VI and VII, esp. pp.118-21). (3) From Ras Shamra in North Syria, a port in close contact with the Mycenaean world, there is documentary evidence for "Canaanite" seafaring (see pp.126-8), and this fact, taken with the last two mentioned, shows that, while clear proof of any oriental settlement at Thebes is lacking, there is historically nothing implausible in the hypothesis. (4) The Cretan interpretation of the legend involves postulating on etymological grounds an additional hypothesis of a change of meaning in the term Φοίνικες, of which there is no trace either in Homer or in later Greek literature. The oriental view on the other hand involves no change of meaning of the term, a derivation from the sense "red" or "purple" is still tenable, and Φοίνιχες is understood in its natural and widely attested sense of *Phoenicians*. (5) The oriental interpretation has the added advantage that the tradition of Kadmos' introduction of Φοινιχήια can be taken as referring to what it most reasonably suggests, namely the introduction of the Phoenician alphabet to Greece (see above pp.174-9 esp. p.179).

To sum up: there is no means of demonstrating that any element in the legend has as its basis the memory of historical events of the Mycenaean Age, but the arguments in favour of regarding Kadmos' oriental origin as a pure invention are inconclusive, and our other sources of information suggest not that the story bears no relation to historical fact, but rather that it is consistent with several possible reconstructions of events, not all of which need be mutually exclusive.[209] Of the main interpretations, the oriental appears to be the most plausible, though the Cretan hypothesis can still be maintained without doing violence to the evidence. As to the precise date of any settlement at Thebes which the story of Kadmos might reflect, only tentative suggestions can be offered (see Ch. VIII, esp. pp.168-74), and it must be emphasised that different parts of the legend may relate to events of more than one period, including post-Mycenaean times. Cogent proof for any particular reconstruction is lacking, and all too often scholars have claimed more for the evidence than it warrants. It must also be borne in mind that new discoveries, especially through archaeological excavation, may at any time cause us to reassess the balance of probability, as has been seen more than once in recent years.

209. For instance, it is not difficult to see how various theoretical interpretations could be devised which combined ideas of Kadmos both as an oriental and as a Cretan, particularly if the meaning of the term *Phoinix* was once ambiguous (cf. Ch. V). Such interpretations might gain in plausibility if the proposed decipherment of Linear A as Semitic (see n. 126) should prove well-founded, or if it should otherwise be established that there were Semites among the population of Minoan Crete. The curious persistence of the Phoenician element in the mythological and other links between Crete and Boeotia (see n. 118) may be worth mentioning here.

What light then does this study of the Kadmos legend cast on the wider problem of the relationship between the Greek legends in general and the Mycenaean Age? It was seen in Chapter I how scholarly attitudes in this matter have changed very greatly over the years, and how even today radically different views are held. In considering the principal ideas which are still being put forward we begin with the view that the Greek legends are an extremely reliable source for the study of prehistory and that it is possible to make detailed reconstructions of events from them. Such a belief is upheld by J. Zafiropulo, whose recent book published in the Budé "Collection d'études anciennes" and entitled *Histoire de la Grèce à l'âge de bronze* (1964) is offered in all seriousness as "un essai sur la valeur historique des mythes de l'Hélladique récent III" and in response to Wace's suggestion that the evidence of Greek legend should be re-examined (op. cit. p.12; cf. above p.14).

Zafiropulo's basic method is to rationalise the supernatural and divine elements in the stories and to regard all the rest as valid material for the reconstruction of events. Though he occasionally makes use of the other available sources, he does not regard corroboration from these as necessary for establishing facts. Greece, according to his reconstruction, was first invaded at the beginning of the LH period by Egyptianised Phoenicians, under the leadership of Danaos; this was followed around 1360 B.C. by an invasion under the Phoenician Kadmos, who arrived with a Tyrian army, conquered Delphi, and made himself master of Thebes. Zafiropulo sees the fortification of the great citadels of the Argolid as the result of an economic and religious conflict between the prosperous, mead-drinking "sectateurs du taureau", originally organised by Danaos, and the poor, wine-drinking "sectateurs du bouc", originally organised by Kadmos, and the destruction of Thebes in LH III as the culmination of this conflict (*HGAB* Chs. I to IV).

The details of this reconstruction of events may be questioned on numerous points, but it is the basic premises of Zafiropulo which we wish to consider here. First, it is assumed throughout that the heroes are *real people*: Kadmos, for instance, is described as "un grand politique et surtout un organisateur de tout premier ordre qui comprit parfaitement le problème de son époque ..." (*HGAB* p.96), and as having "un génie extraordinaire" (*HGAB* p.28); similarly Danaos becomes "un personnage fort remarquable" (*HGAB* p.108), and Amphitryon "un propriétaire de petit bétail", probably descended from "une famille passablement ruinée" (*HGAB* p.115). Now there is reason to believe that the names of certain heroes, particularly some of those in the Homeric epic, may belong to real people. D.L. Page has argued that heroes associated with traditional formulaic epithets are likely to have been historical, and that some of the facts preserved in Homer about them may well be true (*HHI* Ch. VI). Such arguments are especially convincing where the heroes are associated with objects which appear to be Mycenaean, e.g. Aias with his tower-like shield. But it must be confessed that the number of heroes even in epic who can be regarded as certainly real people is very small. Even within Homer some minor characters have the appearance of being invented (cf. Forsdyke, *GBH* p.110), while in later sources one must expect the proportion of invented heroes to be even larger. We cannot therefore agree with Zafiropulo's basic assumption that all the heroes may be regarded as real people: some are fictitious, some invented as personifications of tribes, peoples, places or abstract ideas, and some may be sacral or divine personages.

Secondly, Zafiropulo assumes that a very detailed reconstruction of events is possible, and that facts such as the date of a hero's birth, succession to the throne, marriage and death are recoverable. This seems to stem from a fundamental misunderstanding of the nature of the traditions: the elements of folktale, religious myth, later elaboration, rationalisation and systematisation of the stories are completely ignored. A few examples must suffice: Zafiropulo suggests that Amphitryon's marriage with the beautiful Alkmene may have turned his head (*HGAB* pp. 115f.); but great beauty is a typical quality of all fairytale princesses. He follows a version of the rape of Europê in which the myth is interpreted as a raid on Tyre by an Achaean king of Crete (*HGAB* pp. 24f., 91f.); but the union of Europê with a god in the form of a bull is one of the certain elements of religious myth in the whole story, and the creation of a king called Tauros, whom Zafiropulo naively includes in his reconstruction (*HGAB* pp.27, 92), is but an ancient attempt to explain away a tradition which had become no longer credible.

Thirdly, Zafiropulo's whole chronological scheme, which seems at first sight so neat, is a fantasy. He arrives at an apparent consistency by which the events of the royal houses of Thebes, Crete and Mycenae fit into the same period beginning at 1360 B.C. (see *HGAB*, chart facing p.31); but this is achieved only by ignoring the ancient versions which contradict this reconstruction, and by adopting arbitrary lengths for the reigns of the different kings. Thus, the fundamental difficulty that Kadmos in a well-known tradition lived *six* generations before the Trojan War and Europê only *three* (see Ch. VIII with Table 7) is obviated by laying the genealogies on a Procrustean bed, and assigning reigns of only 15 or 20 years to the rulers of Thebes and much longer reigns, of 30 or 40 years, to the Cretan monarchs. But it is quite ludicrous to attempt to harmonise the traditions in this way.[210] Zafiropulo is throughout making uncritical use of the material, and many of his interpretations are but perpetuating the methods of Konon and Palaiphatos.[211]

210. Two further examples well illustrate the arbitrary nature of Zafiropulo's chronological scheme. (a) *Herakles:* Zafiropulo places the birth of this hero only 40 years after Kadmos' marriage at Thebes (*HGAB* chart facing p.31); this is clearly inconsistent with Herodotos' explicit reference (II. 44) to the birth of Herakles five generations after the search for Europê (even allowing for Herodotos' inclusive method of reckoning here, on which see the commentary of How and Wells, Vol. I p.439). (b) *Amphion and Zethos:* Zafiropulo refers to these heroes as founding Thebes around 1400 B.C., i.e. about 40 years before his date for Kadmos (*HGAB* p.94); but he glosses over the fact that there were two distinct stories, one in which Thebes was founded by the twins Amphion and Zethos, and one in which it was founded Kadmos, and that when the twins were put into a relationship with Kadmos, they were placed at the time of his great-grandson Laios (see Paus. IX. 5.6 and 9; Apollod. III. 5.5).

211. Zafiropulo's book has here been singled out for attention, since it is both recent and far-reaching, but he is not alone in his uncritical approach. One frequently sees isolated details in legend seized upon as historical without regard to their literary genre or the source of their attestation: thus the Cyclops episode of the *Odyssey*, one of the best examples of a folktale theme in Greek literature (see Page, *HO* Ch. I), has been rationalised as "a real encounter with a large and savage native of Sicily" (Bradford, *Ulysses Found* (1963) p.61); for another example cf. n. 205. Particularly regrettable is the uncritical use of material in Graves' Penguin book *The Greek Myths* (1955), which reaches a wide public and abounds in fantastic, unsupported conjectures of a euhemeristic nature. His interpretations of the Kadmos legend have already been

It is obvious that an approach of this kind must be rejected and that one cannot expect to reconstruct such a detailed history of events from the Greek legends. But a crucial question remains: is it still possible to use the legendary material at least to a limited extent in the study of the Mycenaean Age, or should one reject its testimony altogether? Both these views have won support among modern scholars. For example, in the 1930's Martin Nilsson argued that the outlines of the great mythological cycles originated in the Mycenaean period, and he attempted to determine the historical content of many of the major legends (on Nilsson's work see above Ch. I). More recently the belief that it is legitimate to use the legends has been maintained by F.H. Stubbings in his study of the Mycenaean period in the revised edition of the *Cambridge Ancient History*.[212] He writes: "The Greeks of later times inherited an immense body of legends and traditions, often confused or contaminated by myth and folk tale, but *valid in their main sequences* (at least where events are causally linked); valid too in their localizations, since each city had best reason to remember its own past, and so *preserving in rough outline the history of the civilization which we call Mycenaean*" (*CAH* ed. 2, fasc. 18 (1963) p.4; our italics).

In contrast to this view a number of scholars today advocate an extremely sceptical attitude to the Greek legendary traditions, maintaining that they should be discounted as a source for the study of the Mycenaean Age. Thus C.G. Starr repeatedly stresses the unreliability of myth, legend and epic as a source for history, arguing that "the historian has no valid tool by which to separate folk memory from later elaboration" and that it is "hopeless practically and unsound logically" to try to draw historical events out of the legends

---

mentioned in this connexion in Chs. II and III above, and they are typical of his whole approach. Two further examples may be taken at random: Apollo's pursuit of Daphne is understood as referring to a Hellenic occupation of Tempe (*GM* I p.81); Herakles' exploit with the Stymphalian birds is interpreted as the suppression of a college of Arcadian priestesses by an Achaean tribe (*GM* II pp.120f.).

212. *CAH* ed. 2, fasc. 4 (1962) esp. pp.69f., 74 (= ed. 3 Vol. I.1 pp.240f., 245); fasc. 18 (1963) pp.4f. and passim; fasc. 26 (1964) esp. pp.4-9; and fasc. 39 (1965) esp. pp.7-13, 15-19.

(see *OGC* (1962) esp. pp. 46f., 67f., 109f., 156-9). Similarly M.I. Finley has on a number of occasions argued against the historical reliability of the Homeric epic, and believes that "no one in his right mind" would go to it for information about the Trojan War (see esp. *JHS* 84 (1964) p.9). More generally he writes: "The plain fact is that the classical Greeks knew little about their history before 650 B.C. (or even 550 B.C.), and that what they thought they knew was a jumble of fact and fiction, some miscellaneous facts and much fiction about the essentials and about most of the details" ("Myth, memory, and history" in *History and Theory* 4 (1965) p.288).

This whole question of the evidential value of legends needs to be assessed with the utmost care. The view that only the outlines of the legendary stories can be regarded as based on fact has many advantages over the naively literalistic method of interpretation considered earlier in this Chapter. It recognises the complexity of the traditional material, and the fact that this contains non-historical elements. But it must be admitted that this approach also encounters considerable difficulties. One of these is the impossibility of obtaining from the legends a satisfactory chronological framework, which means that any outline of events obtained from them must remain very rough indeed (on the difficulties of arriving at even an approximate chronology from the genealogical evidence see Ch. VIII with nn. 177 and 180). A more important objection is that, however reliable the legends are thought to be in their outlines or main sequences, *it is exceedingly difficult to determine what these main sequences are,* and almost impossible to avoid being subjective in one's choice of the essential elements of a story. The Kadmos legend has well illustrated this point: is the hero's Phoenician origin essential, in which case the legend might be explained by relations between Greece and Canaan? Is his Egyptian connexion essential, and the story explicable by relations with the Hyksos? Is merely his foreignness essential, in which case the legend might support the Cretan theories? Is his descent from the Argive Io a basic element, in which case the legend might reflect the return of Phoenicianised Mycenaeans from the East? Clearly each legend needs to be examined on its own merits for any possible historical content. But one must guard against the supposition that the legend of Kadmos raises special difficulties; when other legends are investigated in detail, similar problems repeatedly arise.[213]

Does this mean that the testimony of legend is totally valueless for the study of the Mycenaean Age? Here it seems that we must agree with the sceptics to this extent: if our aim is to establish accurate historical facts, then the only safe and certain course is to ignore the legendary evidence. The material is lacking to establish proof of events sufficient to satisfy the stringent tests of a historian, and, as Forsdyke has aptly remarked, "the historical content of any particular legend must finally be established by historical knowledge, which is not yet available for the Greek Heroic Age" (*GBH* p.162). Nevertheless, there are reasons which make it seem proper not to reject the evidence of legend entirely. If the origins of Greek mythology extend back to the Mycenaean period (cf. above Ch. I), then it is reasonable to assume that it has preserved at least some memory of the events of that age, and even the more sceptical scholars acknowledge that it may contain kernels of historical fact. It is easy to exaggerate the ancient Greeks' ignorance of their own past: for instance, A. Jardé writes that "of the early history of the lands which became Greece the Greeks themselves knew nothing", and that "the sole interest of legend is to tell us how

---

213. See esp. n. 208 on the legend of Danaos. Two further examples may be considered: (a) *Traditions of the Perseids.* It is not clear whether the essential sequence of the Perseus story concerns the *foundation* of Mycenae, which might be referred to LH I (so tentatively Stubbings, *CAH* ed. 2, fasc. 18 p.27) or its *fortification,* which might be placed in LH III (so Mylonas, *AMyc* p.15, suggesting a 14th cent. date). It is also obscure whether Elektryon belongs to Midea, Tiryns or Mycenae; there are difficulties over the traditional localisation of Herakles (Thebes or Tiryns), and it is uncertain whether the connexion between Alkmene and Amphitryon and the Argolid is organic or invented to explain Herakles' relation to Eurystheus (on these problems cf. Nilsson's brief discussion, *MOGM* pp.206f. with his n.37).

(b) *The Attic traditions.* Here it is especially difficult to distinguish the main outlines from later systematisation and elaboration. It is, for instance, questionable whether the versions of Egyptian origins for the heroes Erechtheus and Kekrops (see Diod. I. 28-9) are genuine ancient traditions or mere late inventions. There are curious duplications of Kekrops, Pandion and Erechtheus/Erichthonios in Apollodoros and the chronographers (cf. Myres, *WWG* p.326). The position of Theseus and the Theseids also presents special problems: see my general discussion in *QT* esp. p.50, and, in full detail, Herter, *RhM* 85 (1936) pp.177-91 and 193-239; on the relation of Menestheus to the Theseids see also Page, *HHI* p.146 with his nn.78 and 79.

the Greeks of classical times imagined their beginnings; we must not ask it for any real facts" (*FGP* pp.55, 59). But how can we be sure that the Greeks knew nothing? It is important to remember that while it is exceedingly difficult to demonstrate that any given legend rests on a basis of fact, it is also exceedingly difficult to prove that it is entirely fictional. We saw this in our study of the Kadmos legend, and the same point is borne out by other examples. Starr for instance believes that the tradition of Minos' thalassocracy is "a myth, and an artificial one to boot", and Finley argues that the narrative of the Trojan War must "be removed *in toto* from the realm of history and returned to the realm of myth and poetry"; but when the arguments for these views are examined,[214] they are found to be no more probable than the idea that

214. (a) *Minos' thalassocracy.* For Starr's view see *Historia* 3 (1954-5) pp.282-91, esp. p.283; for criticisms of this, and for arguments in favour of accepting a historical basis see Cassola, *PP* 12 (1957) pp.343-52, and R.J. Buck, *Historia* 11 (1962) pp.129-37. We may note: (1) Starr successfully attacks the picture of an imperialistic thalassocracy coloured by the concept of a British naval empire, and the old hypothesis of a Cretan conquest of the mainland in LM I; but his proposal that the whole idea of a Minoan sea power is an Athenian invention designed to glorify Theseus is a singularly weak explanation of the tradition and does not win conviction. (2) There is nothing historically improbable in the idea of widespread Minoan trade and seafaring; indeed this is surely what the archaelogical record itself suggests with its indications of settlement or at least substantial trading contact in MM III/LM I on Rhodes, Melos, Thera, Kythera and Keos. Starr considerably underestimates the extent of the archaeological evidence for Minoan trade abroad. See further Scholes, *BSA* 51 (1956) pp.9-40, esp. pp.37-9; Huxley, *CL* esp. pp.2f.; Warren, *PPS* 33 (1967) pp.37-56, esp. p.53; id., *PCA* 67 (1970) p.34.

(b) *The Trojan War.* For Finley's view see *JHS* 84 (1964) pp.1-9, esp. p.9. Counter-arguments and criticisms are put forward by Caskey, Kirk and Page (ib. pp.9-20), and only the chief points need here be summarised: (1) Finley relies heavily on analogies from other sources, but the material he cites does not bear out his conclusion, first because the conditions of transmission are not truly comparable, and second, because our knowledge of the events with which these other traditions (e.g. the *Nibelungenlied*) are ultimately concerned is so incomplete that one is in danger of attempting to elucidate the *obscurum per obscurius* (cf. Kirk, op. cit. pp.12-15). (2) The archaeological record tells of a destruction of Troy in a period consistent with the traditional evidence; it does not provide proof of who or what destroyed the city, but but proof of the type required by Finley cannot be expected from purely archaeological sources (cf. Caskey, op. cit. pp.9-11). (3) Finley's alternative hypothesis of a destruction of Troy VIIA by marauding northerners must remain entirely conjectural; on the other

both traditions are founded on real circumstances or events. Whether it is maintained that the stories are fictional or basically historical, we are equally concerned with hypotheses, not established facts.

This perhaps can lead us to adopt an approach to the problem which takes into account what is reasonable in both the sceptical and the more positive (or optimistic) points of view. We must recognise that in reconstructing the events of the Mycenaean Age, we are dealing not with facts, but with theories and hypotheses; not with proofs but with plausibilities and even mere possibilities. An accurate tool for distinguishing the history from the fiction is not available, but if we are content to recognise the limitations of the legendary evidence, then, as was seen in our study of the Kadmos story, some rough and ready tools are available in the close scrutiny of the various attested versions of a legend and in the comparison with the other potential sources of information.

What we must remember in considering the use of legend is that the problem of the reliability of sources is no new thing for the historian: the same sort of difficulties arise for the student of Anglo-Saxon England with regard to the historical value of the Mediaeval chronicles, or for the ecclesiastical historian in using lives of the saints as source-material for the early history of the church. Greek legend is particularly intractable because there is scarcely any means of reaching a true critical appreciation from internal evidence alone, that is from an assessment of the historical value of the source in which a particular story is found. We may be more inclined to give credence to a statement found in Homer than in Apollodoros or Stephen of Byzantium, but it is clear that on the one hand the oldest epic poetry already includes much fictional material, and on the other that the possibility of isolated facts being preserved even in writings of a relatively late date cannot be completely discounted. In these circumstances it is of paramount importance to consider what contributions may be made by other sources of information, and to

hand there is reason to suppose that Homer's narrative is accurate on a number of significant points (cf. the remark by Page, op. cit. p.20, that Finley here is "substituting the wholly unverifiable for the partly confirmed").

these we now turn.

The three chief sources available, each of which is studied as an intellectual discipline in its own right quite apart from its value to the prehistorian, are archaeology, language and documents. But these, it must be remembered, exist on different levels both from the legendary tradition and from each other, and each must be interpreted within the limits which are imposed by its own intrinsic nature. Thus archaeology is concerned in the first instance only with physical remains, and those remains themselves represent but a fraction of what once physically existed, the rest having perished to a degree which varies according to climatic and other conditions. This very partial nature of the archaeological evidence needs to be strongly emphasised: it does not represent the full picture, and there is much that it can never tell us.[215] Linguistic evidence on the other hand consists for the prehistorian in the survival of a special form of behaviour which is relatively conservative and handed down largely without self-consciousness, thus allowing deductions to be drawn about populations and their movements. But it must not forgotten that these are deductions: the study of language provides direct evidence only for particular modes of speech, and once inferences from these are made, then ambiguities appear and room for variety of opinion.[216] Documents, the last of these

215. For useful discussions of the nature of archaeological evidence and its limitations see Childe, *PPIA* (1956); Piggott, *ApA* (1959) Ch. I, esp. pp.8-12; and Wainwright, *APNH* (1962) pp.30-7. The debt of the present Chapter to Wainwright's lucid consideration of principles will be readily recognised by those familiar with his work.

216. On the particular contribution of language study to Greek prehistory see above Ch. I with n. 5. The linguistic evidence has not always been sufficiently taken into account by critics of the conventional reconstructions of Greek prehistory: for example Renfrew implies that the Greek language might have "developed of its own accord ... from the pre-Greek substratum", and questions "whether all Indo-European languages must really derive, ultimately, from a remote land to the north-east", concluding that "it may be that the Greeks did not come from anywhere" (*Kret. Chron.* 18 (1964) pp.107-141, esp. 138, 141). But the existence of a common source from which all the IE languages are shown by their structure to have evolved is a firmly established conclusion from the evidence of comparative philology. No one suggests that Greece could be the original home of Indo-European, and it follows that the Greek language, in some form, was introduced to Greece by outsiders. McNeal similarly is unsatisfactory in his treatment of the linguistic evidence (see *Antiquity* 46 (1972) esp. pp.22-4, with Sir Gerald Clauson's criticisms, ib. 47 (1973) esp. p.39).

three sources, convey information verbally, but in a non-historical period their evidence has special limitations. Thus in the Mycenaean Age we are not dealing with narrative historical texts, originating in and contemporary with the period itself (which would transform it from prehistory or protohistory into history), but either with very occasional references in historical texts from other areas of culture, i.e. the oriental documents, or with texts from our own area which are concerned only with minor transactions and records, i.e. the Linear B documents. When one also recalls the ambiguities and obscurities of the Bronze Age documents from both Greece and the orient, it is easy to see how they have only a limited significance for reconstructing the events of the Mycenaean period.[217]

It is sometimes assumed by those who urge us to disregard legend and concentrate on these other sources that they are in some way more *objective* than the traditions.[218] But we must emphasise that archaeology, language and documents are objective only within a very restricted compass, in fact only so long as they are concerned with the mere observation and description of data. Once they aspire to

217. The problems of historical interpretation with the Linear B documents are too well known to need illustration here (for a recent attempt to collate the documentary and archaeological data see Stella, *CMDC* (1965), and compare the criticisms made by Chadwick in *JHS* 86 (1966) pp.214f.).

The chief hazard with the oriental texts arises from the difficulty of identifying with certainty any references to the peoples of Greece: see for example Page's discussions of the *Ahhijawa* question (*HHI* Ch. I) and of the problem of the Sea Peoples (ib. pp.21f. n. 1); and, on *Keftiu*, see Vercoutter, *EMEP*. Identification is all the more difficult in the case of possible references to individual persons, where often the proposed interpretations are little more than unverifiable guesswork based upon a vague similarity of name (cf. above p.154 on Kadmos and Kidin-Marduk, and Gurney, *The Hittites* p.49 on Tawagalawas and Eteokles).

218. See for example Lowie's article "Oral tradition and history", originally published in *Journal of American Folk-Lore* 30 (1917) pp.161-7 and reprinted in *LSPA*, ed. Du Bois (1960) pp.202-10. Lowie writes: "We cannot substitute primitive tradition for scientific history. Our historical problems can be solved only by the objective methods of comparative ethnology, archaeology, linguistics, and physical anthropology" (*LSPA* p.210). One is bound to agree that legend must not be treated as history; but however objective are the methods of the sciences named here by Lowie *when applied within their own fields,* this objectivity does not extend to the solution of historical problems.

interpretation, a subjective element enters in. This is particularly worth illustrating with regard to the archaeology: the same assemblage of artefacts, the very same destruction levels, may be interpreted in different ways by different archaeologists.[219] There is moreover a tendency for archaeological interpretations to run in fashions. Thus in British prehistory it was customary in the first part of this century for certain changes in material culture to be explained by invasion; today this view is generally rejected in favour of explanations through indigenous development.[220] Similarly in Greek prehistory we can see

219. It is illuminating here to compare Gordon Childe's comments in *Prehistoric Migrations in Europe* (1950), where he writes: "Inevitably a great deal of my subject is highly controversial. The data provided by prehistoric archaeology do not suffice to determine with scientific accuracy a large number of questions. On many points there are two or three views that are almost equally likely. Which of them any author chooses, may depend largely on *a priori* assumptions or quite subjective prejudice" (op. cit. p.2; cf. also p.9 and the whole of Childe's Ch. I "Archaeological postulates").

This ambiguity in the interpretation of archaelogical evidence may be illustrated by specific examples: the discovery of similar or identical pottery in two different areas may mean the migration of people from one area to another, or the arrival of the same new people in the two areas, or it might be solely the result of trade. Likewise the appearance of a burnt level at a site could be a destruction arising from external invasion, or from internal conflict, or on the other hand it need be only the result of accidental fire. Thus in Greek prehistory there are several possible explanations of the occurrence of Grey Minyan ware in both MH Greece and at Troy VI (see Page, *HHI* pp.54-7, and compare carefully his nn. 94, 98, 103 on pp.87-91 on the views of Schachermeyr and Bittel). Similarly the destructions which are attested in the LH IIIB period are interpreted by Desborough as the work of invaders, while Hammond writing in the same fascicle maintains that they resulted from internal upheaval: see *CAH* ed. 2, fasc. 13 p.5 (Desborough) and pp.48f. (Hammond); cf. also Rhys Carpenter's suggestion that the collapse of Mycenaean civilisation was due not to invasion but to a worsening of climatic conditions, and that the palaces were destroyed at a time of drought by a hungry populace (*DGC* (1966) esp. pp.39-41, 68-70). For further examples of variety in possible interpretation of the archaeological evidence see above Ch. V on how the Cretan theory came to be accepted and abandoned; Ch. VI on the possible interpretations of the oriental seals from Thebes; and n. 181 to Ch. VIII on the various explanations of the cultural change at the beginning of the LH period.

220. Cf. Clark, "The invasion hypothesis in British archaeology" in *Antiquity* 40 (1966) pp.172-89; cf. also Adams, "Invasion, diffusion, evolution?" in *Antiquity* 42 (1968) pp.194-215, on the wider problems concerning the postulation of invasion in prehistory, with special reference to Nubia.

how up to the 1890's there was a tendency to interpret many Bronze Age achievements as the work of Phoenicians or other orientals (cf. above Ch. III with n.57); how shortly afterwards the Cretan hypothesis became almost universally accepted, and how at the present time the independence of mainland Greece is generally stressed.[221] The other sources then are not in themselves objective *for the purpose of reconstructing prehistory;* they are subject to limitations of precisely the same order as the legendary tradition. The prehistorian is always working from imperfect and ambiguous material, and there is, *pace* Starr (see above p.195), nothing basically illogical or unsound about using legendary evidence, provided that one recognises what one is doing.

But how in practical terms may one seek to combine the different sources? In the first instance each of them should be pursued in isolation, kept scrupulously apart, and examined without preconceptions. But it is unreasonable to expect such a rigorous separation to go on for ever, since this would lead only to a narrow and sterile concern with the increasingly detailed study of unrelated facts. Eventually one must compare the conclusions reached from the different disciplines, and attempt to use them to modify, supplement or elucidate each other. Often much that is valuable can be learned from such a comparison. For example, archaeology alone cannot tell us the nationhood of the people whose artefacts are being studied. The archaeologist has to label them with such names as "Battle-axe folk",

---

221. It is to be noted also how the current interpretations in archaeological and documentary study have influenced ideas about mythology: today with the excavation and publication of so many Near Eastern documents there is a tendency to look for comparisons between the Greek and the Ugaritic, Hittite and Babylonian myths and legends; but in the last century, when the discovery of Sanskrit texts was still fresh, scholarly interest was centred on the relationship of Greek and Indian mythology, and it was even postulated on the basis of the Kadmos legend that there were once Indians in Greece. Thus E. Pococke writes: "There can remain no shadow of a doubt to those who are acquainted with the missionary efforts of the early Bud'hists ... that this settlement of Cadmus in Greece, was the vanguard of a series of Bud'histic propagandism" (*India in Greece; or, Truth in Mythology* (1852) p.280). It is obviously right that new material should constantly influence interpretation, but one must always be careful to keep the mind open to all the possibilities.

"Broch-builders" or "Urnfield people". But it can sometimes happen that, when documentary or linguistic evidence is brought to bear on a problem, then a theoretical identification may be made which, though it may not be proved beyond all possible doubt, will nevertheless have a high degree of probability. Thus in Greek prehistory it now seems almost certain, thanks to the decipherment of Linear B, that the Mycenaeans were Greeks. The problems of correlation are great because our sources are fundamentally different, and it is certainly an oversimplification to suppose that archaeology has provided a direct means of testing the truth of legend.[222] But the challenge of combining the different sources cannot lightly be ignored. However scientifically and objectively Troy has been excavated, the work of the prehistorian is incomplete until he has attempted to relate the archaeological evidence to the literary sources: in Caskey's words "Homer will not let us rest" (*JHS* 84 (1964) p.10). This then is the real answer to the

---

222. Hammond writes that "archaeological discovery has now provided a touchstone, by which the validity of Greek legend can be measured" (*HGHam* p.58), and Wace remarks that "the archaeological approach ... provides a testing of the truth or probability of legend" (*CH* p.332). But as we have already seen, archaeology and the legendary traditions are sources on fundamentally different levels, and much of the subject-matter of legend is such that corroboration from strictly archaeological sources can never be expected; even with events such as wars and immigrations, for which one might reasonably look for a reflection in the material record, archaeology can often provide only an aid to the assessment of their plausibility, not actual confirmation of historical truth (cf. earlier in this Chapter on the legend of Kadmos). It is here worth comparing the conclusions which have been reached in a very different field of study. In evaluating the Biblical traditions of the patriarchal period as a historical source, John Bright writes: "Nor are we to overbid archaeological evidence. It cannot be stressed too strongly that in spite of all the light that it has cast on the patriarchal age, in spite of all that it has done to vindicate the antiquity and authenticity of the tradition, archaeology has not proved that the stories of the patriarchs happened just as the Bible tells them. In the nature of the case it cannot do so. .. The witness of archaeology is indirect. It has lent to the picture of Israel's origins as drawn in Genesis a flavor of probability, and has provided the background for understanding it, but it has not proved the stories true in detail, and cannot do so. We know nothing of the lives of Abraham, Isaac, and Jacob save what the Bible tells us, the details of which lie beyond the control of archaeological data" (*AHI* (1960) p.67). Much of what Bright says here of the Biblical material might well be applied to the Greek heroic tradition.

204

sceptical view: the literary evidence is there, and will not let us ignore it.

There has in recent years been a tendency for archaeology to become more and more scientific; to concern itself increasingly with the collection and classification of data and with the detailed description of material culture. But if archaeology is to have any contribution to make to society, if in the long run it is to achieve a worth-while purpose, it must stimulate us to explain as well as to observe, even though an ideal standard of accuracy in interpretation is unattainable. This point was made by Rhys Carpenter in his lectures entitled *The Humanistic Value of Archaeology* (see *HVA* (1933) esp. pp.32-4, 109, 127f.); it has more recently been re-emphasised by Sir Mortimer Wheeler in "What *matters* in archaeology?" (an address originally written in 1950 and reprinted in 1966 in *Alms for Oblivion* pp.99-115). Wheeler speaks of the need to use the imagination in re-creating the past in spite of the inadequacy of the information at our disposal: "We must do what we can with the material vouchsafed to us, in full consciousness of its incompleteness. But try we must, always with the thought that archaeology and history are alike frustrate unless they contribute to a vital *reconstruction of man's past achievement,* in other words aspire to interpretation as well as to mere transliteration."[223] With Greece in the Mycenaean period we have an unusual opportunity to re-create the past in that our stones, pots and tombs belong to a context which is not entirely nameless; we have in legend information about persons, peoples and events, evidence for which is imperfect or non-existent in the other sources. If there is an intellectual risk involved in interpretation, so is there too in using other types of evidence.

As far as legend is concerned, this risk may be minimised by the observance of a few simple rules, and perhaps one of the most useful results of the present work may be to suggest some principles of study:

(1) Before any use can be made of legend to reconstruct history or

---

223. Wheeler, *AFO* p.115 his italics; see also ib. p.112. We may compare here Jacquetta Hawkes' plea that the more humanistic and interpretative approach to archaeology should not be neglected in the face of the development of so many technical and scientific aids ("The proper study of mankind" in *Antiquity* 42 (1968) pp.255-62).

interpret archaeology, the sources of the legend must be carefully studied. Late versions cannot automatically be excluded, but if interpretations are to be based on these alone, some attempt must be made to see why these alone have preserved the tradition and whether some other explanation is not available. The testimony of any author must be carefully assessed according to what is known of his personal characteristics, the particular purpose of his work, his use of sources and his general attitude to history. This basic examination is necessary both for the study of social conditions[224] and for the reconstruction of historical events.

(2) One must then endeavour to isolate the elements which are *prima facie* likely to be historical, and those which may more plausibly be regarded as fiction, whether myth, folktale, rationalisation or any other form of elaboration, since even early and well attested elements may never have been a reflection of historical truth. The means of isolating these elements may admittedly be less accurate than one could wish, but it is not an entirely arbitrary process. Myths are traceable by their aetiological function, by their obvious association with cult, and by the divine origin of their characters; elements of folktale on the other hand may be identified by the universality of their themes, which serve no purpose other than to entertain and frequently involve the marvellous (cf. the end of Ch. II above, and on the role of folktale in the Greek traditional stories in general see Rose, *HGM* Ch. X, and Halliday, *IEFT* esp. Ch. VI on Perseus). Late elaboration and rationalisation can often be detected by a careful study of the development of the legend within classical times. These criteria are not infallible, but they serve as a guide.

(3) The results of this study may be compared with conclusions

224. The fact that a criticism of sources is necessary for sociological interpretation as well as for the reconstruction of events should be self-evident, but is often overlooked. Thus E.A.S. Butterworth in his recent book puts forward many rash conjectures about matrilineal order and prehistoric Greek society without any serious source-criticism of the myths, relying for example on the evidence of Apollodoros alone for details of Niobe's children (a matter on which ancient tradition was very varied), and making use of the testimony of such late and notoriously unreliable writers as Diktys of Crete (see *STPW* (1966) esp. pp.8, 14).

reached from other sources, most notably archaeology, language and documents, which must all have been carefully scrutinised. Here the major contribution will undoubtedly be from archaeology,[225] but inferences drawn from the other sources must also be taken into account, including any obtained from examining religious cult, parallels in motif or historical analogy, though such evidence must clearly play a subsidiary role. In analysing and comparing all this material one must try to take as whole a view as possible, not forgetting that more than one interpretation may fit the facts. The first possible combination of legendary and archaeological evidence should not be adopted unless the alternatives have been considered, and it needs to be frankly recognised that even after this study there will be little certainty or positive proof of the occurrence of events, since this is inevitable with a prehistoric period.

One final point must continually be borne in mind: the true course of events is likely to have been very much more complicated than modern reconstructions based on our partial evidence might lead us to believe. This thought has been well expressed by the late F.T. Wainwright in his book *Archaeology and Place-Names and History* (1962). Wainwright's chief field of interest was Britain in the centuries before the Norman Conquest, an obscure period which presents difficulties of co-ordination by no means unlike those confronting us in the study of the Mycenaean Age. He writes (op. cit. p.123): "What most requires emphasis is the extreme complexity of the problems we are trying to solve and of the pictures we are trying to recapture. All human activity in its several dimensions is inextricably complicated, and each of our conceptions offers at best only a faint reflection of one aspect of it. Simple solutions are to be suspected, and it should be remembered that any picture of the past recaptured by our inadequate techniques from the fragmentary evidence available to us cannot be more than a rough approximation to the truth, a fleeting glimpse of conditions and developments to a great extent outside the range of recovery."

225. I include here the evidence of physical anthropology and of the scientific study of other natural remains, though the inferences that can be drawn from these about historical events are generally very limited.

BIBLIOGRAPHY OF WORKS CITED

Abbreviations for books and articles are given in the right hand margin. For other abbreviations, including names of periodicals, see the list of Abbreviations, above pp. xi-xiii.

W.Y. ADAMS, "Invasion, diffusion, evolution?" in *Antiquity* 42 (1968) pp. 194-215.

F.M. AHL, "Cadmus and the palm-leaf tablets" in *AJPh* 88 (1967) pp. 188-94.

J. AISTLEITNER, *Wörterbuch der ugaritischen Sprache.*   *WUS* Berlin, 1963.

W.F. ALBRIGHT, *"Notes on early Hebrew and Aramaic epigraphy"* in *JPOS* 6 (1926) pp. 75-102.

—, "The role of the Canaanites in the history of civilization"; ed. 1 in *Studies in the History of* *RCHC* *Culture* (the Waldo H. Leland volume), Menasha, Wisc., 1942, pp. 11-50; ed. 2 in *The Bible and the Ancient Near East* (ed. G.E. Wright), London, 1961, pp. 328-62.

—, *The Archaeology of Palestine.* Harmondsworth, *AP* 1949 (here cited in the rev. ed. of 1960).

—, "Some oriental glosses on the Homeric problem" in *AJA* 54 (1950) pp. 162-76.

—, "Syria, the Philistines, and Phoenicia" in *CAH* ed. 2 fasc. 51, 1966 (= ed. 3 Vol. II, Ch. XXXIII).

—, and T.O. LAMBDIN, "The evidence of language" in *CAH* ed. 2 fasc. 54, 1966 (= ed. 3 Vol. I, Ch. IV).

E. AKURGAL, *The Birth of Greek Art.* London, 1968. *BGA*

P. ÅLIN, *Das Ende der mykenischen Fundstätten auf* *EMFF* *dem griechischen Festland (SMA* I). Lund, 1962.

W. ALY, *"Lexikalische Streifzüge"* in *Glotta* 5 (1914) pp.

57-79.

R. AMIRAN, *Ancient Pottery of the Holy Land.* New Brunswick, 1970.   *APHL*

P.B.S. ANDREWS, "The myth of Europa and Minos" in *G&R* 2nd ser. 16 (1969) pp. 60-6.

P.E. ARIAS and M. HIRMER, *A History of Greek Vase Painting.* London, 1962.   *HGVP*

P. ARNOULD, *Étude sur l'origine du nom phénicien* (Mémoire présenté pour l'obtention du grade de licencié en Philosophie et Lettres, Université Catholique de Louvain, 1963). Not published: see n. 86.   *EONP*

M.C. ASTOUR, "Greek names in the Semitic world and Semitic names in the Greek world" in *JNES* 23 (1964) pp. 193-201.

—, "The origin of the terms 'Canaan,' 'Phoenician,' and 'purple' " in *JNES* 24 (1965) pp. 346-50.

—, *Hellenosemitica: An Ethnic and Cultural Study in West Semitic Impact on Mycenaean Greece.* Leiden, ed. 1, 1965; ed. 2, 1967.   *HS*

—, "Aegean place-names in an Egyptian inscription" in *AJA* 70 (1966) pp. 313-7.

P. ÅSTRÖM, "Three Tell el Yahudiyeh juglets in the Thera Museum" in *Acta of the First International Scientific Congress on the Volcano of Thera,* Athens, 1971, pp. 415-21.

C. AUTRAN, *"Phéniciens." Essai de contribution à l'histoire de la Méditerranée.* Paris, 1920.

J. BABELON, "Le voile d'Europè" in *RA* 6ᵉ sér. 20 (1942-43) pp. 125-40.

J. BAIKIE, *The Sea-Kings of Crete.* London, 1910.   *SKC*

H.C. BALDRY, "The dramatization of the Theban legend" in *G&R* 2nd ser. 3 (1956) pp. 24-37.

A. BANIER, *The Mythology and Fables of the Ancients explain'd from History.* 4 vols., London, 1739-40, translated from the French original, Paris, 1738-40.   *MFA*

210

D. BARAMKI, *Phoenicia and the Phoenicians*. Beirut, 1961.   *PhPh*

R.D. BARNETT, "Early Greek and oriental ivories" in *JHS* 68 (1948) pp. 1-25.

—, "Early shipping in the Near East" in *Antiquity* 32 (1958) pp. 220-30.

G.F. BASS, "Cape Gelidonya: a Bronze Age shipwreck" in *Trans. Amer. Philos. Soc.* n.s. 57 (1967) pt. 8.   *CGBS*

—, (ed.), *A History of Seafaring based on Underwater Archaeology*. London, 1972.   *AHS*

A.J. BEATTIE, "Aegean languages of the Heroic Age" in *CH* (ed. Wace and Stubbings) 1962, pp. 311-24.

R.L. BEAUMONT, "Greek influence in the Adriatic Sea before the fourth century B.C." in *JHS* 56 (1936) pp. 159-204.

J.D. BEAZLEY, *Etruscan Vase-Painting*. Oxford, 1947.   *EVP*

—, *Paralipomena*. Oxford, 1971.

(K.) J. BELOCH, *Griechische Geschichte*. Strassburg, ed. 1, 3 vols. in 4, 1893-1904; ed. 2, 4 vols. in 8, 1912-27.

—, "Die Phoiniker am aegaeischen Meer" in *RhM* 49 (1894) pp. 111-32.

J. BÉRARD, *Recherches sur la chronologie de l'époque mycénienne*. Paris, 1950.   *RCEM*

—, "Les Hyksôs et la légende d'Io" *Syria* 29 (1952) pp. 1-43.

—, "Écriture pré-alphabétique et alphabet en Italie et dans les pays égéens" in *Minos* 2 (1953) pp. 65-83.

V. BÉRARD, *Les Phéniciens et l'Odyssée*. Ed 1, 2 vols., Paris, 1902-3.   *Ph. Od.*

H. BERGER, article s.v. Europe (2) in *RE* VI (1909) cols. 1287-1309.

M. BESNIER, article s.v. purpura in Daremberg and Saglio, *Dictionnaire des Antiquités* IV. 1. Paris, n.d. (ca. 1907) pp. 769-78.   *DA*

E. BETHE, *Thebanische Heldenlieder.* Leipzig, 1891.

—, *Homer. Dichtung und Sage.* 3 vols., Leipzig and Berlin, 1914-27.

M. BIEBER, *The History of the Greek and Roman Theater.* Ed. 2, Princeton, 1961.   *HGRT*

H. BIESANTZ, "Mykenische Schriftzeichen auf einer böotischen Schale des 5. Jahrhunderts v. Chr." in *Minoica. Festschrift J. Sundwall* (ed. E. Grumach), pp. 50-60. Berlin, 1958.

A. BIRAN, "A Mycenaean charioteer vase from Tel Dan" in *IEJ* 20 (1970) pp. 92-4.

A.M. BISI, *Il grifone; storia di un motivo iconografico nell' antico Oriente Mediterraneo.* Rome, 1965.

J. BLAIR, *The Chronology and History of the World, from the Creation to the year of Christ, 1753.* London, 1754.

C.W. BLEGEN, "Excavations at Troy, 1937" in *AJA* 41 (1937) pp. 553-97.

—, "Preclassical Greece — a survey" in *BSA* 46 (1951) pp. 16-24.

—, see also under Wace.

J. BOARDMAN, "Early Euboean pottery and history" in *BSA* 52 (1957) pp. 1-29.

—, (and L.R. Palmer), *On the Knossos Tablets.* Oxford, 1963.   *OKT*

—, *The Greeks Overseas.* Harmondsworth, 1964.   *GO*

—, "An orient wave" (review of Astour, *HS*) in *CR* n.s. 16 (1966) pp. 86-8.

—, "The Khaniale Tekke tombs, II" in *BSA* 62 (1967) pp. 57-75.

—, *Greek Gems and Finger Rings.* London, 1970.

S. BOCHART, *Geographiae Sacrae pars altera: Chanaan, seu de coloniis et sermone Phoenicum.* Cadomi, 1646.   *Chan.*

G.H. BODE, *Scriptores rerum mythicarum Latini.* 2 vols., Cellis, 1834.   *SRML*

E. BOISACQ, *Dictionnaire étymologique de la langue*

grecque. Ed. 3, Heidelberg and Paris, 1938.

G. BONFANTE, "The name of the Phoenicians" in *CPh* *NaPh*
  36 (1941) pp. 1-20.

R.C. BOSANQUET, "Excavations at Palaikastro II" in
  BSA 9 (1902-3) pp. 274-89.

—, "Some 'Late Minoan' vases found in Greece" in
  JHS 24 (1904) pp. 317-29.

—, "Dicte and the temples of Idaean Zeus" in *BSA*
  40 (1939-40) pp. 60-77.

C.M. BOWRA, *Heroic Poetry.* London, 1952. *HP*

—, *The Meaning of a Heroic Age.* Newcastle-upon-
  Tyne, 1957.

E. BRADFORD, *Ulysses Found.* London, 1963.

J. BRANDIS, "Die Bedeutung der sieben Thore
  Thebens" in *Hermes* 2 (1867) pp. 259-84.

J. BRIGHT, *A History of Israel.* London, 1960. *AHI*

L.H. BROCKINGTON, "I and II Samuel" in *Peake*
  (1962) pp. 318-37.

R. van den BROEK, *The Myth of the Phoenix according* *MythP*
  to Classical and early Christian Traditions.
  Leiden, 1972.

F. BROMMER, *Vasenlisten zur griechischen Helden-* *VGH*
  sage. Ed. 2, Marburg/Lahn, 1960.

P. BRUNEAU, review of Vian, *Or. Theb.* in *REG* 78
  (1965) pp. 382f.

—, "Documents sur l'industrie délienne de la
  pourpre" in *BCH* 93 (1969) pp. 759-91.

J. BRYANT, *A New System, or, an Analysis of Antient* *NSAM*
  Mythology. London, ed. 1, 3 vols., 1774-6; ed. 3,
  6 vols., 1807.

—, *A Dissertation concerning the War of Troy etc.*
  (see above pp. 1f.). Ed. 1, 1796; ed. 2, London,
  1799.

C.D. BUCK, "The language situation in and about
  Greece in the second millennium B.C." in *CPh*
  21 (1926) pp. 1-26.

R.J. BUCK, "The Minoan thalassocracy re-examined" in

Historia 11 (1962) pp. 129-37.

—, "The Middle Helladic period" in *Phoenix* 20 (1966) pp. 193-209.

W. BÜHLER, *Europa. Ein Überblick über die Zeugnisse des Mythos in der antiken Literatur und Kunst.* Munich, 1968.

E.D. van BUREN, "The god Ningizzida" in *Iraq* 1 (1934) pp. 60-89.

A.R. BURN, *Minoans, Philistines, and Greeks.* London, 1930. *MPG*

—, review of Cloché, *TBOC* in *JHS* 73 (1953) p. 173.

—, *The Lyric Age of Greece.* London, 1960. *LAG*

R.M. BURROWS, *The Discoveries in Crete and their Bearing on the History of Ancient Civilization.* London, 1907. *DC*

A. BURTON, *Diodorus Siculus Book I. A Commentary.* Leiden, 1972. *DSC*

J.B. BURY, *A History of Greece.* London, ed. 1, 1900; ed. 2, 1913; ed. 3, revised by R. Meiggs, 1951. *HGBur*

—, *The Ancient Greek Historians.* London, 1909. *AGH*

G. BUSOLT, *Griechische Geschichte bis zur Schlacht bei Chaironeia.* 3 vols., Gotha, 1885-1904. *GG*

E.A.S. BUTTERWORTH, *Some Traces of the Pre-Olympian World in Greek Literature and Myth.* Berlin, 1966. *STPW*

G. CADOGAN, review of Bass, *CGBS* in *JHS* 89 (1969) pp. 187-9.

G. CAPOVILLA, "Aegyptiaca. L'Egitto e il mondo miceneo" in *Aegyptus* 39 (1959) pp. 290-339.

A. CARNOY, *Dictionnaire étymologique de la mythologie gréco-romaine.* Paris, n.d. (ca. 1957). *DEMG*

R. CARPENTER, *The Humanistic Value of Archaeology.* Cambridge, Mass., 1933. *HVA*

—, "The antiquity of the Greek alphabet" in *AJA* 37 (1933) pp. 8-29.

—, "Letters of Cadmus" in *AJPh* 56 (1935) pp.

5-13.

—, "Origin and diffusion of the Greek alphabet" (summary of a paper) in *AJA* 42 (1938) p. 125.

—, "Phoenicians in the West" in *AJA* 62 (1958) pp. 35-53.

—, *Discontinuity in Greek Civilization.* Cambridge, 1966.   *DGC*

T.H. CARTER, "Western Phoenicians at Lepcis Magna" in *AJA* 69 (1965) pp. 123-32.

M. CARY, *The Geographic Background of Greek and Roman History.* Oxford, 1949.   *GBGH*

J.L. CASKEY, "Excavations in Keos, 1960-61" in *Hesperia* 31 (1962) pp. 263-83.

—, "Greece and the Aegean islands in the Middle Bronze Age" in *CAH* ed. 2 fasc. 45, 1966 (= ed. 3 Vol. II, Ch. IVa).

—, see also under Finley.

F. CASSOLA, *La Ionia nel mondo miceneo.* Naples, 1957.   *IMM*

—, "La talassocrazia cretese e Minosse" in *PP* 12 (1957) pp. 343-52.

L. CASSON, *Ships and Seamanship in the Ancient World.* Princeton, 1971.   *SSAW*

H.W. CATLING, E.E. RICHARDSON and A.E. BLIN-STOYLE, "Correlations between composition and provenance of Mycenaean and Minoan pottery" in *BSA* 58 (1963) pp. 94-115.

—, and A. MILLETT, "A study of the inscribed stirrup-jars from Thebes" in *Archaeometry* 8 (1965) pp. 3-85.   *SIST*

—, and —, "Theban stirrup-jars: questions and answers" in *Archaeometry* 11 (1969) pp. 3-20.

—, "Archaeology in Greece, 1971-72" in *AR* for 1971-72 pp. 3-26.

H.M. CHADWICK, *The Heroic Age.* Cambridge, 1912.   *HA*

—, and N.K. CHADWICK, *The Growth of Literature.* 3 vols., Cambridge, 1932-40.   *GL*

215

J. CHADWICK, "The Greek dialects and Greek pre-history" in *G&R* 2nd ser. 3 (1956) pp. 38-50.

—, *The Decipherment of Linear B.* Cambridge, ed. 1, 1958; ed. 2, 1967. DLB

—, "Minoan Linear A: a provisional balance sheet" in *Antiquity* 33 (1959) pp. 269-78.

—, "The prehistory of the Greek language" in *CAH* ed. 2 fasc. 15, 1963 (= ed. 3 Vol. II, Ch. XXXIX).

—, review of Stella, *CMDC* in *JHS* 86 (1966) pp. 214f.

—, "Greekless archaeology" (review of Hood, *HH*) in *Antiquity* 41 (1967) pp. 271-5.

—, "Linear B tablets from Thebes" in *Minos* n.s. 10 (1969) pp. 115-37.

—, see also under Ventris.

P. CHANTRAINE, *La formation des noms en grec ancien.* Paris, 1933. FNG

—, "À propos du nom des Phéniciens et des noms de la pourpre" in *Studii Clasice* 14 (1972) pp. 7-15. NPNP

S.V. CHAPMAN, "A catalogue of Iron Age pottery from the cemeteries of Khirbet Silm, Joya, Qrayé and Qasmieh of South Lebanon" in *Berytus* 21 (1972) pp. 55-194.

F. CHAPOUTHIER, "De l'avenir des études sur la mythologie grecque" in *Actes du premier Congrès de la Fédération internationale des Associations d'études classiques* pp. 259-67. Paris, 1951. AEMG

G. CHARLES-PICARD and C. CHARLES-PICARD, *Daily Life in Carthage at the time of Hannibal.* London, 1961. DCH

V.G. CHILDE, *Prehistoric Migrations in Europe.* Oslo, 1950.

—, *Piecing together the Past: the Interpretation of Archaeological Data.* London, 1956. PPIA

G. CLARK, "The invasion hypothesis in British archaeology" in *Antiquity* 40 (1966) pp. 172-89.

G. CLAUSON, "Philology and archaeology" in *Antiquity* 47 (1973) pp. 37-42.

H.F. CLINTON, *Fasti Hellenici. The Civil and Literary Chronology of Greece.* 3 vols., Oxford, 1824-34. — *FH*

P. CLOCHÉ, *Thèbes de Béotie dès origines à la conquête romaine.* Namur, 1952. — *TBOC*

J.N. COLDSTREAM, *Greek Geometric Pottery.* London, 1968. — *GGP*

—, "The Phoenicians of Ialysos" in *BICS* 16 (1969) pp. 1-8.

—, and G.L. HUXLEY (eds.), *Kythera. Excavations and Studies.* London, 1972.

—, see also under Huxley.

A.B. COOK, *Zeus. A Study in Ancient Religion.* 3 vols. in 5, Cambridge, 1914-40.

J.-C. COURTOIS, "Les cités états de Phénicie au IIème millénaire" in *Archeologia* 20 (1968) pp. 15-25.

G.W. COX, *A Manual of Mythology.* Ed. 1, London, 1867 (here cited from ed. 6, 1892).

—, *The Mythology of the Aryan Nations.* 2 vols., London, 1870. — *MAN*

O. CRUSIUS, article s.v. Kadmos II in *Roscher* II (1890-7) cols. 824-93.

W. CULICAN, *The First Merchant Venturers: the Ancient Levant in History and Commerce.* London, 1966. — *FMV*

E. CURTIUS, *The History of Greece.* 5 vols, London, 1868-73, transl. from the German original of 1857-67. — *HGCur*

G. DANIEL, *The Idea of Prehistory.* London, 1962 (here cited in the Pelican ed., Harmondsworth, 1964). — *IP*

G. DAUX, "Chronique des fouilles" annually in *BCH* 88 (1964) to *BCH* 93 (1969).

R.M. DAWKINS, "Excavations at Palaikastro IV" in *BSA* 11 (1904-5) pp. 258-92.

J. DAY, "The letters of Cadmus" (summary of a paper) in *AJA* 42 (1938) p. 125.

V.R. d'A. DESBOROUGH, *Protogeometric Pottery.* Oxford, 1952.   *PgP*

—, and N.G.L. HAMMOND, "The end of Mycenaean civilization and the Dark Age" in *CAH* ed. 2 fasc. 13, 1962 (=ed. 3 Vol. II, Ch. XXXVI).

—, *The Last Mycenaeans and their Successors.* Oxford, 1964.   *LMS*

A. DESSENNE, *Le sphinx. Étude iconographique I. Dès origines à la fin du second millénaire.* Paris, 1957.

—, "Le griffon créto-mycénien" in *BCH* 81 (1957) pp. 203-15.

P. DEVAMBEZ, *Greek Painting.* London, 1962.

E. DHORME, *Les religions de Babylonie et d'Assyrie* in E. Dhorme and R. Dussaud, *Les anciennes religions orientales* II. Paris, 1949.   *LRBA*

D. DIRINGER, *The Alphabet.* Ed. 3, 2 vols., London, 1968.

E.R. DODDS (ed.), *Euripides, Bacchae.* Oxford, ed. 2, 1960.

W. DÖRPFELD and others, *Alt-Olympia.* 2 vols., Berlin, 1935.

R.M. DORSON, "Theories of myth and the folklorist" in *Myth and Mythmaking* (ed. H.A. Murray), pp. 76-89. New York, 1960.   *TMF*

M. DOTHAN and D.N. FREEDMAN, *Ashdod I* (*'Atiqot,* Eng. ser. 7). Jerusalem, 1967.

—, *Ashdod II-III* (*'Atiqot,* Eng. ser. 9-10). Jerusalem, 1972.

S. DOW, "The Greeks in the Bronze Age" in *Rapports du XIe Congrès international des Sciences historiques* II, pp. 1-34. Stockholm and elsewhere, 1960.   *TGBA*

H. DRAGENDORFF (ed.), *Thera II. Theräische Gräber.* Berlin, 1903.

G. R. DRIVER, *Canaanite Myths and Legends.*   *CML*
Edinburgh, 1956.

M.S. DROWER, "Ugarit" in *CAH* ed. 2 fasc. 63, 1968   *Ugarit*
(=ed. 3, Vol. II, Ch. XXI (b) iv and v).

G. DUMÉZIL, "Λάβρυς" in *JA* 215 (1929) pp. 237-54.

M. DUNAND, *Fouilles de Byblos.* 2 vols. in 4, Paris,   *FB*
1937-58.

T.J. DUNBABIN, *The Greeks and their Eastern*   *GEN*
Neighbours (*JHS* suppl. pap. 8). London, 1957.

M. DUNCKER, *Geschichte des Alterthums.* 7 vols., ed.   *GADun*
4, Leipzig, 1874-82.

—, *History of Greece.* 2 vols., London, 1883-86,   *HGDun*
transl. from vols. V-VII of the above.

R. DUSSAUD, *Les civilisations préhelléniques dans le*   *CivP*
bassin de la mer Égée. Paris, 1910.

—, "Victor Bérard" (Nécrologie) in *Syria* 12 (1931)
pp. 392-4.

—, "Le sanctuaire et les dieux phéniciens de Ras
Shamra" in *RHR* 105 (1932) pp. 245-302.

—, "Égypte et Égée dans les textes de Ras Shamra"
in *CRAI* for 1938 pp. 536-40.

—, "Rapports entre la Crète ancienne et la
Babylonie" in *Iraq* 6 (1939) pp. 52-65.

—, *Les découvertes de Ras Shamra (Ugarit) et*
l'Ancien Testament. Ed. 2, Paris, 1941.

—, *L'art phénicien du IIe millénaire.* Paris, 1949.

G.P. EDWARDS and R.B. EDWARDS, "Eratosthenes
and the date of Cadmus" in *CR* 24 (1974) pp.
181 f.

—, and —, "Red letters and Phoenician
writing" in *Kadmos* 13 (1974) pp. 48-57.

I.E.S. EDWARDS, *The Pyramids of Egypt.* Har-   *PE*
mondsworth, 1947.

R.B. EDWARDS, "The story of Theseus" and "The
growth of the legend" in *The Quest for Theseus*   *QT*
(ed. A.G. Ward), pp. 7-50. London, 1970.

—, "Some traditional links between Crete and

Boiotia" in *Teiresias* 2 (1972) pp. 2-5.

—, see also under G.P. Edwards.

O. EISSFELDT, article s.v. Phoiniker und Phoinikia in *RE* XX. 1 (1941) cols. 350-80.

—, article s.v. Tyros (3) in *RE* 2nd ser. VII. 2 (1948) cols. 1876-1908.

J.A. EMERTON, "The meaning of the root 'mzl' in Ugaritic" in *JSS* 14 (1969) pp. 22-33.

J. ESCHER, article s.v. Europe (1) in *RE* VI (1909) cols. 1287-98.

A.J. EVANS, "A Mycenaean system of writing in Crete and the Peloponnese" in *The Athenaeum* No. 3478 for June 23rd 1894 pp. 812f.

—, "Knossos" (Report of the Palace excavations in 1900) in *BSA* 6 (1899-1900) pp. 3-70.

—, "The Palace of Knossos" (Report of the excavations in 1902) in *BSA* 8 (1901-2) pp. 1-124.

—, *Scripta Minoa* I. Oxford, 1909.   *SM*

—, "The Minoan and Mycenaean element in Hellenic life" in *JHS* 32 (1912) pp. 277-97.

—, "The new excavations at Mycenae" in *The Times Literary Supplement* for July 15th 1920 p. 454.

—, "The ring of Nestor. A glimpse into the Minoan after-world" in *JHS* 45 (1925) pp. 1-75.

—, *The Palace of Minos.* 4 vols. in 6 and index,   *PM*
London, 1921-36.

A. FALKENSTEIN, "Zu den Siegelzylindern aus Theben" in *Kadmos* 3 (1964) pp. 108f.

L.R. FARNELL, *The Cults of the Greek States.* 5 vols., Oxford, 1896-1909.

—, "The value and the methods of mythologic study" in *PBA* for 1919-20 pp. 37-51.

—, *Greek Hero Cults and Ideas of Immortality.*   *GHC*
Oxford, 1921.

J.G. FÉVRIER, "Les origines de la marine phénicienne" in *RHPh* n.s. fasc. 10 (1935) pp. 97-124.

—, "L'ancienne marine phénicienne et les découvertes récentes" in *La Nouvelle Clio* 1 (1949) pp. 128-43.

A. FICK, *Vorgriechische Ortsnamen als Quelle für die Vorgeschichte Griechenlands verwertet.* Göttingen, 1905.   *VO*

D. FIMMEN, "Die Besiedlung Böotiens bis in frühgriechische Zeit" in *Neue Jahrbücher für das klassische Altertum* 29 (1912) pp. 521-41.   *BBFZ*

M.I. FINLEY, J.L. CASKEY, G.S. KIRK and D.L. PAGE, "The Trojan War" in *JHS* 84 (1964) pp. 1-20.

—, "Myth, memory, and history" in *History and Theory* 4 (1965) pp. 281-302.

J. FONTENROSE, *Python. A study of Delphic Myth and its Origins.* Berkeley and elsewhere, 1959.

—, review of Vian, *Or. Theb.* in *CPh* 61 (1966) pp. 189-92.

(E.) J. FORSDYKE, "Minoan pottery from Cyprus, and the origin of the Mycenean style" in *JHS* 31 (1911) pp. 110-18.

—, "The pottery called Minyan ware" in *JHS* 34 (1914) pp. 126-56.

—, *Greece Before Homer. Ancient Chronology and Mythology.* London, 1956.   *GBH*

H. FRANKFORT, "Gods and myths on Sargonid seals" in *Iraq* 1 (1934) pp. 2-29.

P.M. FRASER, "Archaeology in Greece" annually in *AR* for 1968-69 to *AR* for 1970-71.

J.G. FRAZER, *The Golden Bough.* Ed. 1, 2 vols., 1890; ed. 3, 12 vols., London, 1907-15.   *GB*

—, (ed.), *Apollodorus, The Library* (Loeb ed.). 2 vols., London, 1921.   *ApLoeb*

P. FRIEDLÄNDER, *Herakles. Sagengeschichtliche Untersuchungen (Philologische Untersuchungen* 19). Berlin, 1907.   *Herak.*

—, "Kritische Untersuchungen zur Geschichte der

Heldensage I. Argonautensage" in *RhM* 69 (1914) pp. 299-317.

J. FRIEDRICH, "Zum Phönizisch-Punischen" in *ZS* 2 (1924) pp. 1-10.

—, *Phönizisch-punische Grammatik.* Rome, 1951.

H. FRISK, *Griechisches etymologisches Wörterbuch.* 3 vols., Heidelberg, 1960-72.   *GEW*

A. FURUMARK, *The Chronology of Mycenaean Pottery.* Stockholm, 1941.   *CMP*

—, *The Mycenaean Pottery. Analysis and Classification.* Stockholm, 1941.   *MP*

—, "The settlement at Ialysos and Aegean history c. 1550-1400 B.C." in *AIRRS* 15 (1950) pp. 150-271.   *SIAH*

A.H. GARDINER, *Egypt of the Pharaohs.* Oxford, 1961.   *EP*

T.H. GASTER, "A Phoenician naval gazette" in *PalEQ* for 1938 pp. 105-12.

—, "Ras Shamra, 1929-39" in *Antiquity* 13 (1939) pp. 304-19.

—, *Thespis. Ritual, Myth, and Drama in the Ancient Near East.* Ed. 1, New York, 1950; ed. 2, Garden City, N.Y., 1961 (here cited in ed. 1 unless otherwise stated).   *Thesp.*

H. von GEISAU, article s.v. Kadmos in *Der kleine Pauly* Vol. III, cols. 40f. Stuttgart, 1969.

G. GESENIUS, *Scripturae Linguaeque Phoeniciae Monumenta.* Leipzig, 1837.   *SLPM*

J. GILLIES, *The History of Ancient Greece.* London, 1786.   *HAG*

G. GLOTZ, *The Aegean Civilization.* London and New York, 1925.   *AegC*

A.W. GOMME, "The topography of Boeotia and the theories of M. Bérard" in *BSA* 18 (1911-12) pp. 189-210.   *TBTB*

—, "The legend of Cadmus and the logographi" in *JHS* 33 (1913) pp. 53-72, 223-45.   *LCL*

—, *A Historical Commentary on Thucydides.* Vol. I,   *HCT*

222

Oxford, 1956.

C.H. GORDON, *Ugaritic Grammar.* Rome, 1940.   *UG*

—, *Ugaritic Handbook.* Rome, 1947.   *UH*

—, *Ugaritic Literature.* Rome, 1949.   *UL*

—, *Ugaritic Manual.* Rome, 1955.   *UM*

—, "Notes on Minoan Linear A" in *Antiquity* 31 (1957) pp. 124-30.

—, "Akkadian tablets in Minoan dress" in *Antiquity* 31 (1957) pp. 237-40.

—, "Minoan Linear A" in *JNES* 17 (1958) pp. 245-55.

—, "Minoica" in *JNES* 21 (1962) pp. 207-10.

—, *Ugaritic Textbook.* Rome, 1965.   *UT*

—, *Evidence for the Minoan Language.* Ventnor, N.J., 1966.

—, *Forgotten Scripts. The Story of their Decipherment.* Rev. ed., Harmondsworth, 1971.

V.R. GRACE, "The Canaanite jar" in *The Aegean and*   *AegNE* *the Near East* (Studies presented to H. Goldman, ed. S.S. Weinberg), pp. 80-109. Locust Valley, N.Y., 1956.

Mary GRANT (ed.), *The Myths of Hyginus* (Univ. of Kansas Publications, Humanistic Studies No. 34). Kansas, 1960.

Michael GRANT, *Myths of the Greeks and Romans.*   *MGR* London, 1962.

H. GRASSL, "Herodot und die griechische Schrift" in *Hermes* 100 (1972) pp. 169-75.

R. GRAVES, *The Greek Myths.* 2 vols., Harmondsworth,   *GM* 1955.

J. GRAY, *The Krt Text in the Literature of Ras Shamra.*   *KTL* Leiden, ed. 1, 1955; ed. 2, 1964.

—, "Israel's neighbours - III. The Levant" in *Peake* (1962) pp. 109-14.

—, *The Canaanites.* London, 1964.   *Can.*

P. GRIMAL, *Hellenism and the Rise of Rome.* London,   *HRR* 1968.

G. GROTE, *A History of Greece.* 12 vols., London, 1846-56.   *HGGro*

E. GRUMACH, "Theben und das Alter von Linear B" in *Kadmos* 4 (1965) pp. 45-57.

—, "The coming of the Greeks" in *Bulletin of the John Rylands Library* 51 (1968-69) pp. 73-103, 400-430.   *TCG*

M. GUARDUCCI, "La culla dell'alfabeto greco" in Γέρας 'Αντωνίου Κεραμοπούλλου pp. 342-54. Athens, 1953.   *GK*

—, *Epigrafia greca* I. Rome, 1967.   *EpG*

O.R. GURNEY, *The Hittites.* Harmondsworth, 1952.

—, see also under Palmer.

W.K.C. GUTHRIE, "The religion and mythology of the Greeks" in *CAH* ed. 2 fasc. 2, 1961 (= ed. 3 Vol. II, Ch. XL).

W. HALES, *A New Analysis of Chronology.* 3 vols., London, 1809-12.

H.R. HALL, "The discoveries in Crete and their relation to the history of Egypt and Palestine" in *Proc. Soc. Bibl. Arch.* 31 (1909) 135-48, 221-38, 280-5, 311-8.

—, *The Ancient History of the Near East.* London, 1913 (here cited in ed. 3, 1916).   *AHNE*

—, *The Civilization of Greece in the Bronze Age.* London, 1928.   *CGBA*

W.R. HALLIDAY, *Indo-European Folk-Tales and Greek Legend.* Cambridge, 1933.   *IEFT*

N.G.L. HAMMOND, *A History of Greece to 322 B.C.* Oxford, ed. 1, 1959; ed. 2, 1967.   *HGHam*

—, see also under Desborough.

V. HANKEY, "Late Helladic tombs at Khalkis" in *BSA* 47 (1952) pp. 49-95.

—, "Mycenaean pottery in the Middle East: notes on finds since 1951" in *BSA* 62 (1967) pp. 107-47.   *MPME*

D. HARDEN, *The Phoenicians.* London, 1962.   *Phoen.*

J.P. HARLAND, "The Peloponnesus in the Bronze Age"   *PelBA* in *HSPh* 34 (1923) pp. 1-61.

J.E. HARRISON, *Prolegomena to the Study of Greek Religion*. Ed. 3, Cambridge, 1922.   *PSGR*

P. HARVEY, *The Oxford Companion to Classical Literature*. Oxford, 1937.   *OCCL*

H.W. HAUSSIG (ed.), *Götter und Mythen im vorderen Orient (Wörterbuch der Mythologie I)*. Stuttgart, 1965.   *GMVO*

C.F.C. HAWKES, *The Prehistoric Foundations of Europe to the Mycenaean Age*. London, 1940.   *PFE*

J. HAWKES, "The proper study of mankind" in *Antiquity* 42 (1968) pp. 255-62.

D.E.L. HAYNES, *An Archaeological and Historical Guide to the pre-Islamic Antiquities of Tripolitania*. Tripoli, n.d. (ca. 1956).   *AT*

A.H.L. HEEREN, *A Sketch of the Political History of Ancient Greece*. Oxford, 1829, transl. from the German original of 1823.   *SPAG*

W. HELBIG, *Sur la question mycénienne (Mém. de l'Acad. des inscr. et belles-lettres 35.2)*. Paris, 1896.   *SQM*

B. HEMBERG, *Die Kabiren*. Uppsala, 1950.   *Kab.*

B. HEMMERDINGER, "Trois notes. I. Kadmos. II. Emprunts du grec mycénien à l'akkadien. III. L'infiltration phénicienne en Béotie" in *REG* 79 (1966) pp. 698-703.

A. HERMANN, "Das Motiv der Ente mit zurückgewendetem Kopfe im ägyptischen Kunstgewerbe" in *ZASA* 68 (1932) pp. 86-105.

H. HERTER, "Theseus der Ionier" in *RhM* 85 (1936) pp. 177-91, 193-239.

W.A. HEURTLEY, "Notes on the harbours of S. Boeotia, and sea-trade between Boeotia and Corinth in prehistoric times" in *BSA* 26 (1923-25) pp. 38-45.

—, and others, *A Short History of Greece*. Cambridge, 1965.   *SHG*

R.A. HIGGINS, *Greek and Roman Jewellery*. London, 1961. GRJ

G.F. HILL, *Catalogue of the Greek Coins of Phoenicia in the British Museum*. London, 1910. CGCP

J.H.B. HILLER VON GAERTRINGEN, *Thera I. Die Insel Thera in Altertum und Gegenwart*. Berlin, 1899.

L.B. HOLLAND, "The Danaoi" in *HSPh* 39 (1928) pp. 59-92.

E. HOMANN-WEDEKING, *Archaic Greece*. London, 1968.

S. HOOD, *The Home of the Heroes. The Aegean before the Greeks*. London, 1967. HH

—, *The Minoans*. London, 1971.

S.H. HOOKE, *Middle Eastern Mythology*. Harmondsworth, 1963. MEM

HOPE SIMPSON, see under Simpson.

W.W. HOW and J. WELLS, *A Commentary on Herodotus*. 2 vols., Oxford, 1912.

R.W. HUTCHINSON, *Prehistoric Crete*. Harmondsworth, 1962. PC

G.(L.) HUXLEY, *Crete and the Luwians*. Oxford, 1961. CL

—, and J.N. COLDSTREAM, "Kythera, first Minoan colony" in *ILN* for August 27th 1966, pp. 28f.

—, review of Vian, *Or. Theb.* in *JHS* 85 (1965) pp. 220f.

—, see also under Coldstream.

S.E. IAKOVIDIS, Περατή. τὸ νεκροταφεῖον. 3 vols., Athens, 1969-70.

J.W. JACKSON, "The geographical distribution of the shell-purple industry" in *Memoirs of the Manchester Lit. and Philos. Soc.* 60 (1915-16) no. 7, pp. 1-29. GDSP

F. JACOBY, article s.v. Hellanikos (7) in *RE* VIII (1913) cols. 104-53.

—, "The first Athenian prose writer" in *Mnemosyne* AGGFJ

3rd ser. 13 (1947) pp. 13-64 (cited here from the reprint in *Abhandlungen zur griechischen Geschichtschreibung von Felix Jacoby* (ed. H. Bloch), Leiden, 1956, pp. 100-43).

T.H.G. JAMES, "The Egyptian-type objects" in *Perachora* II (ed. T.J. Dunbabin) pp. 461-516. Oxford, 1962.

A. JARDÉ, *The Formation of the Greek People.* London, 1926.   *FGP*

R.C. JEBB (ed.), *Bacchylides. The Poems and Fragments.* Cambridge, 1905.

L.H. JEFFERY, *The Local Scripts of Archaic Greece.*   *LSAG* Oxford, 1961.

—, "Writing" in *CH* (ed. Wace and Stubbings), 1962, pp. 545-59.

—, "'Αρχαῖα γράμματα: some ancient Greek views" in *Europa. Festschrift Ernst Grumach* (ed. W.C. Brice) pp. 152-66. Berlin, 1967.

—, and A. MORPURGO-DAVIES, "Ποινικαστάς and ποινικάζεν: BM 1969. 4-2.1, a new archaic inscription from Crete" in *Kadmos* 9 (1970) 118-54.

L.B. JENSEN, "Royal purple of Tyre" in *JNES* 22 (1963) pp. 104-18.

N. JIDEJIAN, *Byblos through the Ages.* Beirut, 1968   *Byblos* (here cited in ed. 2, 1971).

—, *Tyre through the Ages.* Beirut, 1969.   *Tyre*

—, *Sidon through the Ages.* Beirut, 1972.   *Sidon*

A. JIRKU, *Kanaanäische Mythen und Epen aus Ras*   *KME* *Schamra-Ugarit.* Gütersloh, 1962.

H.J. KANTOR, "The Aegean and the Orient in the   *AegO* second millennium B.C." in *AJA* 51 (1947) pp. 1-103.

—, "Syro-Palestinian ivories" in *JNES* 15 (1956) pp. 153-74.

C.P. KARDARA, "'Αθηνᾶ Φοινίκη" in *AAA* 3 (1970) pp. 95-7.

G. KARO, *Die Schachtgräber von Mykenai.* 2 vols.,   *SchM*
Munich, 1930-3.

T. KEIGHTLEY, *The Mythology of Ancient Greece and*   *MAGI*
Italy. London, 1831.

J. KENRICK, *Phoenicia.* London, 1855.

K.M. KENYON, *Amorites and Canaanites.* London,
1966.

A.D. KERAMOPOULLOS, " Ἡ οἰκία τοῦ Κάδμου" in
AE for 1909, cols. 57-122.

—, "Μυκηναϊκοὶ τάφοι ἐν Αἰγίνῃ καὶ ἐν Θήβαις" in
AE for 1910, cols. 177-252.

—, "Θηβαϊκά" in *AD* 3 (1917) pp. 1-503.

—, further reports on excavations at Thebes in
PAAH and *AE;* for details see n. 101.

C. KERÉNYI, *The Heroes of the Greeks.* London, 1959.   *HG*

O. KERN, article s.v. Kabeiros und Kabeiroi in *RE* X. 2
(1919) cols. 1399-1450.

J.T. KILLEN, "The wool industry of Crete in the Late
Bronze Age" in *BSA* 59 (1964) pp. 1-15.

G. KINKEL (ed.), *Epicorum Graecorum Fragmenta.*   *EGF*
Vol. I, Leipzig, 1877.

G.S. KIRK and J.E. RAVEN, *The Presocratic*   *PreP*
. *Philosophers.* Cambridge, 1957.

—, *Myth. Its Meaning and Functions in Ancient and*   *MMF*
other Cultures. Cambridge, 1970.

—, see also under Finley.

K.A. KITCHEN, "Theban topographical lists, old and
new" in *Orientalia* n.s. 34 (1965) pp. 1-9.

—, "Aegean place names in a list of Amenophis III"
in *BASO* 181 (1966) pp. 23f.

A. KLEINGÜNTHER, "Πρῶτος εὑρετής. Untersuchungen zur Geschichte einer Fragestellung"
in *Philologus Supplementband* 26.1. Leipzig,
1933.

W.F. Jackson KNIGHT, *Many-Minded Homer.* London,   *MMHom*
1968.

J.A. KNUDTZON, *Die El-Amarna-Tafeln.* 2 vols.,

Leipzig, 1915.

M. KOCHAVI, "Tel Aphek" in "Notes and News" in *IEJ* 22 (1972) pp. 238f.

L. KOEHLER and W. BAUMGARTNER, *Lexicon in Veteris Testamenti Libros.* Leiden, 1958.   *LVTL*

G. KONSTANTINOPOULOS, "Ροδιακὰ III. Σκέψεις περὶ τῶν πρώτων ἐν Ρόδῳ ἐγκαταστάσεων" in *AD* 24 (1969) A (*Meletai)* pp. 76-80.

CH. KOUKOULI-CHRYSANTHAKI, "Δύο προϊστορικοὶ συνοικισμοὶ εἰς Θάσον" in *AAA* 3 (1970) pp. 215-22.

A.H. KRAPPE, "Les Chananéens dans l'ancienne Afrique du Nord et en Espagne" in *Am. Journ. Sem. Lang. and Lit.* 57 (1940) pp. 229-43.

W.G. LAMBERT, "The reading of a seal inscription from Thebes" in *Kadmos* 3 (1964) pp. 182f.

S. LAMBRINO, *CVA* France fasc. 10. Paris — Bibliothèque Nationale fasc. 2. Paris, 1931.

B. LANDTRÖM, *Ships of the Pharaohs.* London, 1970.

S.H. LANGDON, *The Mythology of All Races* (ed. L.H.   *MARS* Gray and J.A. MacCulloch) Vol. V, *Semitic.* Boston, Mass., 1931.

M.T. LARSEN, letter to *Nestor,* July 1st 1964, pp. 335f.

K. LATTE, article s.v. Kadmos (4) in *RE* X.2 (1919) cols. 1460-72.

M. LAUNEY, *Études thasiennes I. Le sanctuaire et le*   *ET I* *culte d'Héraklès à Thasos.* Paris, 1944.

C. LAVIOSA, "La marina micenea" in *ASAA* 47-48 (1969-70) [1972] pp. 7-40.

J. LEIBOVITCH, "Le griffon dans le moyen-orient antique" in *'Atiqot* 1 (1955) pp. 75-88.

M. LEJEUNE, *Traité de phonétique grecque.* Ed. 2,   *TPG* Paris, 1955.

F. LENORMANT, *Les premières civilisations.* 2 vols.,   *LPC* Paris, 1874.

A. LESKY, *A History of Greek Literature* (transl. from   *HGL* the German original (ed. 2) of 1963). London, 1966.

I. LEVY, "L'origine du nom de la Phénicie" in *RPh* 29 (1905) pp. 309-14.

H. LEWY, *Die semitischen Fremdwörter im Griechischen.* Berlin, 1895.   *SFG*

H.G. LIDDELL and R. SCOTT, *A Greek-English Lexicon.* Ed. 9, Oxford, 1940.

M. LIVERANI, *Storia di Ugarit nell'età degli archivi politici.* Rome, 1962.   *SUEA*

S. LLOYD, *Early Anatolia.* Harmondsworth, 1956.

H.L. LORIMER, *Homer and the Monuments.* London, 1950.   *HM*

R.H. LOWIE, "Oral tradition and history" in *Journal of American Folk-Lore* 30 (1917) pp. 161-7 (cited here from the reprint in *Lowie's Selected Papers in Anthropology* (ed. C. Du Bois), Berkeley, 1960, pp. 202-10).   *LSPA*

J.V. LUCE, *The End of Atlantis.* London, 1969.   *EAt*

A.M. McCANN, review of Bass, *CGBS* in *AJA* 74 (1970) pp. 105f.

W.A. McDONALD, *Progress into the Past.* New York, 1967.   *PITP*

R.A. McNEAL, "The Greeks in history and prehistory" in *Antiquity* 46 (1972) pp. 19-28.

T.A. MADHLOOM, *The Chronology of Neo-Assyrian Art.* London, 1970.

J.P. MAHAFFY, *Prolegomena to Ancient History.* London and Dublin, 1871.

B. MAISLER, "Canaan and the Canaanites" in *BASO* 102 (1946) pp. 7-12.

B. MALINOWSKI, *Sex, Culture, and Myth.* London, 1963.   *SCM*

L. MALTEN, *Kyrene. Sagengeschichtliche und historische Untersuchungen (Philologische Untersuchungen* 20). Berlin, 1911.

S. MARINATOS, "La marine créto-mycénienne" in

BCH 57 (1933) pp. 170-235.

—, review of Reusch, *ZRF* in *Gnomon* 29 (1957) pp. 533-7.

—, "Γραμμάτων διδασκάλια" in *Minoica. Festschrift J. Sundwall* (ed. E. Grumach) pp. 226-31. Berlin, 1958.   GD

—, and M. HIRMER, *Crete and Mycenae.* London, 1960.   CM

—, *Excavations at Thera* I-IV. Athens, 1968-71.

—, "Ἑλίκη, Θήρα, Θῆβαι" in *AAA* 1 (1968) pp. 1-17.

—, "An African in Thera (?)" in *AAA* 2 (1969) pp. 374f.

—, "Thera. Summary of the 1971 excavations" in *AAA* 5 (1972) pp. 1-15.

—, "Some features of 'Minoan' Thera" in *AAA* 5 (1972) pp. 445-50.

E. MASSON, *Recherches sur les plus anciens emprunts sémitiques en grec.* Paris, 1967.   RESG

F. MATZ, *Crete and Early Greece.* London, 1962.   CEG

—, "Minoan civilization: maturity and zenith" in *CAH* ed. 2 fasc. 12, 1962 (= ed. 3 Vol. II, Chs. IV(b) and XII).

A.H.S. MEGAW, "Archaeology in Greece" annually in *AR* for 1962-63 to *AR* for 1967-68.

A. MENTZ, "Die Urgeschichte des Alphabets" in *RhM* 85 (1936) pp. 347-66.

E. MEYER, *Geschichte des Alterthums.* Stuttgart, 5 vols., ed. 1, 1884-1902; ed. 3, 1910-39.   GAMey

J.-P. MICHAUD, "Chronique des fouilles" annually in *BCH* 94 (1970) to *BCH* 96 (1972).

W. MITFORD, *The History of Greece.* 5 vols., London, ed. 1, 1784; ed. 2, 1789; rev. ed., 10 vols., 1820-22.   HGMit

M. MODIANO, "History in Bronze Age pictures" in *The Times* for March 23rd, 1973.

J. MONEY, "The destruction of Acrotiri" in *Antiquity* 47

(1973) pp. 50-3.

P. MONTET, *Byblos et l'Égypte.* 2 vols., Paris, 1928-29.

B. MOON, *Mycenaean Civilization, Publications since 1935 (BICS* suppl. 3). London, 1957.

—, *Mycenaean Civilization, Publications 1956-60 (BICS* suppl. 12). London, 1961.

A. MORPURGO-DAVIES, see under Jeffery.

S. MOSCATI, *The World of the Phoenicians.* London,   *WPh*
1968.

F.C. MOVERS, *Die Phönizier.* Vol. I, Bonn, 1841; Vol. II, Berlin, 1849-56.

J.D. MUHLY, "Homer and the Phoenicians" in *Berytus*   *HAP*
19 (1970) pp. 19-64.

H.D. MÜLLER, *Mythologie der griechischen Stämme.* 2   *MGS*
vols., Göttingen, 1857-69.

K.O. MÜLLER, *Orchomenos und die Minyer* (Vol. I of   *OM*
Geschichten hellenischer Stämme und Städte. 3
vols., Breslau, 1820-4).

—, *Prolegomena zu einer wissentschaftlichen Mythologie.* Göttingen, 1825.

—, *Introduction to a Scientific System of Mythology* (Eng. transl. of the above by J. Leitch). London, 1844.

G. MURRAY, *The Rise of the Greek Epic.* Oxford, 1907.

G.E. MYLONAS, "'Ο ἐνεπίγραφος ἑτερόστομος ἀμφορεὺς τῆς Ἐλευσῖνος καὶ ἡ Ἑλλαδικὴ γραφή" in *AE* for 1936 pp. 61-100.

—, *Ancient Mycenae.* London, 1957.   *AMyc*

—, *Aghios Kosmas. An Early Bronze Age Settle-*   *AK*
ment and Cemetery in Attica. Princeton, 1959.

—, "The Luvian invasion of Greece" in *Hesperia* 31 (1962) pp. 284-309.

—, *Mycenae and the Mycenaean Age.* Princeton,   *MMA*
1966.

J.L. MYRES, review of Helbig, *SQM* in *CR* 10 (1896) pp. 350-7.

—, "Prehistoric archaeology" in *YWCS* for 1911 pp.

21-37.

—, *Who were the Greeks?* Berkeley, 1930.   *WWG*

A. NAUCK (ed.), *Tragicorum Graecorum Fragmenta.*   *TGF*
Ed. 2, Leipzig, 1889.

J. NAVEH, "Some Semitic epigraphical considerations
on the antiquity of the Greek alphabet" in *AJA*
77 (1973) pp. 1-8.

Sir Isaac NEWTON, *The Chronology of Ancient
Kingdoms Amended etc.* London, 1728.

M.P. NILSSON, *The Mycenaean Origin of Greek*   *MOGM*
Mythology. Cambridge, 1932.

—, *The Minoan-Mycenaean Religion and its Survi-*   *MMR*
val in Greek Religion. Lund, ed. 1, 1927; ed. 2,
1950.

—, *Cults, Myths, Oracles, and Politics in Ancient
Greece (Acta Instituti Atheniensis Regni
Sueciae* 1). Lund, 1951.

D.E. NINEHAM, *The Gospel of St Mark.* Har-   *GSM*
mondsworth, 1963.

I.G. NIXON, *The Rise of the Dorians.* Puckeridge,   *TRD*
Herts., 1968.

A.D. NOCK, review of Launey, *ET* I in *AJA* 52 (1948)
pp. 298-301.

J. NOUGAYROL, *Le Palais royal d'Ugarit III. Textes*   *PRU* III
*accadiens et hourrites des archives est, ouest et
centrales.* 2 vols., Paris, 1955.

—, *Le Palais royal d'Ugarit IV. Textes accadiens des*   *PRU* IV
archives sud (archives internationales). 2 vols.,
Paris, 1956.

—, "Nouveaux textes accadiens de Ras-Shamra" in
CRAI for 1960 pp. 163-71.

—, "Du bon usage des faux" in *Syria* 42 (1965) pp.
227-34.

—, *Le Palais royal d'Ugarit VI. Textes en*   *PRU* VI
*cunéiformes babyloniens des archives du grand
palais et du palais sud d'Ugarit.* Paris, 1970.

A.K. ORLANDOS (ed.), Τὸ ἔργον τῆς Ἀρχαιολογικῆς   *Ergon*

Ἑταιρείας κατὰ τὸ *1971.* Athens, 1972.

D.L. PAGE, *The Homeric Odyssey.* Oxford, 1955. HO

—, *History and the Homeric Iliad.* Berkeley and Los HHI
Angeles, 1959.

—, *The Santorini Volcano and the Desolation of* SVDC
Minoan Crete (JHS Suppl. Paper 12). London,
1970.

—, see also under Finley.

L.R. PALMER, "Luvian and Linear A" in *TPhS* for 1958
pp. 75-100.

—, *Mycenaeans and Minoans.* London, 1961. M&M

—, (and J. Boardman), *On the Knossos Tablets.* OKT
Oxford, 1963.

—, and O.R. GURNEY, "New light thrown on
ancient Crete" in *The Times* for July 17th 1964.

—, "Mycenaean inscribed vases" in *Kadmos* 10
(1971) pp. 70-86; and ib. 11 (1972) pp. 27-46.

A. PARRY (ed.), *The Making of Homeric Verse: the*
collected papers of Milman Parry. Oxford, 1971.

L.B. PATON, article s.v. Phoenicians in *Encyclopaedia of* PhHa
Religion and Ethics (ed. J. Hastings), Vol. 9 pp.
887-97. Edinburgh, 1917.

L. PEARSON, *Early Ionian Historians.* Oxford, 1939. EIH

H. PEDERSEN, *Linguistic Science in the Nineteenth* LSNC
Century. Cambridge, Mass., 1931.

O. PELON, review of Raison, *VIPA* in *REG* 81 (1968)
pp. 562-7.

J.D.S. PENDLEBURY, *Aegyptiaca. A Catalogue of*
Egyptian Objects in the Aegean Area. Cambridge, 1930.

—, *The Archaeology of Crete.* London, 1939. AC

G. PERROT and C. CHIPIEZ, *History of Art in*
Primitive Greece. 2 vols., London, 1894, transl.
from *Histoire de l'art dans l'antiquité VI.* Paris,
1894.

A.W. PERSSON, *The Royal Tombs at Dendra near* RTD
Midea. Lund and elsewhere, 1931.

R. PFEIFFER, *History of Classical Scholarship*. Oxford, 1968.   *HOCS*

E. PFUHL, "Der archaische Friedhof am Stadtberge von Thera" in *Ath. Mitt.* 28 (1903) pp. 1-290.

N. PHARAKLAS, "Θῆβαι: ἀνασκαφὴ οἰκοπέδου Λιακοπούλου-Κύρτση" in *AAA* 1 (1968) pp. 241-4.

—, "Ἀρχαιότητες καὶ μνημεῖα Βοιωτίας" in *AD* 23 (1968) B.1 (*Chronika*) pp. 207-24; and *AD* 24 (1969) B.1 (*Chronika*) pp. 173-9.

—, see also under Philippaki.

B. PHILIPPAKI, S. SYMEONOGLOU and N. PHARAKLAS, "Ἀρχαιότητες καὶ μνημεῖα Βοιωτίας" in *AD* 22 (1967) B.1 (*Chronika*) pp. 225-57.

A. PHILIPPSON, *Die griechische Landschaften*. 4 vols.,   *DGL* Frankfurt-am-Main, 1950-9.

K.M. PHILLIPS Jr., "Perseus and Andromeda" in *AJA* 72 (1968) pp. 1-23.

Charles PICARD, *Les religions préhelléniques*. Paris,   *RP* 1948.

Gilbert PICARD and Colette PICARD, see under Charles-Picard.

S. PIGGOTT, *Approach to Archaeology*. London, 1959.   *ApA*

M. PLATNAUER (ed.), *Euripides, Iphigenia in Tauris*. Oxford, 1938.

N. PLATON and E. STASSINOPOULOU-TOULOUPA, "Oriental seals from the Palace of Cadmus: unique discoveries in Boeotian Thebes" in *ILN* for Nov. 28th 1964 pp. 859-61; "Ivories and Linear-B from Thebes" in *ILN* for Dec. 5th 1964 pp. 896f.

E. POCOCKE, *India in Greece; or, Truth in Mythology*. London, 1852.

M. POPE, "The Linear A question" in *Antiquity* 32 (1958) pp. 97-9.

M.R. POPHAM, "Two Cypriot sherds from Crete" in

235

BSA 58 (1963) pp. 89-93.

—, and L.H. SACKETT, *Excavations at Lefkandi,*   *ELE*
Euboea, 1964-66. London, 1968.

—, *The Destruction of the Palace at Knossos.*   *DPK*
Pottery of the Late Minoan IIIA Period (*SMA*
12). Göteborg, 1970.

E. PORADA, "Cylinder seals from Thebes; a preliminary
report" (summary of a paper) in *AJA* 69 (1965)
p. 173.

—, "Further notes on the cylinders from Thebes"
(summary of a paper) in *AJA* 70 (1966) p. 194.

J. POUILLOUX, *Recherches sur l'histoire et les cultes de*   *ET* III
Thasos I (*Études thasiennes III*). Paris, 1954.

N.J.G. POUNDS, *An Historical Geography of Europe,*   *HGE*
450 B.C.-A.D. 1330. Cambridge, 1973.

J.U. POWELL (ed.), *The Phoenissae of Euripides.*   *PhE*
London, 1911.

J.B. PRITCHARD (ed.), *Ancient Near Eastern Texts*   *ANET*
relating to the Old Testament. Ed. 3, Princeton,
1969.

A.F. RAINEY, "Business agents at Ugarit" in *IEJ* 13
(1963) pp. 313-21.

—, "The Kingdom of Ugarit" in *The Biblical
Archaeologist* 28 (1965) pp. 102-25.

J. RAISON, *Les vases à inscriptions peintes de l'âge*   *VIPA*
mycénien. Rome, 1968.

G. RAWLINSON, *History of Herodotus.* Ed. 4, 4 vols.,   *HHer*
London, 1880.

—, *Phoenicia* (in the series *The Story of the Nations*).
London, 1889.

—, *History of Phoenicia.* London, 1889.   *HPhoen*

S. REINACH, "Le mirage oriental" in *L'Anthropologie* 4
(1893) pp. 539-78; 699-732.

—, "Les Cabires et Mélicerte" in *RA* 3ᵉ sér. 32
(1898) pp. 56-61.

C. RENFREW, "Crete and the Cyclades before
Rhadamanthus" in Κρητικὰ Χρονικά 18 (1964)

pp. 107-41.

—, *The Emergence of Civilisation. The Cyclades and*   *ECCA*
the Aegean in the Third Millennium B.C.
London, 1972.

H. REUSCH, "Ein Schildfresko aus Theben (Böotien)"
in *AA* for 1953 cols. 16-25.

—, *Die zeichnerische Rekonstruktion des Frauen-*   *ZRF*
frieses im böotischen Theben. Berlin, 1956.

T. Talbot RICE, *Everyday Life in Byzantium.* London,   *ELB*
1967.

G.M.A. RICHTER, *The Furniture of the Greeks,*   *FGR*
Etruscans and Romans. London, 1966.

A. de RIDDER, "Vases archaïques à reliefs" in *Mélanges
Perrot* pp. 297-301. Paris, 1903.

W. RIDGEWAY, *The Early Age of Greece.* Vol. I,
Cambridge, 1901.

P.J. RIIS, "The first Greeks in Phoenicia and their
settlement at Sukas" in *Ugaritica* VI (see under
Schaeffer) pp. 435-50. Paris, 1969.

—, *Sukas I. The North-East Sanctuary and the First
Settling of the Greeks in Syria and Palestine.*
Copenhagen, 1970.

G. RODENWALDT, "Fragmente mykenischer Wand-
gemälde" in *Ath. Mitt.* 36 (1911) pp. 221-50.

—, "Mykenische Studien I" in *JDAI* 34 (1919) pp.
87-106.

H.J. ROSE, *A Handbook of Greek Mythology.* Ed. 6,   *HGM*
London, 1958.

G. ROUX, *Ancient Iraq.* London, 1964 (here cited in the   *AI*
Pelican ed., Harmondsworth, 1966).

S. RUNCIMAN, *Byzantine Civilization.* London, 1933.   *ByzC*

B. RUTKOWSKI, "The origin of the Minoan coffin" in
BSA 63 (1968) pp. 219-27.

I.A. SAKELLARAKIS, "Ἐλεφάντινον πλοῖον ἐκ
Μυκηνῶν" in *AE* for 1971 (1972) pp.188-233.

M.B. SAKELLARIOU, *La migration grecque en Ionie.*   *MGI*
Athens, 1958.

F. SALVIAT, "Lions d'ivoire orientaux à Thasos" in *BCH* 86 (1962) pp. 95-116.

—, and J. SERVAIS, "Stèle indicatrice thasienne trouvée au sanctuaire d'Aliki" in *BCH* 88 (1964) pp. 267-87.

J.M. SASSON, "Canaanite maritime involvement in the second millennium B.C." in *JAOS* 86 (1966) pp. 126-38.

T. SÄVE-SÖDERBERGH, *The Navy of the Eighteenth Egyptian Dynasty.* Uppsala, 1946.

F. SCHACHERMEYR, "Welche geschichtlichen Ereignisse führten zur Entstehung der mykenischen Kultur?" in *Archiv Orientální* 17.2 (1949) pp. 331-50.

—, *Die minoische Kultur des alten Kreta.* Stuttgart, 1964.   *MKAK*

C.F.A. SCHAEFFER, "Die Stellung Ras Shamra-Ugarits zur kretischen und mykenischen Kultur" in *JDAI* 52 (1937) pp. 139-65.

—, *The Cuneiform Texts of Ras Shamra-Ugarit.* London, 1939.   *CTRS*

—, *Ugaritica.* Paris, Vol. I, 1939; II, 1949; III, 1956; IV, 1962; V, 1968; VI, 1969.

—, *Stratigraphie comparée et chronologie de l'Asie Occidentale.* Oxford, 1948.   *SCCA*

—, "Reprise des recherches archéologiques à Ras Shamra-Ugarit. Sondages de 1948 et 1949 et campagne de 1950" in *Syria* 28 (1951) pp. 1-21.

—, "Une industrie d'Ugarit — la pourpre" in *AAS* 1 (1951) pp. 188-92.

—, "Les fouilles de Ras Shamra-Ugarit. Quinzième, seizième et dix-septième campagnes (1951, 1952 et 1953)" in *Syria* 31 (1954) pp. 14-67.

K. SCHEFOLD, *Myth and Legend in Early Greek Art.* London, 1966.   *MLGA*

H₍ SCHLIEMANN, *Ilios: the City and Country of the Trojans.* London, 1880.

K. SCHNEIDER, article s.v. purpura in *RE* XXIII. 2 (1959) cols. 2000-20.

F. SCHOBER, parts A and B of article s.v. Thebai (Boiotien) in *RE* 2nd ser. V (1934) cols. 1423-92.　　　　　　*RE(T)*

K. SCHOLES, "The Cyclades in the later Bronze Age: a synopsis" in *BSA* 51 (1956) pp. 9-40.

A. SEVERYNS, *Bacchylide*. Liège and Paris, 1933.

H. SEYRIG, "Quatre cultes de Thasos" in *BCH* 51 (1927) pp. 178-233.

G. SHARPE, *Two Dissertations: I. Upon the Origin, Construction, Division and Relation of Languages. II. Upon the Original Powers of Letters.* London, 1751.　　　　*DUOP*

R. Hope SIMPSON, *A Gazetteer and Atlas of Mycenaean Sites* (*BICS* suppl. 16). London, 1965.　　*GMS*

—, and J.F. LAZENBY, *The Catalogue of Ships in Homer's Iliad*. Oxford, 1970.　　　　*CSHI*

W. Stevenson SMITH, *Interconnections in the Ancient Near East. A study of the relationships between the arts of Egypt, the Aegean and Western Asia.* New Haven, 1965.　　　　*IANE*

W. von SODEN, *Akkadisches Handwörterbuch*. Vol. I, Wiesbaden, 1965.

E.A. SPEISER, "The name *Phoinikes*" in *Language* 12 (1936) pp. 121-6.　　　　*NP*

TH. G. SPYROPOULOS, "Πλακίδιον μὲ ἐγχαράκτους παραστάσεις ἐκ Θηβῶν" in *AD* 24 (1969) A (*Meletai*) pp. 47-50.

—, "'Αρχαιότητες καὶ μνημεῖα Βοιωτίας" in *AD* 24 (1969) B.1 (*Chronika*) pp. 180-7.

—, "'Ανασκαφὴ εἰς τὸ Μυκηναϊκὸν νεκροταφεῖον τῆς Τανάγρας" in *AAA* 3 (1970) pp. 184-97.

—, "'Ελεφαντίνη γλυπτὴ λαβὴ ἐκ Θηβῶν" in *AAA* 3 (1970) pp. 268-73.

—, "Τὸ ἀρχεῖον τοῦ Μυκηναϊκοῦ ἀνακτόρου τῶν Θηβῶν" in *AAA* 3 (1970) pp. 322-7.

—, "Ἀρχαιότητες καὶ μνημεῖα Βοιωτίας-Φθιώτιδος" in *AD* 25 (1970) B.1 (*Chronika*) pp. 211-45.

—, "The discovery of the palace archives of Boeotian Thebes" in *Kadmos* 9 (1970) pp. 170-2.

—, "Τοπογραφικὰ τοῦ Καδμείου ἀνακτόρου" in *AAA* 4 (1971) pp. 32-7.

—, "Μυκηναϊκὸς βασιλικὸς θαλαμωτὸς τάφος ἐν Θήβαις" in *AAA* 4 (1971) pp. 161-4.

—, "Αἰγυπτιακὸς ἐποικισμὸς ἐν Βοιωτίᾳ" in *AAA* 5 (1972) pp. 16-27.

—, "Mycenaean Tanagra: terracotta sarcophagi" in *Archaeology* 25 (1972) pp. 206-9.

C.G. STARR, "The myth of the Minoan thalassocracy" in *Historia* 3 (1954-55) pp. 282-91.

—, *The Origins of Greek Civilization, 1100-650 B.C.* London, 1962.   OGC

E. STASSINOPOULOU-TOULOUPA, see E. Touloupa; also under Platon.

L.A. STELLA, "Importanza degli scavi di Ras Shamra per il problema fenicio dei poemi omerici" in *ArchClass* 4 (1952) pp. 72-6.

—, *Il poema di Ulisse.* Florence, 1955.

—, *La civiltà micenea nei documenti contemporanei.*   CMDC
Rome, 1965.

F.H. STUBBINGS, "The Mycenaean pottery of Attica" in *BSA* 42 (1947) pp. 1-75.

—, *Mycenaean Pottery from the Levant.* Cambridge,   MPL
1951.

—, "Communications and trade" in *CH* (ed. Wace and Stubbings), 1962 pp. 539-44.

—, (with W.C. Hayes and M.B. Rowton), "Chronology... The Aegean Bronze Age" in *CAH* ed. 2, fasc. 4, 1962 (= ed. 3 Vol. I, Ch. VI).

—, "The rise of Mycenaean civilization" in *CAH* ed. 2, fasc. 18, 1963 (= ed. 3 Vol. II, Ch. XIV).

—, "The expansion of Mycenaean civilization" in

CAH ed. 2, fasc. 26, 1964 (= ed. 3 Vol. II, Ch. XXIIa).

—, "The recession of Mycenaean civilization" in *CAH* ed. 2, fasc. 39, 1965 (= ed. 3 Vol. II, Ch. XXVII).

F. STUDNICZKA, *Kyrene. Eine altgriechische Göttin.* Leipzig, 1890.

C.H.V. SUTHERLAND, *Gold.* London, 1959.

S. SYMEONOGLOU, see under Philippaki and Touloupa.

TALBOT RICE, see under Rice.

W. TECHNAU, "Die Göttin auf dem Stier" in *JDAI* 52 (1937) pp. 76-103.

F. THACKERAY, *Researches into the Ecclesiastical and Political State of Ancient Britain.* 2 vols., London, 1843.   *REPS*

C. THIRLWALL, *A History of Greece.* 8 vols., London, 1835-47.   *HGThi*

D'Arcy W. THOMPSON, *A Glossary of Greek Fishes* (St. Andrews Univ. Publ. no. 45). London, 1947.   *GGF*

Stith THOMPSON, *A Motif-index of Folk-literature.* Rev. ed., 6 vols., Copenhagen, 1955-58.   *MIFL*

G. THOMSON, *Studies in Ancient Greek Society I. The Prehistoric Aegean.* London, 1949.   *SAGS I*

F. THUREAU-DANGIN, "Vocabulaires de Ras-Shamra" in *Syria* 12 (1931) pp. 225-66.

—, "Un comptoir de laine poupre à Ugarit d'après une tablette de Ras-Shamra" in *Syria* 15 (1934) pp. 137-46.

M.N. TOD, *A Selection of Greek Historical Inscriptions to the end of the fifth century B.C.* Ed. 2, Oxford, 1946.   *GHI*

J. TOEPFFER, *Attische Genealogie.* Berlin, 1889.

E. TOULOUPA, "'Αρχαιότητες καὶ μνημεῖα Βοιωτίας" in *AD* 19 (1964) B.2 (*Chronika*) pp. 191-203.

—, and S. SYMEONOGLOU, "'Αρχαιότητες καὶ μνημεῖα Βοιωτίας" in *AD* 20 (1965) B.2

(*Chronika*) pp. 228-44; and *AD* 21 (1966) B.1
(*Chronika*) pp. 176-205.

—, see also under Platon.

A.D. TRENDALL and T.B.L. WEBSTER, *Illustrations*   *IGD*
of Greek Drama. London, 1971.

T.G. TUCKER (ed.), *The Seven Against Thebes of*   *AesS*
Aeschylus. Cambridge, 1908.

G. TÜRK, articles s.v. Phoinix in *Roscher* III
(1897-1909) cols. 2401-9.

I.G. TZEDAKIS, "Zeugnisse der Linearschrift B aus
Chania" in *Kadmos* 6 (1967) pp. 106-9.

—, "Λάρνακες Ὑστερομινωϊκοῦ νεκροταφείου
᾽Αρμένων Ρεθύμνης" in *AAA* 4 (1971) pp.
216-22.

F.A. UKERT, *Geographie der Griechen und Römer.* 3   *GGR*
vols., Weimar, 1816-46.

B.L. ULLMAN, "The origin and development of the
alphabet" in *AJA* 31 (1927) pp. 311-28.

—, "How old is the Greek alphabet?" in *AJA* 38
(1934) pp. 359-81.

A.D. URE, "Linear B at Larissa?" in *BICS* 6 (1959) pp.
73-5.

J. USHER, *Annales Veteris Testamenti.* 2 vols., London,
1650-54.

I. VELIKOVSKY, *Ages in Chaos* I. London, 1953.

—, *Oedipus and Akhnaton.* London, 1960.

M. VENTRIS and J. CHADWICK, *Documents in*   *DMG*
Mycenaean Greek. Cambridge, 1956.

J.C. VERCOUTTER, *L'Égypte et le monde égéen*   *EMEP*
préhellénique. Cairo, 1956.

E. (T.) VERMEULE, *Greece in the Bronze Age.* Chicago   *GBA*
and London, 1964.

—, "Painted Mycenaean larnakes" in *JHS* 85 (1965)
pp. 123-48.

—, "Kadmos and the dragon" in *Studies Presented*   *KD*
to George M.A. Hanfmann (ed. D.G. Mitten and
others) pp. 177-88. Mainz, 1972.

A.W. VERRALL (ed.), *The "Seven against Thebes" of Aeschylus.* London, 1887.

F. VIAN, *Les origines de Thèbes: Cadmos et les Spartes.*   *Or. Theb.* Paris, 1963.

R. VIRCHOW, preface to Schliemann, *Ilios,* 1880.

C. VIROLLEAUD, "Six textes de Ras Shamra provenant de la XIVe campagne" in *Syria* 28 (1951) pp. 163-79.

—, *Le Palais royal d'Ugarit II. Textes alphabétiques*   *PRU* II *des archives est, ouest et centrales.* Paris, 1957.

—, *Le Palais royal d'Ugarit V. Textes en cun-*   *PRU* V *éiformes alphabétiques des archives sud, sud-ouest et du petit palais.* Paris, 1965.

A.J.B. WACE and C.W. BLEGEN, "Pottery as evidence   *PET* for trade and colonization in the Aegean Bronze Age" in *Klio* 32 (1939) pp. 131-47.

—, *Mycenae. An Archaeological History and Guide.* Princeton, 1949.

—, "The history of Greece in the third and second millenniums B.C." in *Historia* 2 (1953-54) pp. 74-94.

—, foreword to Ventris and Chadwick, *DMG,* 1956.

—, "The early age of Greece" in *CH* (ed. Wace and Stubbings), 1962, pp. 331-61.

F.T. WAINWRIGHT, *Archaeology and Place-Names*   *APNH* *and History.* London, 1962.

B.H. WARMINGTON, *Carthage.* London, 1960 (here cited in the Pelican ed., Harmondsworth, 1964).

P. WARREN, "Minoan stone vases as evidence for Minoan connections in the Aegean Late Bronze Age" in *PPS* 33 (1967) pp. 37-56.

—, "The thalassocracy of Minos" (summary of a paper) in *PCA* 67 (1970) p. 34.

—, *Myrtos. An Early Bronze Age Settlement in Crete (BSA* Suppl. Vol. 7). London, 1972.

T.B.L. WEBSTER, *From Mycenae to Homer.* London,   *MycH* 1958.

—, see also under Trendall.

R. WEILL, "Phéniciens, Égéens et Hellènes dans la Méditerranée primitive" in *Syria* 2 (1921) pp. 120-44.

F.G. WELCKER, *Über eine kretische Kolonie in Theben, die Göttin Europa und Kadmos den König.* Bonn, 1824.   *UKK*

A. WESTHOLM, "Built tombs in Cyprus" in *AIRRS* 5 (1941) pp. 29-58.

R.E.M. WHEELER, *Alms for Oblivion.* London, 1966.   *AFO*

U. von WILAMOWITZ-MOELLENDORFF, *Homerische Untersuchungen (Philologische Untersuchungen* 7). Berlin, 1884.   *HU*

—, *Pindaros.* Berlin, 1922.

—, "Die griechische Heldensage, II" in *Sitzungsberichte der preussischen Akademie der Wissenschaften* for 1925, pp. 214-42.   *GH*

R.F. WILLETTS, *Cretan Cults and Festivals.* London, 1962.   *CCF*

A.G. WOODHEAD, *The Study of Greek Inscriptions.* Cambridge, 1959.   *SGI*

E. WÜST, article s.v. Phoinix (4) in *RE* XX.1 (1941) cols. 412-14.

J. ZAFIROPULO, *Histoire de la Grèce à l'âge de bronze.* Paris, 1964.   *HGAB*

—, *Mead and Wine* (Eng. transl. by P. Green of *HGAB* with minor revisions). London, 1966.

L. ZIEHEN, part C of article s.v. Thebai (Boiotien) in *RE* 2nd ser. V (1934) cols. 1492-1553.   *RE(T)*

INDEX

This includes material in the footnotes as well
as in the text, but all numbers refer to pages.

247

Lesbos, 12
Lethaios, river, 90
Leviathan, 151
Lévi-Strauss, C., 12
Levy, I., 92
Lewy, H., 58, 157
Libya (geogr.), 57, 180
Libya (heroine), 27f., 50
Lindian Temple Chronicle, 23, 30, 46
Linear A, 7, 101, 120, 176, 191
Linear B, 6, 8, 14, 82, 104, *107f.*, 119f.,
  163, 175-8, 190, 201, 204
Liverani, M., 124, 126
Il, 144, 153
loan-words, 119f., 171, 182
logographers, 18, 36, 55, *66f.*, *69-75*, 83
Lorimer, H.L., 95, 98, 181
Lowie, R.H., 201
Luce, J.V., 101
Lucian, 38, 46, 47
lunar elements, 44
Luwians, 7
Lychnida, -os, 33
Lycia, 77, 88, 93, 127
Lykophron, 30, 48
lyre, 33

McDonald, W.A., 134
McNeal, R.A., 14, 200
Mallia, 106
Malinowski, B., 11
Malten, L., 54
Marduk, 151
Märchen, 42
Mark, gospel of, 155
Malalas, Ioannes, 40, 46, 47, 48
Mari texts, 127
Marinatos, S., 102, 106, 176, 180
Martial, 46, 47
Matz, F., 101, 106, 170
Medeia, 76
Μεγάλοι Θεοί, 81, 146
Megara, 130, 151
megaron, 100, 107
Melos, 101, 102, 180, 198

Membliaros, 19, 31, 54, 78, 164
Memphis, 27, 50
Menestheus, 197
Mentz, A., 163, 175
Mesopotamia, 96, 123
Messenia, 102
Mestor, 165
metalwork, precious, 118, 125
metope, 145
Meyer, E., 53, 116, 129
Middle Helladic, 7, 14, 100, 103, 165,
  169f., 202
Midea, 197
migration, *see* immigration
Miletos, 12, 55, 75, 76, 82-4, 86
Millett, A., 103, 105, *108f.*
mines, mining, 30, 32, 44, 180f.
Minet-el-Beida, 123, 124, 125
Minoan civilisation, *see* Crete
Minos, 19, 74, 88, 91f., 111, 165, 166,
  198
Minotaur, 40, 92
Minyae, 56, 88f., 91
Minyan, Grey, 202
"*mirage phénicien*", 76, 85, 175
Mitannians, 123, 132
Mitford, W., 1, 4, 51, 58, 146
Mnaseas, 30
Mnesimachos, 111
moon-goddess, 44
morning-star, 59, 141-4, 157
Moses, 47
motifs, mythological, 68, 139, 141-61,
  190, 207
Mt. Carmel, 51, 92
Mt. Pangaion, 30, 32, 33
Mousaios, 20
Movers, F.C., 58, 95, 115, 157
Müller, F. Max, 9, 10
Müller, K.O., *2, 52*, 58, 68, 75, 129
Muhly, J.D., 65, 79, 94, 96, 97, 117, 120,
  126, 167
murex, *see* dye, purple
Murray, G., 59
Mycenae, 3, 7f., 12, *13*, 62, 107, 118, 125,

165, 194; foundation, 151, 197; frescoes, 95; graves, 7, 88, 100, 118, 125, 189

Mycenaean Age, culture, 8, 11-15, 34, 62, 64, 80, 112, 117f., 139f., 158f., 169f., 176, 184f., 187-207 *passim;* interpreted as Cretan, 99f., 117; —as Phoenician, 53f., 60, 203

Mycenaean Greek, 6, 14, 96, 126; *see also* Linear B

Mykalessos, 31, 37

Mylonas, G.E., 7, 97, 105, 125, 134, 164, *175-7,* 197

Myres, Sir J., 54, *57, 89f.,* 92, 98f., *163f.,* 171, 197

Myrtos, 98

mystery cults, 30, 38, 80

myth, 35, 76, 85f., 189, 198, 203, 206; definition of, 10f.; aetiological, 43; combat, 151; foundation, 169; religious, 43, 187, 193; *see also* motifs

mythographers, 30, 39, 46, 69, 154

names, *see* proper names

Naron, river, 33, 34

"naval gazette", 126f., 129

Naveh, J., 175, 179

Neilos, Nile, 26-8, 70, 73

Neolithic, 4, 90, 103, 169

"New Kadmeion", 104, 132

New Testament, cited, 82, 155

Nicander, 34, 46, 47

Nikomachos, 33

Nilsson, M.P., 11-13, 35, 83, 86, 88, 169, 188, 189, 195, 197

Nineham, D., 155

Ningišzida, 141, 150-3, 154

Niobe, 206

Niqmed, 61

Nixon, I.G., 163

Noah, 37

Nock, A.D., 80

Nonnos, 24, 27, 29, 30, 31, 32, 34, 35, 46, 47, 48

"Norsemen", 146

Nougayrol, J., 123, 131, 132

Nubia, 202

Nuzi, 96

Ochrid, Lake, 33

Odyssey, *see* Homer

Ogygos, 49, 50, 90

Oidipous, 10, 21, 61, 166, 178

oil-store, 104, 106

Okaleai, 111

Old Testament, 1, 5, 204; cited, 37, 68, 146, 155, 157, 158

Onga (Onka), 48, 49

onomastics, *see* proper names

Oppian, 46, 47

oracle, 19, 23, 31f., 157

Orientalising, 60, 181, 182

Orpheus, 41

Orthosia, 92

Osiris, 41

Ovid, 18, 31, 32, 35, 46, 47, 85

ox-chariot, 22, 23

Page, Sir D.L., 15, 130, 180, 189, 193, 194, 197, 198, 201, 202

Palaeolithic, 4

Palaikastro, 97

Palaiphatos, 39, 41, 46, 47, 136, 194

Palamedes, 66

Palestine, 118, 180, 183

Pallene, 41

Palmer, L.R., 7, 8, 62, 109, 134, 170

palms, 176, 180

Pandion, 167, 197

Pangaion, Mt., 30, 32, 33

Parian Marble, 167

Parry, Milman, 14

Parthenius, 33

Pasiphae, 1

Paul, St., 82

Pausanias, 24, 31, 32, 38, 46, 47, 48, 81, 83, 85, 111, 135, 136, 165, 194

Pelagon, 31, 113

Pelasgians, 57, 113

Pelon, O., 109

Simonides, 66
Simpson, R.H., 108, 130, 131
Sisyphos, 151
Skaios, 178
Skylax, 34
Şml, 141
snake-god, *see* gods
snakes, 20, 22, 34, 43, 141, 151-4; *see also* dragon-fight
solar symbolism, 9f., 43f., 53, 116, 141-6, 153,
Solinus, 90
Solymoi, 93
Song of Roland, 168
Sophokles, 19, 21, 165, 166
sowing (of dragon's teeth), 20, 31f., 36, 66, 69
Spartoi (Sown Men), 20, 33, 36, 40, 42, 66, 76 *187*
Speiser, E.A., 94, 96, 98
sphinx, 118
Spyropoulos, Th.G., 51, 103, 104, 107, 108, 110, *173*
Starr, C.G., 195f., 198, 203
Stassinopoulou-Touloupa, E., 104, 132f.
Statius, 32, 35, 47
Stella, L.A., 201
Stephen of Byzantium, 19, 30, 31, 33, 34, 46, 47, 48, 78, 81, 101, 102, 199
Stesichoros, 22, 66, *69,* 74
stirrup-jars, 104, 105, 107-9, 170
stone-quarrying, 32
stone-throwing, 42, 187
storax, 111
Strabo, 30, 34, 46, 68, 83, 84, 92, 111
Stubbings, F.H., *62,* 100, 101, 105, 119, 121, 126, 130, 131, *169f.,* 180, 189, *195*
Studniczka, F., 52, 79
Suda, the, 46, 49
Sumerian, 5, 124, 141, 150-2
Suppiluliumas, 124, 136
Sutherland, C.H.V., 179
symbolism, *see* solar symbolism
syncretism, religious, 38, 42, 81, 145

Syria(ns), 7, 29, 37, 62, 92, 97, 113, 118, 122-8, 135f., 158-60, 171, 173, 177, 180f., 190
Syros, 28, 29, 37

Tacitus, 23, 46, 136
Tammuz, 152
Tanagra, 68, 110f., 112, 170
Taphians, 30, 37
Taurus, -os, 1, 39f., 193
Tawagalawas, 201
teeth, *see* sowing
Teiresias, 154, 165, 188
Tektamos, 154, 157
Telephassa, 25, 50
Telephe, -ae, 25, 28, 30, 36
Tell Abu Hawam, 121
Tell el-Yahudiyah, 172
Tell Sukas, 119, 158
Teos, 23
Teumessos, 111
textiles, 182
thalassocracy, 91, 115, 117f., 126, 198
Thales, 92f.
Thasos (hero), 19, 25-9, 78, 90
Thasos (island), 19, 30, 37, 41, 45, 49, 62, 179, 183f.
Thebes (Boeotian), 32, 62, 65, 80, 151, 172, 178; and Crete, 56-8, 89, 92, *105-13,* 131, *170f.,* 190; destruction, 8, 104, 106, 132, 192; excavations, 54, 57, 86, 89, 102-12, 117, 129, 131-7; foundation, *see* Kadmos; geog. position, 116f., 130f., 134f.
Thebes (Egyptian), 38, 41, 47, 49, 50, 172
Thebes (Hypoplacian), 188
Theodaisia, 111
Theognis, 20
Theognostos, 33
Theophrastos, 32
Thera, 8, 19, 31, 32, 45, *54,* 62, 101, 102, *179-182,* 190, 198
Theseus, 92, 197, 198
Thirlwall, C., 1, 58, 172

MAPS

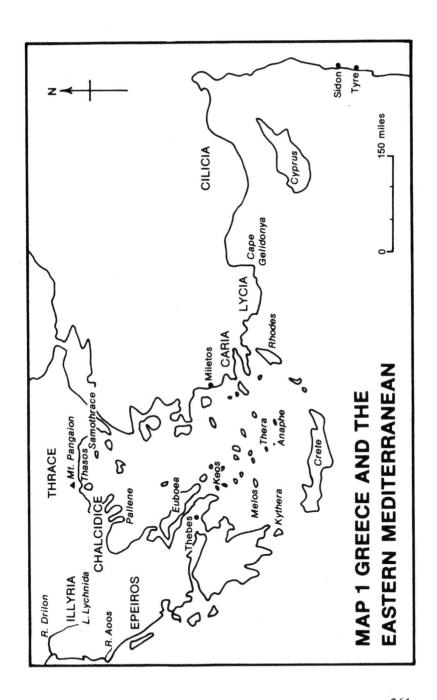

MAP 1 GREECE AND THE
EASTERN MEDITERRANEAN

THRACE

Mt. Pangaion
Thasos
Samothrace

CHALCIDICE

Pallene

ILLYRIA

R. Drilon

L. Lychnida

R. Aoos

EPEIROS

Euboea

Thebes

Keos

Melos

Kythera

Thera

Anaphe

Crete

Miletos

CARIA

Rhodes

LYCIA

Cape
Gelidonya

CILICIA

Cyprus

Sidon

Tyre

N

0   150 miles

261

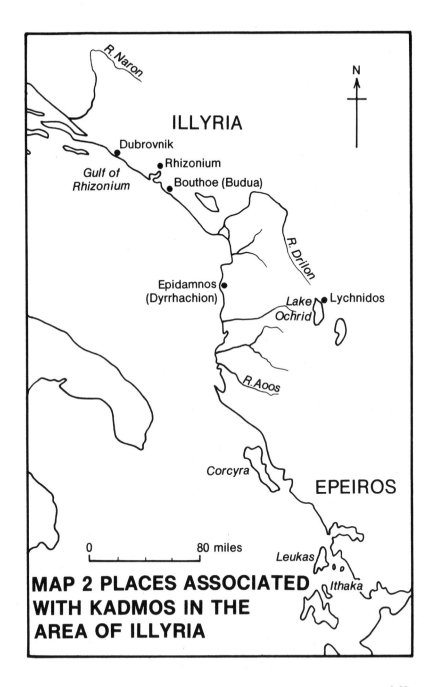

MAP 2 PLACES ASSOCIATED
WITH KADMOS IN THE
AREA OF ILLYRIA

CILICIA

Cape Gelidonya

CYPRUS

Alalakh
Al Mina

R. Orontes

Ras Shamra
(Ugarit)

Tell Sukas

Arados

N

Orthosia

Byblos

Beirut
Gharifeh

Nahr
Litany

Sidon

Sarepta

Tyre

Hazor

Tell Abu Hawam

Mt. Carmel

Megiddo

0   100 miles

R. Jordan

Amman

Ashdod

Pelusium

Lachish

NILE DELTA

MAP 3 PHOENICIA AND
ADJACENT AREAS

265

LIBRARY OF DAVIDSON COLLEGE

Books on regular loan may be checked out for **two weeks.** Books must be presented at the Circulation Desk in order to be renewed.

A fine is charged after date due.

Special books are subject to special regulations at the discretion of the library staff.